CHRIST THE FORM OF BEAUTY

CHRIST THE FORM OF BEAUTY

A Study in Theology and Literature

Francesca Aran Murphy

T&T CLARK
EDINBURGH

T&T CLARK LTD
59 GEORGE STREET
EDINBURGH EH2 2LQ
SCOTLAND

First published 1995

0 567 09708 0

British Library Cataloguing-in-Publication Data
A catalogue record for this book is available from the British Library

Typeset by Hewer Text Composition Services, Edinburgh
Printed and bound in Great Britain by Bookcraft, Avon

**For
Christina Moss
&
David Cooke**

Contents

1

Introduction: Imagining

This book is about the Christological imagination. It argues that our ability to enter into the Incarnation is in proportion to our willingness to imagine realistically. What 'imagining' means, and whether it is an activity in which theologians ought to engage, are questions which have been answered in different ways. We shall begin by noticing some of answers.

Thomas Aquinas: The Earthbound Imagination

St Thomas considered that the embodied mind approaches reality through sense, imagination and intellect. Knowing begins in the sensation of particular things. Although imagining and thinking are based in their work, true knowledge is beyond the scope of the senses. It is the intellect which understands and judges the causes which drive things. The intellect transcends the physical conditions which it deploys.[1] A judgement cannot fully be described in terms of the physical events which initiate it. In the course of its quest for universal truths, the theological intellect transverses, and then ascends beyond the objects of sense and imagination.

Thinking requires phantasms, or images. Imagining is its necessary prerequisite. To imagine well is to create an image of a fact in a perspective which best displays its meaning. The act of understanding needs an image. But it can be replaced by others which reveal alternative perspectives of the object: all images are subsidiary to the mind's ascent toward universal

1

truth. If true judgement is a grasp of cause, imagination is incapable of it. The theologian's imagination must be quiescent when he or she seizes the causes which bind created being together, and which connect created and self-subsistent Being. Thomas says that theology culminates in judgements which employ, but ultimately supersede the imagination.[2]

His view advances on the basis that thinking is nourished by images which are drawn from physical facts. This is valuable, for it grips the bond between knowledge and a given world. Although imagination does not aspire to the highest reaches of thought, its images circumscribe and delimit that human energy which leaps toward God. Even the prophetic vision is grounded in a concrete phantasm – made transparent to meaning by the Holy Spirit.[3] Human thought depends upon imagination because thinking is mediated by a body. 'Originary thinking' is for Thomas a receptivity.[4] Imagination limits thought in two ways. First, it requires that it feed upon physical things. Second, and, following from this, image-based thought cannot be purely creative. The imagination must reshape the data which it receives from sensation. Whatever we add to this, we will retain the principle that imagination is a channel to the objective world because it plays upon concrete facts.

Immanuel Kant: The Synthesizing Imagination

Kant also locates the imagination between a physical and an immaterial faculty, that is, the sensibility and the understanding. The sensibility provides the data of apprehension. The understanding supplies the a priori rules by which presentations are related. These rules are the categorical laws which underpin the possibility of experience. The imagination synthesizes the material representations of the sensibility with the categorial conceptions of understanding. The imaginative synthesis is delimited by the facts which the sensibility garners, and by obedience to the universal guidelines laid down by the understanding.[5] Kant distinguishes the reproductive and the productive imagination.[6] The former associates and synthesizes the images to which it gives rise. It is 'retrospective', or bound by physical causality. The productive imagination has not this constraint: it is 'prospective'. It creates schemata. These are procedures which relate abstract concepts to specific instances. Productive imagination 'translates'. It places the wayward fact within its type or genre. When it comes upon some new thing, it is able to see it as an extension of a known genre: it detects in the fountain pen a primitive keyboard. Apprehension thus relies on the imagination's organization of experience. Its ordered images enable us to regard nature as a unity.[7] Imagining regulates our experience and makes it comprehensible.

Kant's theory of aesthetic judgement provides a new type of imagination: one which is intuitive or creative.[8] The aesthetic imagination sees and produces form. The forms which it creates are autonomous aesthetic worlds. The aesthetic imagination is not dominated by the tight associative bonds which the understanding sets up.[9] The part which the understanding plays in aesthetic judgements is limited: the adjustment of imagination to understanding is not automatic but freely chosen. The freedom of the aesthetic judgement ensures its creativity. The rational tram-lines which gird the world fabricated by the understanding impinge upon it only in so far as it wishes. Because they are non-conceptual, aesthetic judgements build their own world, a playful kingdom whose rules are set apart from those which govern the 'non-aesthetic' reality in which we ordinarily live and love.

Kant often uses 'imagination' to *create* order rather than to reflect it. His 'reproductive imagination' responds to the senses: but the organizing network which it extrudes does not inhere within facts. The form in which Kant's aesthetic imagination is said to uncover beauty is the perfect fit of understanding and imagination.[10] The perfectly adjusted forms which it intuits reside within the subject. The kingdom of the aesthetic dream, that is, is literally within us, not around and about us.

Romanticism: The Creative Imagination

Goethe contended in his *Theory of Colours* that each colour in the spectrum educes its opposite. It follows that

The appearances of colour . . . seen in their juxtaposition,
produce a whole. This whole is harmony to the eye. . . .
nature tends to emancipate the sense from confined
impressions by . . . producing the whole . . . a natural
phenomenon immediately applicable to aesthetic purposes.[11]

The Romantics were to underscore the unities in nature in
order to show that poetic forms are 'wholes'. In August
Schlegel's Vienna Lectures of 1809–1811, Romanticism defined itself in terms of the opposition between the art of 'organic
form' and that of 'mechanical regularity'.[12] Kant had dimin-
ished the role of the regulative understanding in aesthetics, and
enlarged that of imagination. His Romantic successors elaborate upon this. They contrast the automatic machinations of
understanding with the free movement of imagination. They
were perturbed by the fissures which seemed to them to have
separated God from the world, humanity from nature, and the
human faculties one from another. They regarded the mechanistic philosophies of the eighteenth century as a source of these
dismemberments, and not without due cause. The co-ordinat-
ing power of imagination is their vehicle of reintegration.
Schelling transforms Kant's 'creative imagination' into *Einbildungskraft*. He defines *Einbildungskraft* as the power by which
diverse things are made to coalesce into a whole.[13] For
Coleridge, beauty is 'that in which the many, still seen as
many, becomes one'.[14] The intricate structure of the beautiful
form gives the human imagination a well-organized model.[15]
   Imagining is taken to be the authentically human way of
knowing.[16] The human self is the first object to which it lends
cohesion. Imagination is a counterpoise to the mechanism
which eliminates self-determination. As Coleridge noted, if
the subject is determined by matter, it disappears. It does
not create: it watches the process of creation flow through
it.[17] For Coleridge, it is imagination which makes the human
self distinct from its environment. 'Imagination' not only
'reconciles' the faculties: it also makes human beings into real
subjects.[18]
   Coleridge goes on to define imagination as the power

through which the human 'I' repeats the I AM of the Creator. Imagination is said to grasp and to imitate the pulsing heart of nature. For Schelling, as for Coleridge, the imagination that knows the forms of nature participates in the creative energy through which God is making the universe.[19] The highest unity that imagination achieves is that between the finite and the infinite. The unity of divine and human energy is represented in a symbol. When Coleridge said that symbols express the compenetration of God and nature, he gave to beauty a value which neither Thomas' theology nor Kant's philosophy had accorded it.[20] The mind is anchored in reality by the beautiful symbol. Such symbols imitate God's creation of the world.[21]

The unity which imagination discerns informs an extended object. It is captured in the object's 'mid-point': in the centre which each of the parts imitate, and with which they are causally inbound.[22] That form may become, as Coleridge said, 'a mid-point, in which the historical and the spiritual meet.'[23] For Coleridge, Christ is the perfect Image, who holds one arm out to humanity and the other to God, joining the two.

And yet, as Philippe Lacoue-Labarthe observes, the Romantic 'organon easily becomes organization'.[24] Romanticism is dazzled by the *production* of form. Kant had aligned productive imagination with human spontaneity. The Romantics envisage creative imagination as the source of personal autonomy.[25] If the result is the absolutization of human freedom, then imagining is propelled by a *will* which is empowered wholly to reformulate reality. Voluntarism is an inalienable element of the Idealism which was the Romantics' philosophical inspiration. They are therefore fascinated by *poiesie*, as something which we *do*, and thus by 'putting-into-form', or *Bildung*.[26]

To some extent, then, the Romantic mind was guided by the energy of the will. Its 'imagination' invents its own world. Whilst Schelling, for example, says that *poiesie* engages with nature, he believes that the beauty which it represents is extrasensory, or non-factual. He also has little sense of nature as an entity existentially distinct from the Creator. His 'nature' is not autonomous enough to mediate between the poet and the Maker. Its 'unveiling' becomes a direct vision of the 'archetypes' within God.[27]

Postmodernism: Imagining Within Language

The Romantics' mantle has been taken up by Postmodernist theologians and philosophers. Lacoue-Labarthe says that August Schlegel's '*Lectures* make language . . . the original poiesy . . . by way of a reformulation of the concept of mimesis (henceforth equated with poiesis . . . [they] lead to a general linguistics.'[28] The image which fills the Postmodernist imagination is that of speech as both encompassing the human world, and yet perpetually retreating from engagement with the things and persons 'within' or 'beyond' it. Language then becomes the originary human environment, within which words are creative rather than imitative. Such words are not 'of' or 'about' the real. The seeds of the downfall of the Romantic attitude are prepared within it. For it brings about the Postmodern sense of the 'opacity of language, [its] incapacity . . . to serve the purpose of representation'.[29] Thus, Kevin Hart says that the principle that words refer to beings in their presence is the original sin of philosophy.[30] Such an apprehension underlies Michael Edwards' notion of a 'Christian Poetics'. His diagram circles the arch between Fall and ultimate redemption. He suggests that language itself, the vehicle of story, is fallen. It can no longer achieve the perfect mirroring of reality with which prelapsarian language was gifted. But there was no story-telling in Eden: 'The oneness of Eden excludes story; when evil enters to corrupt the oneness . . . story is born, as another world to be reached for, out of this one.'[31] In this engaging theory, the task of story is 're-creation', as imagination strains forward to a future paradise.

I will be both less and more optimistic. My interpretation is *less* optimistic in that it treats language as a medium of analogy, not of univocity. As one of many meaning relations between self and world, language co-operates with the multiplicity of being itself. Being is dramatic: ever multiplying its inner differences. Language must be mobile and many-sided if it is to cope with such a shifting and opaque reality. To bind the arts of imagination to the given is not to reduce it to a one-dimensional mirroring, but to present it as properly creative. I will be *more* optimistic in contending that imagination plays upon concrete facts. The moralist who finds her way out of two apparently absolute alternatives, or the businessman who invents an unnoticed need, draw upon a fallen, but still imagining humanity. We need imagination in order to make our way through the world: it need not leap forward into a future paradise in order to find meaning.

The Realistic Imagination

The realistic imagination is unlike fantasy in that it is of or about something. Imagining is a way of being related to facts. It is a means of knowing facts through images. Such images are inbuilt perspectives on reality. Experience is filtered through images. The type of world which we experience is determined by their frame. We need those images which focus upon the full density of facts. Our ways of imagining should allow us to enter the world as concrete, and individual; to know the pottery vase on the table. And so the image must have a narrow range. Specific details are the imagination's clue to the whole: it finds through them the thing's centre of action. A pattern is created: things are seen to be related to one another because each is part of an interlocking path to this centre. To experience the world through narrow images is to be directed to particular facts. Imagination thus turns facts into humanly apprehensible forms. It does not construct an internalized film of reality. Its images engage in the world. Imagining transforms the mass of mundane facts into a human world, in which order can be discovered. Images give shape to the relation between the self and the world. The image is relative to its creator because the intuition flows from a human personality. But the reality of some object is compressed into this image. The imagination is both creative and receptive. Its shapings are neither a neutrally objective record, nor simply projections. They lie between the mind and its world, holding the two together.

The imagination is adventurous when it reshapes experience into new patterns. It *need not* be so. It can close the door, and replay the old patterns. Then it will take us away from rather than toward the world. The imaginative impulse can be fantasial. But it can also be realistic: it can break with the neurotic web of certainties. It is realistic when its images are used to work with reality, by giving it definite boundaries. The imagination which *has* succeeded in engaging with the world becomes ever more optimistic. It takes chances. It invents unforeseen linkages which it turns into figurative forms by joining one link to another. It wants to do this so that experience will hang together. Imagination touches and reproduces the specific movements of concrete individuals. It uncovers the meaning of facts, and expresses it in terms which draws the self into the world. The image constructs a relation between the self and its world. It creates symbolic forms.

To find meaning in ordinariness takes imagination. All of us, even the most ascetic, do this: a well-dressed young woman becomes a princess; a less beautifully accoutred middle-aged man is the professor; an eyesore of concrete and glass is the university. Such imaginative magnifying, or embellishing, enlarges facts and persons beyond their natural confines. As opposed to the literal vision, an imaginative seeing extends its objects. Is it then, just imbuing what is there with an oversized meaning? Does the imaginative eye simply project significance on otherwise dreary facts: does it project a costume of glamour so as to conceal the naked power at the heart of things? The question, and its possible answers, tells us three things about the imagination. In the first place, an imagined person, or place, is a *humanized* fact. That is, the imagined thing has lost its neutrality, as one object amidst a thousand others: it has been given a relation to subjectivity. Second, it gains its 'archetypal' enlargement by dint of being given its situation within a human schema, or narrative. Placed within an imagined narrative, physical forces and the elements which they drive, the processes of nature and the powers wielded by human beings, are given subjective meaning: they do not simply lie about us, but lie 'toward us'; they are gathered around a human focus. The as yet unhumanized world is the cosmos of things, a dense, resistant mass of moving energies. From this the imagination shrinks back: then the sphere of human meaning and the cosmos of things become two separate trajectories which never meet. This is what Allen Tate calls 'the separation of subject and vision'.[32] Imaginative seeing joins the 'subject' with their 'vision': it finds the world within the cosmos. Third, it is an open question whether such potentially infinite imaginative enlargment and 'enworlding' can be justified: the answer is, only if this world itself contains such a depth.

The Realistic Imagination and Christology

The aim of this book is to show how such a realistic imagination can provide the human context, the subjective roots, of faith in the Incarnation of Christ. By way of the realistic imagination, I shall set out the metaphysical and epistemic presuppositions of the Incarnation. To envisage the person of Christ in the light of imagination is to comprehend him as *transcendental beauty*. Our metaphysics shall have largely to do with beauty and our epistemology will be an aesthetics.

My exposition will be guided by six figures: the philosopher Jacques Maritain, three of the leaders of the Southern literary renaissance, namely, John Crowe Ransom, Allen Tate and Caroline Gordon, and two theologians, William Lynch and Hans Urs von Balthasar. These men and women did not form a single self-conscious school. It is nonetheless my belief that their several visions are linked at the core in the fact that each finds out at the heart of things a moving, specific, and realistic analogy. It will help us both to begin to indicate what these writers have in common, and to develop our presentation of 'imagination', if we pause to note their views of the Thomistic, the Romantic, and the Postmodernist conceptions of what imagination can do.

Maritain, the Southerners, Lynch and von Balthasar believed that when imagining is not rooted in facts it merely projects fantasies. For them, as for Thomas, we have to imagine because we are embodied and 'enworlded'. They do not exaggerate the imagination's power to know absolutes. Allen Tate prefers to speak of the 'limits' of imagination than of its extents.[33] He deploys Thomas' view of imagination against what he sees as the abstraction of Romantic and post-Romantic writing. Drawing upon Maritain's *The Dream of Descartes*, Tate castigates the 'angelic intellect', which dreams of imageless thought.

These writers also consider that Romanticism has an overly subjective bias.[34] They argue that the Romantic belief that poetic energy imitates Divine creativity transforms the poet into the projector of the material world. This view of Romanticism is part of the genealogy of ideas which these analogically minded authors constructed in order to state their own positions. Von Balthasar seems to invert what he thinks is a purely creative view of imagination within the Romantic tradition, when he writes that,

> the *Einbildungskraft* ('imagination') which primarily projects from within toward the exterior, ought rather to be called *Ausbildungskraft* ('power to externalise images') whereas the process of *Ausbildung* ('education', 'formation', 'development'), in which the objective content of images is assimilated from the outside toward the exterior ought rather to be called *Einbildung* ('imaging' or 'imag-ining', that is, interiorising external images).[35]

If we are to interiorize images, the world outside of us must present them to us. These authors' view of imagination is primarily metaphysical. Von Balthasar says that Goethe's 'morphology' was one seed of his work: he is drawn by its 'piety' before the given.[36] But, without depreciating Thomas' contention that the philosopher's quest for truth transcends sensible images, the authors of whom I speak extend the place which he gave to imagination. Having given the first weight to being, they incorporate the Kantian or Romantic conception of aesthetic objects as subsistent forms. These forms are structured wholes, not simply Thomistic 'phantasms'. It is the imagination which apprehends such wholes, for it knows things in their figurative extension. Aesthetic form provides a right relation to reality. If so, then imagining is as much a way of knowing as is thinking. Thus, for the Southerners, literature is a means of knowledge; Lynch and von Balthasar can give a role to imagination in theology. Tate, who sharply criticizes Coleridge's psychological emphasis, also says that he owes 'most of all' to the poet-theologian of English Romanticism.[37] For the

Southerners and for Lynch, imagination witnesses against modern variants of 'mechanism'. The 'realistic imagination' knows that facts are not exhausted in a list of their discrete components. It discerns figures within reality, and lifts the world into meaning through them.

Frank Burch Brown indicates in his *Religious Aesthetics* a sharp disinclination for the revelational foundation of von Balthasar's theological aesthetics. He urges that the data of aesthetics may not be extrapolated from Christian doctrine. But his commitment to the complexities of aesthetics does not seem to be founded in an equally profound attachment to the reality of form. He is also disquieted by what he sees as the 'formalist' bias in the aesthetics of both Maritain and the Southern writers.[38] Once one begins to take artistic form seriously, as they do, one must ask what its ultimate basis is. Should the basis be found in a form which is buried so deep within reality that it can only be apprehended when it reveals itself, this need not be taken to undercut the givenness of the created forms in which it flowers.

The Postmodernist suspicion of form, and of representation, binds itself up with the rejection of metaphysical theologies, taken as grandiose supra-experiential designs. Drawing out the implications of Heidegger's thought, O'Leary says that metaphysical theologies superimpose a totalizing metanarrative upon experience. Kevin Hart disavows 'the attempt to unify heaven and earth by means of one structure'.[39] How would our 'analogical imaginers' respond to such negations? I think that they would begin by affirming form: for it is in the perception of form that faith is touched by the *other*.

On the other hand, they would add a 'negation' upon which Hart and O'Leary do not dwell. Created form makes existence present, but is not its ground. The 'it is' of each fact is present, not as a heavy or systematizable polyfiller, but lightly, or contingently. For von Balthasar, where the lacunae between a thing and its being is understood analogically, the

hovering within the world between Being and entity, as determined by the metaphysics of Thomas and to some extent again in Heidegger . . . prevents any fixing of beauty to . . . a readily-grasped system of concepts.[40]

This is the ontological difference between things and the being which St Thomas calls *ens*. To grasp it is to open the lacunae between *ens*, being as inherently interwoven with things, and the Being Who is self-subsistent.[41] The theological aesthetic depends upon revelation because it speaks of analogies between God and this world, not of an univocal conjunction of two 'beings' whose story is identical. Von Balthasar admires Heidegger's recognition that speech responds to the 'silence' of a 'supra-conceptual' horizon. But he believes that it is Thomas who preserves the difference and the discontinuity between the beauty of this world, and the glory of the Lord in His fulness of Being. Nor did Thomas move from the verbal negations of speech about God to a negation of the being to which they refer, as von Balthasar considers Heidegger to have done.[42] The outcome of his project will be, not a metanarrative but a 'Theodrama'. If it is interpreted dramatically, the analogy of being maintains the open spaces within existence, without conceding meaning.

How then can the perception of analogy be used to build a Christology? We begin with the mysterious givenness of being. That is, we first require a realistic metaphysics. The 'it is' of each concrete thing is manifested by its form. The existing of beings is revealed by the beautiful form, as an objective reality present both in natural things and in artistic works. The transcendent Being of God is its cause. This metaphysics is founded on the analogizing of being: that is, on the representative action which moves between the Being of God and the created being which depends upon it. Maritain's Thomistic philosophy of being is such a realistic metaphysics.

Our second task is to say how the self is real. Liberal theology thinks to achieve this by separating the objective from the existentially significant, and taking the world of meaning to repose in the latter. With Bultmann, attention to the subjective act replaced concern for its metaphysical basis: faith in Christ becomes a formless interior attitude. In like manner, Joseph O'Leary opposes the 'phenomenality' of 'originary experience' to 'onto-theology'.[43] The endeavour to touch the deepest roots of experience appears to be ever more desperate. Is this because, as Gerardus van der Leeuw argued, 'primal experience' as such is unrecoverable? It can, he suggests, only be known in that third thing which lies between subjectivity and objectivity: that is, meaning.[44] The phenomenology of religion undertakes to excavate religious meanings within the plethora of forms or types, which mediate the experience of the 'Wholly Other'. To strip theology to its existential self-certainty alone is to do justice neither to being, nor to experience. I will argue that the self is unified when it is guided by aesthetic form. The Southern writers claim that, by creating such forms, the imagination finds a centre for experience. I draw on those writings of John Crowe Ransom, Allen Tate and Caroline Gordon which contend that human experience is given meaning by the rounded patterns of form. In order to be whole, experience must be ingathered by aesthetic form.

The implicit dynamism of the imagination tends toward the transcendent basis of natural forms. Thirdly, therefore, we need to see how the imaginative grasp of form is met by One Who comes to meet it from beyond human powers of exploration. The ultimate goal of the imagination's search for meaning lies in the singular form of a supernatural Person. In Lynch and von Balthasar's writings, the Person of Christ is the historical revelation of the Form of beauty. He reveals himself to us from beyond the natural world. At the same time, He impels the human effort imaginatively to unite itself with reality. His shape converges with the patterns of imagination and yet extends infinitely beyond them.

All of these writers draw upon both a realist metaphysics and a creative doctrine of imagination. In this way, they render what is due both to the richness of being as such, and to the way in which it is apprehended. These authors share a dual adherence to a broadly Thomistic metaphysic and to a phenomenological study of the shapes of apprehension. The Thomism grounds their argument in objective being; the phenomenological data allows the person to become the focal point of that reality. The Thomistic philosophy treats being as form, which is one way of saying being as beautiful. The phenomenological aspect examines the perception of form. Both are included in the final, theological stage. Von Balthasar and Lynch point to the only good reason we have for thinking that being is a self-illuminative spectacle, in which forms entwine to construct a metaphysical theatre in which human persons act and find meaning. That is, they look to the person of Christ, as the germinal ground of all natural form. Before we can draw out the implications of such a perception of form for Christology, we must outline two further conceptions which are central to the realistic imagination.

Myth

In the cosmos of things, a struggle for survival is perpetually enacted, between snails and birds, weaker and stronger nations, lecturers and professors. The human world is also a space of conflict, defeat and death. But here, the participants are self-reflective. They assume roles and take on an identity, as characters within a story devised by themselves. A 'world' gains its form by being envisaged as the locus of a story. Only that story need be called a fantasy whose very perfection closes it to uncertainty, to change and to suffering. A genuinely imaginative story, which gives shape, not to day-dreams, but to an unpredictable cosmos, is hard won. That story which is not a magical arena from within which we control our fate, is earned by finding the dream within the facts and persons around us.

Mythic stories are one of the imagination's ways of uncovering order in experience. Mythic images interpret mundane situations. As G. S. Kirk argues, myths make specific events into exemplars for human action.[45] The Greek myths gave typical means of reacting to events; one might say, 'this is like what happened to Odysseus' and respond accordingly. All societies produce representative characters – in our own, the tycoon, the sports star, the journalist, for example – upon whom we model our lives, and which are part fantasial projection and partly a reflection of real human possibilities. Those who create them draw on the traditions, the common language of their culture. Myths are *social* symbols. They embody the 'metaphysical dream' of a society.[46]

The mythic tale is usually about the gods or the heroes. These characters, and their wondrous exploits, express extreme, or ideal types and actions. Because it contains extraordinary characters, the mythic narrative presses to the limits of experience. The myth images the world, and human action, as stretching up to a surpassing meaning. The natural world swells to include the divine. Bultmann disavowed the mythic intermingling of humanity and divinity. John Hick also speaks of a disjunction between the facts which science knows, and the mythical realm[47]. For both, myth-making is the improper ascription of what should be internal to the external world. But the mythic realm, in which the gods journey into human experience and the ordinary range of our behaviour is enlarged, may not be so irreconcilably remote from our own world. Perhaps the imaginative insight which creates mythic stories is sometimes appropriate.

Myth is sometimes said to be an exposition of the categories of the human mind, in a projected, external image.[48] Bultmann is among those who so define it. Myth-making is humanly necessary. But perhaps it reflects both the structure of the mind *and* some real thing. For myths are the means through which the community understands its experience. Consider some elements of the myth of Englishness. In the myth, the English are the island race, whose bulldog valour has consistently withheld the designs of foreigners to dominate them. No such myth would have arisen if England had been situated in the Urals, or if Drake and Nelson had not won their victories. The myth cannot perform its function unless it purports to explain historical, or social or geographical facts.

The myth points to the relation between the self-transcending human reality and a divine, or exemplary world. It may be that the great myths not only describe the congruity of divine and human acts but also effect it. The myth dramatizes the reciprocity between human openness toward the supernatural and the divine itself. Van der Leeuw claims that living myth

> is the reiterated presentation of some event replete with power. . . . Mythical repetition in the form of narrative . . . not only evokes . . . some powerful event, but it also endows this with form.[49]

For van der Leeuw, myth is the re-presentation of the power, or energy, of Being. This affiliates mythic vision to biblical revelation. The two are similar in that each has a shape, which imitates a reality. Both can be historical. When they purport to be so, both point to a specific fact – the defeat of the Armada or Israel's return from exile. The two must not be wholly disassociated: the theological imagination needs the sensitivity which led Patristic authors to compare Odysseus at the mast to Christ upon the Cross.[50] Nor does the difference consist solely in the greater objectivity of revelation, for the biblical historians had to *interpret* their community's experience.

In his *Histories*, Herodotus described the victory of the 'democratic' Greeks over the 'despotic' Persians as a victory for the human spirit which was aided by the gods.[51] It was. But if it is identified with those events in which the Spirit of God is thought to have interceded, the event of revelation becomes indistinguishable from the immanent process of human self-liberation. It is then enclosed in, and wholly defined by, human progress. Revelation transcends myth because its source lies beyond immanent being. The figures of revelation are historical facts in which the finger of God came out and met us.

For Lynch, faith means 'putting on the mind of God, with which to see reality'.[52] The theological imagination first assimilates the events in which God manifested Himself, to Israel, in Christ's life, and in communal religious experience. It then envisages reality through those images. Having considered the objective meaning conveyed by the images, the theologian makes it subjectively accessible to others, by showing how it can be imaginatively interiorized. This requires the indwelling work of Christ. Von Balthasar states that when this happens,

> Christian contemplation becomes an ever deeper . . . living from Christ . . . and . . . both the . . . triune God and the whole of creation enter into this life . . . within the shaping (*Einbildung*) of the image (Bild) of Christ in the contemplative subject. For the theological imagination (*Einbildungskraft* = 'power to shape an image') lies with Christ, who is at once the image (*Bild*) and the power (*Kraft*) of God.[53]

The first motion is the imprinting of the image of Christ in the believer's imagination. His self-revelation issues from the 'future' of the mythic mind. Thus, von Balthasar says that the Old Testament has the immanent aesthetic at its back and the transcendental aesthetic before it, in the New Testament.[54]

Both mythical imagination and revelation are bound to the particular. When the intellect touches a concrete fact, and the senses intuit its meaning, we regain what Edwards is right to see as a lost perfection. Maritain suggests that beauty in art 'has the savour of the terrestrial paradise because it restores . . . the simultaneous peace and delight of the mind and the senses'.[55]

If theology were founded in the definite, historical figure of Christ, such mythical apprehension would be extended toward prophetic vision. In addition to the movement of the mind towards the finite, there is the historical procession of the ultimate individual toward the human mind.

Dramatic Expression

Expressing means displaying. An expression is the presented reality of a feeling, an idea, or an attitude. An object is expressive when its contours and movements overflow from its own directive dynamism. Wittgenstein noted that, in order to find out what it is for someone to understand music, we need not hypothetically construct the internal scenario of their 'understanding'. Rather, we should watch the 'expressive movements' by which it is shown.[56] Whatever is being 'carried forward' in a person or object is drawn by the centrifugal action of meaning to become an expressed form. Further, just as we do not understand others by peering behind their gestures, nor do we capture the meaning of the work of art by looking beyond it. Wittgenstein said that a work of art is 'a felt expression. And . . . in so far as people understand it, they "resonate" in harmony with it . . . the work of art does not aim to convey something else, just itself.'[57] We look to the expressed form in order to find the meaning, for it is this which makes it visible.

Beauty has been described as 'expressive form'.[58] The authors whom I examine consider that beauty is characteristically communicative. Von Balthasar says, for example, that Karl Barth's writings are beautiful because their classical objectivity issues in lucid expression.[59] Beauty is at the heart of these authors' writings because it is expressive.

'Expression' and drama come together in Caroline Gordon's interpretation of Henry James' work: 'the word "scenic" means "dramatic". James conceives of the novel in terms of the scene or picture (something to be . . . watched, not talked about).'[60]

Drama is expressive because it sets a theme into movement, and so manifests its form. We can therefore reply to it in an imaginative way. The imagination can trace out the figure which the drama enacts, and repeat it. Francis Fergusson says that this requires the 'histrionic sensibility', which mirrors a dramatic theme in its own acts. For Lynch, the art of Christian life is the imitation of the dramatic stages of Christ's life. The imagination unifies the corpus of things with which it is faced by gathering them around specific 'scenes'.[61] The 'scenic' imagination can focus on the factual density of the world. Such an imagination is empowered by the figure of Christ. Lynch says that Christ is expressive just because His form is limited by boundaries. His life is a dramatic form, for it can be envisaged in small, communicative 'scenes'.

If we are to imagine a universe in which Christ could reveal Himself, we need to recover the analogizing movement of being between God and the world. For von Balthasar, the analogy of being is not a stable floor, or even an escalator, upon which human beings stand. It is a drama; a thing done. The stage is made in the interplay of human and divine characters. Heaven and earth together create the Theo-drama. What we know of God is given only through His involvement in the divine-human drama.[62] But the play is in His hands. His acts are reiterated, not created, by our narrating. In myth, being is proportioned, or related, to the finite human mind: the drama of revelation unfolds the actions of the God who is the fullness of being.

Comedy and tragedy are the two kinds of dramatic expression which we will consider. Each of these forms is a perspective upon reality. Each creates the world in which its appropriate action can take place. Achieved tragedy and comedy give us a complete vision of life, as does the world of myth. Like a Greek vase, its 'high', perhaps infinite gods are on the rim and finite humanity is in the base. But the dramatic theme is in motion, and so the two must be moving toward one another.

In tragedy, the action is a descent. It is as though the vase were overturned, and the protagonist were being pushed down, into an infinite.[63] Because its protagonist becomes enmeshed in an uncontrollable infinitude, the events in tragedy are inevitable. In comedy, the characters are making an ascent, towards the gods. It celebrates the strange reversal and the lucky chance: the weddings and feasts with which it often concludes are tributes to the contingency and the plurality of existence.

These are two ways of imagining the movement of life, each having a solid base and a transcendent horizon. This movement can be known both poetically and through revelation. I designate Tate and von Balthasar as tragedians, and Ransom, Caroline Gordon and Lynch as masters of comedy.

Conclusion

We are faced with two questions. First, there is the Christological issue: how could a single fact be God? Aesthetics offers us no automatic resolution. It seems perverse to draw upon beauty in order to respond to it. For, second, imagination has become more a vehicle of fantasy than a means of exploring reality. Whilst popular science fiction proliferates, the academy has allowed the beautiful to consume the real. The magical sphere of words replaces hard and refractory reality. Imagining, as pure invention, is taken as a means of control. Our argument thus has two sides. First, that the most fertile locus for imagining is not the possible, but the real. Second, faith in the person of Christ – the simple, literal fact – gives to the imagination its concrete ground.

We will take imagining to be a way of uncovering symbolic form within the world. Such forms are self-communicating actions: scenes from a drama. As such, they lend themselves to story-form, or to the myth, in which the elevation of this world is represented by the contact of divine and heroic persons.

Because the mythic imagination focuses on a specific object, it may be a path toward the God who is not the most abstract of conceptual generalizations, but a Trinity of Persons. But if we refine the imagination's path into a thread which leads only from human self to personal God, we may find that we have lost the world, in which images must be embedded. We turn now to one way of losing the metaphysical basis of theology.

NOTES

1 St Thomas Aquinas, *Summa Theologiae*, Ia, Q. 75, Art. 2, ad 3.
2 St Thomas Aquinas, 'Should We Entirely Abandon the Imagination in Divine Science?', *The Division and Method of the Sciences*, Question VI, Art. 2, Reply.
3 St Thomas Aquinas, *Summa Theologiae*, IIa IIae, Q. 173, Art. 2, 3.
4 St Thomas Aquinas, *Summa Contra Gentiles*, II. 73, 38.
5 Sensibility limits imagination: Robert D. Hume, 'Kant and Coleridge on Imagination', in *Journal of Aesthetics and Art Criticism*, 28 (1969–1970), p. 487. Understanding limits imagination: Theodore Uehling, *The Notion of Form in Kant's Critique of Aesthetic Judgement*, pp. 53–55.
6 W. H. Walsh, *Kant's Criticism of Metaphysics*, pp. 66–69 and 72–73; Kant, *Critique of Pure Reason*, pp. 104–105 and 119.
7 Uehling, *Form*, pp. 55–56.
8 Hume, 'Kant and Coleridge', pp. 388–389.
9 Immanuel Kant, *Critique of Judgement*, Part I: Critique of Aesthetic Judgement, pp. 143 and 176; R. D. Hume, 'Kant and Coleridge', p. 448; Robert L. Zimmerman, 'Kant: The Aesthetic Judgement', in R. P. Wolff (ed.), *Kant: A Collection of Critical Essays*, pp. 388–389.
10 Kant, *Critique of Judgement*, Part I, pp. 58, 71–75, 142–143; James Engell, *The Creative Imagination: Enlightenment to Romanticism* pp. 130–133. Engell notes that Kant moved toward a more objective view.
11 J. W. von Goethe, *Theory of Colours* (1810), pp. 279–280 and 319–320.
12 René Wellek, 'The Concept of Romanticism in Literary History', in *Concepts of Criticism*, pp. 136–137.
13 Schelling defines *phantasie* as reproductive imagination, and *Einbildungskraft* as creative power in *The Philosophy of Art* (The Jena Lectures of 1802–1803), p. 38. See also Engell, *Creative Imagination*, pp. 181–182 and Thomas McFarland, *Coleridge and the Pantheist Tradition* pp. 33–34. For Schelling's idea of *Einbildungskraft* see *The Philosophy of Art*, pp. 31–32 and the selections from his *System of Transcendental Idealism* in David Simpson (ed.), *The Origins of Modern Critical Thought: German Aesthetic and Literary Criticism from Lessing to Hegel*, pp. 226–229. On Schelling's effect on Coleridge's aesthetics: G. N. G. Orsini, *Coleridge and German Idealism: A Study in the History of Philosophy*, pp. 222–229.
14 S. T. Coleridge, 'On the Principles of Genial Criticism Concerning the Fine Arts', in *Biographia Literaria*, edited by J. Shawcross, Volume II, p. 232. Whilst Coleridge was fascinated by Schelling's *Einbildungskraft*, he retained

the distinction between divine and human imagination: Orsini, *German Idealism*, pp. 223–225.

15 Coleridge, the 'Fragment of An Essay on Taste', in Shawcross (ed.), p. 248.

16 Coleridge's imagination is 'the whole mind harmonized by its . . . aesthetic intention'. Kenneth Millar, *The Inward Eye: A Re-evaluation of Coleridge's Psychological Criticism*, p. 348.

17 Coleridge, *Biographia Literaria*, edited by James Engell and W. Jackson Bate Vol. II, pp. 15–16.

18 Ibid. p. 304.

19 As with Coleridge's 'primary imagination': *Biographia Literaria*, edited by James Engell and W. Jackson Bate, Vol. I, p. 304.

20 Schelling, *The Philosophy of Art*, pp. 29, 45–46, and 166; S. T. Coleridge 'On Poesy or Art', in Shawcross (ed.), p. 259; M. H. Abrams, *The Mirror and The Lamp: Romantic Theory and the Critical Tradition*, pp. 294–296.

21 Coleridge, *Biographia Literaria*, Vol. I. p. 304.

22 Coleridge, 'On Poetry or Art', in Shawcross (ed.), p. 255 and 'On the Principles of Genial Criticism', ibid, p. 232.

23 Coleridge, *Confessions of an Inquiring Spirit*, edited by Henry Nelson Coleridge, p. 42; Engell, *Creative Imagination*, pp. 220–222 and 253.

24 Philippe Lacoue-Labarthe and Jean-Luc Nancy, *The Literary Absolute: The Theory of Literature in German Romanticism*, p. 36.

25 Edward S. Casey, *Imagining: A Phenomenological Study*, pp. 183–185.

26 Lacoue-Labarthe, *The Literary Absolute*, p. 104.

27 Schelling, *The Philosophy of Art*, pp. 7, 32, 129, 133.

28 Lacoue-Labarthe and Nancy, *The Literary Absolute*, p. 93.

29 Hayden White, *Tropics of Discourse: Essays in Cultural Criticism*, p. 244.

30 Kevin Hart, *The Trespass of the Sign: deconstruction, theology and philosophy* p. 18.

31 Michael Edwards, *Towards a Christian Poetics*, pp. 9–13 and 73.

32 Allen Tate, 'Introduction to *White Buildings* by Hart Crane', in *Memories and Essays: Old and New: 1926–1974* p. 111.

33 Robert Dupree, *Allen Tate and the Augustinian Imagination: A Study of the Poetry*, p. 9.

34 William Lynch, *Christ and Apollo: The Dimensions of the Literary Imagination*, pp. 158–159; Allen Tate, 'Literature as Knowledge', in *Collected Essays*, pp. 35–40.

35 Hans Urs von Balthasar, *The Glory of the Lord: A Theological Aesthetics: Volume I. Seeing the Form*, pp. 178–179.

36 Hans Urs von Balthasar, *The Glory of the Lord: A Theological Aesthetics: V: The Realm of Metaphysics in the Modern Age*, pp. 362 and 408.

37 Radcliffe Squires, *Allen Tate: A Literary Biography*, p. 194 (unattributed).

38 Frank Burch Brown, *Religious Aesthetics: A Theological Study of Making and Meaning*, pp. 5–6, 19–20 and 28.

39 Joseph O'Leary, *Questioning Back: The Overcoming of Metaphysics in Christian Tradition*, pp. 20, 25; Hart, *The Trespass of the Sign*, p. 110.

40 Von Balthasar, *Glory: V*, p. 598.

41 Hans Urs von Balthasar, *The Glory of the Lord: A Theological Aesthetics: IV: The Realm of Metaphysics in Antiquity*, pp. 374, 395.

42 Von Balthasar, *Glory: V*, pp. 438–447.

43 O'Leary, *Questioning Back*, pp. 11–12 and 94.

44 Gerardus van der Leeuw, *Religion in Essence and Manifestation: A Study in Phenomenology*, p. 673.

45 G. S. Kirk, *The Nature of Greek Myths*, pp. 289–291.

46 Richard Weaver, *Ideas Have Consequences*, p. 88.

47 Rudolf Bultmann, 'New Testament and Mythology', in Hans Werner Bartsch (ed.), *Kerygma and Myth*, pp. 1–44 (pp. 1–2 and 6–7); John Hick, 'Jesus and the World Religions', in Hick (ed), *The Myth of God Incarnate*, p. 178.

48 Karl Philipp Moritz held that 'Narcissus and Eros were part of the expression of archetypal human nature'. Quoted in Engell, *Creative Imagination*, pp. 113–114.

49 van der Leeuw, *Religion in Essence*, pp. 413–414.

50 Hugo Rahner, *Greek Myths and Christian Mystery*, pp. 371–383.

51 Herodotus, *The Histories*, translated by Aubrey de Selincourt, e.g. pp. 487–490.

52 William Lynch, *Images of Hope: Imagination as Healer of the Hopeless*, p. 249.

53 Von Balthasar, *Glory: I*, p. 490.

54 Ibid. pp. 331–338. This parallels St Thomas' view, as cited by Victor White: 'at the . . . end of St Thomas' *De Prophetica* (*De Ver.* xii. 14 ad 5). . . He writes: 'When Moses is said to be superior to the other prophets, this is to be understood of prophets of the Old Testament; for to that epoch, while Christ . . . was still awaited, prophecy . . . belongs. But . . . in the New Testament a clearer revelation was made, on account of which the Apostle in II Corinthians 3:18 sets himself . . . above Moses.' . . . Revelation is . . . now . . . an event of recognition of the interior image . . . in the exterior.' *God and the Unconscious* pp. 152–153.

55 Jacques Maritain, *Art and Scholasticism and Other Essays* (Paris, 1922), p. 24.

56 Ludwig Wittgenstein, *Culture and Value*, edited by G. H. von Wright, pp. 51–52

57 Ibid. p. 58.

58 Suzanne Langer, *Feeling and Form*, p. 396.

59 Hans Urs von Balthasar, *The Theology of Karl Barth*, pp. 22–23.

60 Caroline Gordon, *How to Read a Novel*, p. 118.

61 Francis Fergusson, *The Idea of a Theatre: A Study of Ten Plays. The Art of Drama in Changing Perspective* p. 236 and 238.

62 Hans Urs von Balthasar, *Theo-Drama: Theological Dramatic Theory: II: Dramatis Personae: Man in God*, pp. 173–183 and 196.

63 Comedy contrasted with tragedy: Allardyce Nicoll, *The Theatre and Dramatic Theory*, pp. 104–106, 136; Langer, *Feeling and Form*, pp. 331–334 and Robert Dupree, 'The Copious Inventory of Comedy', in *The Terrain of Comedy*, edited by Louise Cowan, p. 170.

Chapter 2

Learning from Kant's Mistakes

This chapter describes the theological effects of Kant's 'Copernican revolution'. These extend from the elucidation of Christology in what George Lindbeck terms 'experiential-expressive' categories, to the 'public' criteria which govern postliberal theology.[1] During the seventeenth century the model of science became descriptive rather than explanatory. In response to the challenge of Humean empiricism, Kant takes up the task of describing the a priori conditions of human experience. He argues that they are provided by the categorializing activity of the understanding. The understanding is not wholly constructive, for it reacts on the senses. But, for us, the given is that which our minds have framed in categorical unity, not the world as it is in itself. The mind is circumscribed by the reality which a subject can experience. We only know phenomena, or things in relation to our perspective. Beyond this lies the noumenal realm, the world of things as they are in themselves.[2] The noumenal realm guarantees the objectivity of thought, because it is beyond the scope of the mind. It is, Kant tells us, 'an unbounded, but, also, inaccessible field'.[3] Critical philosophers, such as Kant himself, describe how we experience the world. They will not purport to explain it.

God as the Source of Moral Action

How does Kant portray the existence of the Being Who wholly transcends our perspective? Pure reason cannot show that God exists for, as Kant considers, its principles are 'immanent in experience'.[4] When pure reason regards its ideas as objective rather than regulatory, it creates illusions. Practical reason is the source of moral activity. Ethical behaviour finds a ground, and an essential stimulant in the idea of God.[5] God is the goal of the practical, willed endeavour to be good.

When I rise to a specific situation which requires a moral attitude, I step out of my materially conditioned behaviour, and act within the noumenal realm. Having been given access to the noumenal realm by the exercise of moral reason, I may say that God exists. Only an 'I' can make this affirmation. The proposition 'God exists' must be the 'belief' of a self. It cannot hold good in abstraction from a human subject.

Such a God is primarily the ground of good behaviour. We need only be concerned with those of His attributes which affect how we ought to live. Instead of naming God as 'Creator' we may entitle Him the 'Holy Legislator'. The good, like being or truth, might overspill our capacity to conceive it. But since, here, the good is known through reflection on our own moral reason, it is not seen as an element of outward reality. As Maritain says, Kant's ethic appears to be 'a-cosmic'.[6] Kant's God, as a guarantor of right deeds, exists in reference to moral decision. If God's reality is affirmed as a requirement for human actions, He may appear to be constituted by them. By envisaging God as the source of free ethical action, rather than as that which receptive contemplation discovers, Kant seems to make His existence dependent upon a choice of the human will. Even sympathetic commentators concede that it is difficult to say that it is 'true' that God exists on the volitional grounds which Kant supplies.[7]

Kant's Christology and Its Aftermath

In his *Religion Within the Limits of Reason Alone*, Kant posits an 'archetype of moral perfection'. The archetype exists in our reason. It is a requirement of moral life, setting up an ultimate goal towards which we may strive. The conditions of human thought – and these alone – make it necessary for us to imagine the archetype of moral perfection in human form. This is the place of the person of Christ. But the significance of the archetype is its existence in our moral reason, not its manifestation in the external world of appearances.[8] Even if it had occurred, an historical incarnation of the archetype would be an irrelevance. It is not meaning-bearing things, but moral decisions, pivoting on an effort of the will, which propel us into the noumenal world. Phenomenal facts are not its vehicles. For the noumenal is not only the sphere of objectivity: it is also that of freedom. Moral activity frees us from confinement in the categorialized world, to which space and time belong. When we enter the noumenal realm, we lift the carapace of phenomena, and so transcend the conditions of time.[9] Having separated objective meaning from both facticity and temporality, Kant cannot enmesh the idea of Christ as the symbol of universal moral perfection with that of Christ as a historical figure.

Kant believed that the moral 'archetype' is known introspectively. From this flows the major problem of modern Christology: the Christ of faith and the historical Jesus are taken to be separable. Those who choose the earthly half think of Jesus as the man with the mission ethically to uplift our hearts[10]. Kant was not an 'exemplarist'[11]. But his moralized theology, and his closure of history, shutting out the noumenal, opened the way to the image of Jesus as a moral teacher. There followed the many reconstructions of Jesus' life, assembled from sources believed to lie behind the New Testament. But, as Martin Kahler observed, 'the Gospels are the . . . opposite of the embellishing, rationalizing, psychologizing rhetoric of the . . . biographies of Jesus.' [12]

Kant's endeavour to enable the human subject ethically to 'legislate for itself' is one source of modern 'Prometheanism'.[13] For much of classical and medieval thought, the moving principle of reality is being: for the post-Kantian Idealists, it is *will*. The human subject will soon be imagined as an animal which survives by manipulating rather than as a creature which knows by responding. For some philosophers, the self as will takes the throne of God. And yet, each increasingly grandiose attempt to expand the subject is succeeded by an anti-metaphysical reaction.

A form of Neo-Kantianism emerged at Marburg University at the turn of this century. Its protagonists were Hermann Cohen, Wilhelm Hermann, and Paul Natorp.[14] For these men, Kant had erred by excess, in allowing that external sense impressions impinge on the mind, and in granting the existence of the transcendent noumenon. The Neo-Kantians were not slow to attenuate still further the threads binding the subject to an objective world. They eliminated both sense impressions and the thing-in-itself. Left without a given world, the subject must produce its own, not at random, but in obedience to law.

This extension of Kant's philosophy lies behind Bultmann's demythologization programme. He regards 'knowledge' as an 'objectification', that is, as the projection of a cohesive world-picture. As the construction of human rationality, theology's 'cosmological' myths obscure genuine faith. Such 'objectivity' must be stripped from the New Testament story.[15] Bultmann inverts the 'Prometheanism' of Neo-Kantianism. Conceived as power, or Absolute Will, exteriority threatens the subject. Bultmann divests us of our world-projecting powers, so to recover our authentic dependence on God.[16]

He was proceeding along the well-trod path of what Lindbeck calls 'experiential-expressivist' theology. Schleiermacher was its first advocate. Such theology subscribes both to Kant's turn to the experiencing subject and to the naturalism noted by Kahler. The religious core experience is said to be naked: the story which it tells is a secondary accretion. The reconstruction of Christ's inward experience now becomes the focus of research. The experiential-expressivist seeks to plumb His interiority. Thus, Schleiermacher based his Christology in Jesus' supreme feeling of dependence upon God.[17] Edward Schillebeeckx likewise bases his Christology in the 'unprecedented depth' of Jesus' 'Abba experience'. This is said to give rise to a 'disclosure experience' in His disciples.[18] The model is descriptive: it looks first to how Christ's experience was constituted.

The gospels provide a thin resource for the undertaking. Mark shows us Jesus rushing into the fray against the demonic powers. The gospels' turning points, as the Baptism, the incident at Caesarea Philippi, the final week in Jerusalem, are depicted as stages in a journey, not as moments of interior crisis. In the Synoptic gospels, his mission is to preach the kingdom. As in the Old Testament, it is the characters' speech, their interchange with others, which tells us who they are.[19] John's gospel, in particular, is moved along by dialogue. Anything we may gather from the gospels about Jesus' inner experience is as much an interpretative inference as were the schemas of classical Christology. Indeed, as much a theological inference: E. P. Sanders properly castigated those who think they have discovered proof of Jesus' unique self-consciousness in His apocalyptic pronouncements. As empirical evidence, such data is vulnerable to the question whether other first-century charismatics might not equally have believed themselves to be inaugurating the Kingdom.[20] The evidence of experience will not produce proof of universality. The Evangelists went beyond the biographical imperative when they arranged their material within a story structured by a theological claim. If that tale is one of journeying, contestation and healing, it is more closely linked to the Christologies whose metaphysical affirmation is primary, than to those which replace statements about the forms of existence with analyses of the texture of experience.

Whilst many who follow Kant's lead underscore the value of experience, they seldom envisage it as having a form: shapeliness belongs to objectivity, which is inimical to existential significance. Interiority is left in a vacuum, with no finite fact to draw it out into reality. Such is the thought of Bultmann, and of *The Myth of God Incarnate*.[21] That text is half forgotten. But experiential-expressivism dies hard in an empirical culture. This may, as Lindbeck says, be due to the sociological effect of the privatization of the forms of faith.[22] On his analysis, such theologies reflect a subjectivized religiosity. But it may be that Post-Kantian thought does not intensify the subject. Rather, it noughts it. The Kantian 'self' has no substantial form: it is a position through which perceptions pass. For the Romantics, 'all that remains of the "subject" is an "empty form" (a purely logical necessity, said Kant; a grammatical exigency, Nietzsche will say) that "accompanies my representations".'[23] Bultmann's 'self', as a pure faculty of putting-into-decision, is likewise chimerical. The post-Kantian subject is easily undermined.

The result is a continuing recoil from fact and event. Hence, the reassertion of objectivity is not sufficient. The subject must not be abandoned to a world of objective forms which have no sense for them. If we are not to follow Joseph O'Leary in giving up all 'metaphysical names' for Christ, we require a Christology both objective and phenomenological.[24] The theological aesthetic both speaks of metaphysical foundations and includes human experience within them.

Kant's Aesthetic: Private and Public

Kant's view of beauty, and of the sublime, lie behind the Romantic faith in the redemptive quality of art. He believed that, when it is aligned to symbols of the good, beauty gives us access to the noumenal world.[25] Kant links the formal representation of beauty to the thing in itself; some critics claim that he allows facts and values to coinhere in beautiful form, if nowhere else. Others recognize that Kant regards the noumenal realm as being latent within the artist's nature.[26] Beauty is said to reveal the supra-material basis of the artist's subjectivity.[27] We are again referred back into the depths of the subject. Moreover, Kant excludes both knowledge and practical intentions from aesthetic judgements. Aesthetic judgements are non-referential. They are not true, since artistic objects are said to make no affirmation about the world, nor good, since they do not lead to action.[28] Such aesthetic judgements appear to take place in an existential vacuum. This idea of beauty neither supplies a bond to the external world, nor provides a path leading to a meaning outside the self.

This is not to say that Kant regards beauty as a private matter. Judgements about beauty depend upon a 'common public sense'. We have, he says, a right to expect that there be a parallel between the pleasure which I take in the harmony of understanding and imagination and that which every one else enjoys: it is to this parallelism that the universality of aesthetic judgements is due. Our judgement moves around the circle of individuals, without also passing through an objective artistic form. Kant calls the universality which he ascribes to beauty a 'subjective universal communicability'.[29]

The two forms of relativism which have marked the course of aesthetic theory until the present day are both present in Kant's work. His aesthetic has two thrusts. The first focuses so intently on the formal qualities of art that it loses sight of beauty's participation in reality. It is for this offence that von Balthasar names Kant as 'the first theoretician of abstract art.'[30] As Frank Burch Brown notes, Kant is the 'fountainhead' of the 'formalism' which is the precursor of the 'absurdist' refusal to find any objective meaning in artistic works.[31]

Kant's second thrust locates the validity of judgements about art in the judging community. Now, it would be impossible to tell someone that one is an absurdist unless one's interlocutor were not, since the statement of the relativism of aesthetic judgements requires a shared understanding of the meaning of the sentences in which it is posed. Thus, Burch Brown's means of avoiding relativism is to define the aesthetic object in terms of its relation to a community.[32] His 'aestheticon' is to be understood in terms of the 'aesthetic milieu' in which it is perceived: as and when the context varies, so too will our perception of the object. As he has it, an object is or becomes 'aesthetic' only if it can be 'publicly recognizable' as such. Although perhaps necessary, such a criterion is, as I take it, insufficient, if it is intended to safeguard the objectivity of meaning. For this requires a distinction, such as that made by Roman Ingarden, between the 'artistic' and the 'aesthetic object'.[33] The 'artistic' object is a form sprung with potential meanings. When an audience puts those meanings into motion, or actualizes them, it creates the aesthetic object. There is one 'Water Music', as an artistic object. Many and various are the performances in which audience and orchestra bring it to aesthetic life. The aesthetic object is a concretization of this one work if it draws upon the finite range of meanings which the artistic object intends. If we try to do without the artistic object as a guide to the multitude of responses, these latter cease to be given back to itself. To locate the reality of the art work in a responding community, is to leave the field open to the 'absurdists', for it is now the endless interpretations of the audience which lend meaning to the work.

Burch Brown's project reflects the atmosphere of Postliberal theology.[34] It was Hans Frei who first argued, against the experientialism of Bultmann, that the unique '. . . identity of Jesus . . . is not given simply in his inner intention, as a kind of story behind the story. It is given, rather, in the enactment of his intentions.'[35] Under Frei's influence, Postliberalism seized upon the verbal narrative as the key to theology. Just as we know no Christ 'outside the story', so our own experience is conformed to, rather than expressed by, the given religious narrative. In addition, Postliberalism underlines the public framework of meaning. Lindbeck claims that a 'cultural-linguistic' formulation of doctrine will be based in language – which is necessarily public – rather than in the private experience to which liberal theology has recourse.[36] For Christian theology, the common language is that of Scripture. Lindbeck's Postliberalism is an 'intra-textual' theology. Because the public narrative of Scripture defines for believers the whole of reality, they need not – and cannot – consider whether it refers to something beyond itself. Lindbeck carefully distinguishes his position from that of the 'propositionalists', who judge doctrine by its correspondence to external reality.[37] The biblical stories are foundational for doctrine because they have become a *shared* narrative. This is the parallel to Kant's 'public aesthetics argument'.

Lindbeck says rightly that Christian theology has been entrusted with a set of stories. To interpret the life of Christ is to move with a narrative, not to home in on an essence. Lynch and von Balthasar equally reject propositionalism, if this is what it is taken to imply. But they go one step further: the tale informs 'extra-textual' reality. The story binds the community because it is the bond of being. Moreover, they set the 'book' into the free play of history.

Summing up; and an Alternative Path

Just as Descartes mislaid the dialogic quality of human life, so Kant denies the reciprocity between God and the world. His ethical God, set outside the categories of space and time, is singularly immobile. Classical Christian metaphysics believed that God transcends space and time. It was yet able to imagine being as a moving space, founded in God's free causality and travelling its round of procession and return to Him. There is no such mobile, and ontological, path between God and persons in Kant's philosophy. Here God and world are external one to the other. They may never invade the self-enclosed laws of the other. Having disavowed the analogy of being, Kant loses the category of *representation*, which is found in the true proposition, the beautiful form and the ethical role: that is, where one being stands for another. This makes the 'Christological dilemma' insoluble.

Each of the post-Kantian philosophers built on different aspects of his thought, taken as absolutes in themselves, and as separate one from another. Fichte argued that it is ethical duty which compels us to acquiesce in the reality of the world.[38] When theology looks solely to 'orthopraxis' it has Fichte as its ancestor. Schelling, for his part, made the beautiful the ground of reality.[39] When theology, or biblical criticism, envisage the realm of story either as a paradisial poetics or as a self-regulatory grammar, which do not inform the world in which we live, they are indebted to Schelling's belief that beauty could stand alone, without reference to being or to truth.

Our authors agree with Kant that the purpose of artistic form is neither to direct us to ethical deeds, nor to supply pictorial illustrations of philosophical truths. But, on the other hand, Maritain, the Southern writers and von Balthasar all recognized that truth, goodness, and beauty are part of the fabric of being. It is only thus that a beautiful image can contain and transmit the call of the good, the affirmation of the true and the 'is-ing' of being. In this, their work stands in contrast to Kantian formalism.

For they consider that truth, beauty and the good are each objective realities. Beauty is reality under the aspect of form, known by imaginative intuition. Truth is reality as best known propositionally. The good is that which is to be done; it is a reality touched upon in the course of action upon the stage of human life. Both the good and the beautiful are given by recreating their shape, in practice. They thus depend upon a communal code of action, or upon a myth. For Allen Tate, myth is 'a dramatic projection of heroic action, or of the failure of heroic action, upon the reality of the common life of a society, so that the myth is the reality.'[40]

Truth, beauty and the good belong to the same world, manifesting itself in distinct but related ways. The departure from formalism lies in the contention that artistic forms entwine in the energies of real being. As dramatic actions, artistic forms are joined to the movement of life. These authors place beauty within a structure of analogy. For Maritain, beauty is an analogous property of being which is present in all things. The Southerners argue that the literary image *is* a reality: this is the 'is' of generative analogy. The image is related to real actions. When her perception is informed by the image, the reader becomes one with it: to be 'caused' on this level is to be elevated to a unifying vision of meaning. I shall present the Southerners' writings as mythic renditions of the unity of being. In Lynch, human actions are 'inbinded' by the form of Christ. For von Balthasar, Christ is the sovereign analogue of beauty. His form dwells within all created analogues. Without the analogous movement of being from below, the power of form to encapsulate meaning is lost; if we lack the analogizing descent of Form from above, the myths have not their ground.

Maritain describes beauty as the 'radiance of all the transcendentals united'.[41] The largest value of beauty for theology is that it communicates the reality of all of the transcendentals. If being, truth and the good are interpreted in its light, their own reality will shine forth. Beautiful, formed objects are the ingathering, and the outpouring of the intelligibility of *being*. The intrinsic ordering of the artistic image displays the order within reality. The image gives the *true* proposition its place within a synthetic reality. The causal force of the true proposition can then be interpreted as the reciprocity of characters with their world. Beauty gives the *good* a new context. The idea of the good has a particular reference to the identity of the 'I'. For we may only ascribe moral responsibility to an 'I' which is continuously self-identical across time. The good is not the blind effort of an 'a-cosmic' will to create its own world stage. It is, rather, the struggle to wrest a form from the recalcitrant clay of reality. The good is brought to form in the contest of a real self with a real other. Under the aegis of beauty, that is, being is seen as a drama. Beauty reveals the outward depth of being, and that as expressed by a single, personal and historical Image. As the concrete and historical expression of beauty, Christ both holds the transcendentals together and renders them presentable.

Any theology which narrows the scope of its metaphysics to the degree that it must remove individual spatial and temporal incidents in Christ's life from the ground of faith undercuts the reasons it gives for the historical Incarnation as such. The presence of beauty is not disengaged from space or from time. Thus, another facet of the theological significance of beauty is its definite shaping of its external material. The biblical history lives in extensional figures. Christ Himself is a Form: He is an image which appears in the sequential structures of time and in a localized space. His Incarnation issues from an analogizing of being which is personal, and therefore free. He communicates, or effects, an exchange of being between infinite and finite freedom. Here, as von Balthasar says, 'We encounter the mystery of the analogy of personality, which strikes so violently against our Cartesian spirit.'[42]

Through a metaphysics and a poetics of analogy, our three stages have both to rebuild the external world and to show how it is open both to human persons and to Christ.

For beauty is double-sided: it communicates its own, objective existence. In its expressiveness, it gives itself to perceivers. In his study of tragic drama, Aristotle portrays beauty as an inherent property of an object in its relation to an audience:

> Beauty is . . . impossible either 1) in a very minute creature, since . . . perception becomes indistinct as it approaches instantaneity; or 2) in a creature of vast size . . . as in that case . . . the unity and wholeness of it is lost to the beholder . . . in the same way . . . as a beautiful whole . . . must be of a size to be taken in by the eye, so a story must be . . . of a length to be taken in by the memory.[43]

Beauty exists objectively in artistic objects. It is also subjectively accessible: it is open to observers. Basil of Caesarea was the first Christian author to ascribe a dual nature to beauty. This idea became common to Western medieval philosophy and theology. It is illustrated in the formulaic definition of the beautiful which recurs in the writings of the schoolmen. 'The beautiful', they said, is '*id quod visum placet*', 'that which pleases when seen'.[44] We know that we are faced by a beautiful object when we respond to it with pleasure. The pleasure is generated by the object itself.

Why is beauty pleasing? For this tradition, the answer is that the order which shapes beautiful objects reflects the coherence of their perceiver's faculties. As St Thomas has it,

> we call a thing beautiful when it pleases the eye of the beholder. This is why beauty is a matter of right proportion, for the senses delight in rightly proportioned things as similar to themselves, the sense-faculty being a sort of proportion . . . since knowing proceeds by imaging, and images have to do with form, beauty properly involves the notion of form.[45]

If beauty is double-sided, its representation will stand outside, facing us, and yet draw us into itself. Hence, a theology that is based in beauty will be objective whilst including participating subjects. It will be objective without being objectivist. The theological aesthetic is neither a naive objectivism nor a reversion to subjectivism. Its search for a unified experience is anchored in the earth of this world. Aesthetic experience is humanly integrating when it is configured to the forms of beauty. One way of answering Kant's question is to explain the interconnection between persons and outwardness in terms of a figuration which is built into reality. This is the way taken by the writers whose understanding of beauty we shall examine in the chapters which follow.

NOTES

1 George Lindbeck, *The Nature of Doctrine: Religion and Theology in a Postliberal Age* pp. 16 and 20–21.
2 Immanuel Kant, *Critique of Pure Reason*, p. 188.
3 Immanuel Kant, *Critique of Judgement*, Part I, p. 13.
4 Kant, *Critique of Pure Reason*, p. 370.
5 Ibid. p. 469; Kant, *Religion Within the Limits of Reason Alone*, pp. 130–131; E.

Gilson, *The Unity of Philosophical Experience*, p. 238; W. H. Walsh, *Kant's Criticism*, pp. 231–234.

6 Jacques Maritain, *Moral Philosophy* p. 97. The best account is of course Alasdair MacIntyre, *After Virtue: A Study in Moral Theory*, chs. 5–7.

7 W. H. Walsh, *Kant's criticism*, pp. 239–241.

8 Kant, *Religion Within the Limits of Reason*, pp. 54–57 and 109–110; Alister McGrath, 'The Moral Theory of the Atonement', *The Scottish Journal of Theology*, Volume 30 (1985), 205–220 (213–216). Kant counters the criticism of the 'substitutionary' doctrine of atonement, that it would just happen to us from the outside, by cutting the gordian knot: since the archetype is within us, atonement is not performed by someone else.

9 Kant, *Critique of Pure Reason*, pp. 320–321.

10 Karl Barth, *Protestant Theology in the Nineteenth Century: Its Background and History*, pp. 96–97, 104–113 and 436; Albert Schweitzer, *The Quest for the Historical Jesus*, pp. 196–207, and Alister McGrath, *The Making of Modern German Christology: From the Enlightenment to Pannenberg*, pp. 13–17.

11 McGrath, 'The Moral Theory of the Atonement', p. 217.

12 Martin Kahler, *The So-Called Historical Jesus and the Historic, Biblical Christ*, pp. 93, 79, and 53.

13 Jan Patocka, 'Titanism' (1936), in *Philosophy and Selected Writings*, ed. Erazim Kohak, pp. 139–144; Colin Gunton *Enlightenment and Alienation*, Chapter 5.

14 Roger A. Johnson, *The Origins of Demythologizing: Philosophy and Historiography in the Theology of Rudolph Bultmann* pp. 44–54. The phenomenologist Adolf Reinach (1883–1917) describes his experience of studying under the Neo-Kantians as follows: 'we know nothing at all about how things really are – Kant pointed this out too – and the whole world is only in our consciousness, and outside of consciousness there is nothing . . . God forgive them, for they know not what they do.' Letter of 26 Nov., 1907, quoted in Karl Schuhmann and Barry Smith 'Adolf Reinach: An Intellectual Biography', in Kevin Mulligan (ed.), *Speech Act and Sachverhalt: Adolf Reinach and the Foundations of Realist Phenomenology*, p. 10.

15 Johnson, *Origins*, pp. 50–54; Ian Henderson, *Myth in the New Testament*, p. 47. Bultmann says: 'Mythological thought . . . objectifies the divine activity and projects it on to the plane of worldly happenings . . . In faith the closed weft presented or produced by objective observation is transcended.' 'Bultmann Replies to his Critics', in Hans Warner Bartsch (ed.), *Kerygma and Myth*, pp. 197–199.

16 Bultmann, 'New Testament and Mythology', in ibid. p. 11.

17 Friedrich Schleiermacher, *The Christian Faith*, pp. 385–389.

18 Edward Schillebeeckx, *Jesus: An Experiment in Christology*, translated by Hubert Hoskins pp. 46–58; 261–268; 653–655. This is qualified by the penultimate statement that 'deeper than the Abba experience is the Word of God, the self-communication of the Father'. (pp. 666–667).

19 Robert Alter, *The Art of Biblical Narrative*, pp. 63–87

20 E. P. Sanders, *Jesus and Judaism*, pp. 129–141.

21 Nicholas Lash notes that the 'myth-debaters' assume that objectivity means literality, whilst the mythical or symbolic is subjective: 'Interpretation and Imagination', in *Incarnation and Myth: The Debate Continued*, edited by Michael Goulder, p. 21.

22 Lindbeck, *Doctrine*, pp. 21–22 and 77–78.

23 Philippe Lacoue-Labarthe and Jean-Luc Nancy, *The Literary Absolute*, p. 30.

24 O'Leary, *Questioning Back*, p. 74.

25 Kant, *Critique of Judgement*, Part I, pp. 221–224.

26 For the defence: Zimmerman, 'Kant', pp. 385 & 405; for the prosecution, Uehling, *Form*, 94, 103–106 and 112. Uehling concedes that the passages on which his reading is based are extremely difficult to interpret.

27 Kant, *Critique of Judgement*, Part I, p. 212.

28 On the exclusion of understanding: Kant, *Critique of Judgement*, Part I, p. 71; Uehling, *Form*, pp. 38–39. On the exclusion of practical intentions: Kant, *Critique of Judgement*, Part I, pp. 43 and 46–50.

29 Uehling, *Form*, pp. 69–71; Kant, *Critique of Judgement*, Part I, pp. 51, 58–60, 146–147, 153; and Zimmerman, 'Kant', p. 393.

30 Von Balthasar, *Glory V*, p. 506.

31 Burch Brown, *Religious Aesthetics*, pp. 24–27 and 66.

32 Ibid. pp. 54–55, 74–75 and 88.

33 Roman Ingarden, *The Literary Work of Art: An Investigation on the Borderlines of Ontology, Logic and Theory of Literature*, pp. 332, 336–340, 370–372; *The Cognition of the Literary Work of Art*, pp. 376–383.

34 'Postliberal Theology', by William C. Placher, in *The Modern Theologians: An Introduction to Christian Theology in the Twentieth Century: Volume II*, edited by David Ford, pp. 115–128.

35 Hans Frei, *The Identity of Jesus Christ: The Hermeneutical Bases of Dogmatic Theology*, p. 94.

36 Lindbeck, *Doctrine*, pp. 18–20.

37 Ibid, pp. 63–65, 69, 80, 117; but, on the acceptance of moderate, or 'second-order' propositionalism, 47–51, 66.

38 J. G. Fichte, *The Vocation of Man*, pp. 109–111; Josiah Royce, *Lectures on Modern Idealism*, pp. 85–86, and 99–100.

39 René Wellek, *A History of Modern Criticism: 1740–1950 Volume 2. The Romantic Age* pp. 74–75.

40 Allen Tate, 'Faulkner's Sanctuary and the Southern Myth', in *Memories and Essays: Old and New*, p. 151.

41 Jacques Maritain, *Creative Intuition in Art and Poetry*, p. 162.

42 Von Balthasar, *Dieu et l'homme aujourd'hui*, pp. 228–229, quoted in Georges de Schrijver, *Le Merveilleux Accord de L'homme et de Dieu: Étude de l'analogie de l'être chez Hans Urs von Balthasar* p. 58.

43 Aristotle, *Poetics*, Chapter 7, 1450b, 32 – 1451a, 5.

44 See the Appendix on Patristic and Medieval Theories of the Beautiful, on pp. 189–194.

45 St Thomas Aquinas, *Summa Theologiae*, Ia, Q. 5, Art. 4, ad 1.

Chapter 3

Beauty, 'The Cinderella of the Transcendentals': Jacques Maritain's Philosophy of Art

Henri Bergson (1859–1941)

Henri Bergson's philosophy is an indispensable avenue into Maritain's philosophy of art – and also into that of the Southern writers. Bergson's great achievement was to tilt against the grim physicalism of much late nineteenth-century philosophy.[1] He aims his lance toward facets of consciousness which the materialists could not explain. In some respects, his work runs parallel to the emergence of German phenomenology: Edmund Husserl's *Logical Investigations* (1900) contends that the phenomenological investigation of consciousness reveals the implausibility of psychologistic materialism.[2] The data to which Bergson turns is the internal movement, or 'duration', of consciousness. For the physicalist, human consciousness is an immanent motion of loosely associated atoms. For Bergson, it has a direction.[3] He means that consciousness is intentional.

Intuition is Bergson's central notion. It is his means of introspectively examining the flow of a consciousness which is not to be known by generalizations.[4] Consciousness is only to be grasped by an immediate intuition. Intuition can also enter the secret interstices of objects. It reaps its knowledge from concrete facts. It is, Bergson says, the kind of intellectual sympathy by which one places oneself inside an object in

order to coincide with what is unique in it'.[5] Intuition extends
the self into the thing. Intuiting is a stretching or contracting of
oneself, so imaginatively to become the sea or the forest. In
stating that intuition gains real knowledge of things, Bergson
takes issue with the scepticism which is attendant upon materialism.[6]

The Bergsonian intuition is both emotional and cognitive.[7]
But he persistently contrasts intuitive to conceptual knowledge.
Intuition touches the interiority of things; conceptual knowledge
must make do with an external enumeration of their parts.
Having split the thing into its parts, scientific analysis can never
quite reconstruct it. Its scope is too broad adequately to capture
the originality and uniqueness of each fact. It knows only the
kind. Analysis tracks down and nets its prey within typical
schemas. The particular beast eludes it.[8]

The Development of Maritain's Thought

As a student at the Sorbonne at the turn of the century, Jacques
Maritain (1882–1973) was trained in the positivism which then
dominated French philosophy. It did not undermine his love for
Baudelaire's poetry. It was Charles Péguy who led Maritain
'across the street', to the Collège de France where Bergson was
lecturing. Bergson persuaded him that intuitive knowledge is
not the slave of material causality.[9] It knows absolutes.

By 1906, Maritain had recognised that he must depart
further from materialism than Bergson had done. He became
first a Roman Catholic and then emerged as a thoroughgoing
Thomist, and a trenchant critic of his former teacher.[10] He later
composed a neo-Thomistic philosophy of art, *Art and Scholasticism* (1920), critical works about the philosophies of Luther and
of Descartes, and a metaphysics which recasts the scholastic
philosophy of being, *The Degrees of Knowledge* (1932). After the
outbreak of the Second World War, Maritain moved to
America. It was there that he wrote, in English, *Creative Intuition
in Art and Poetry* (1953).

Between the early 1920s and 50s Maritain's philosophy of art
developed, as he slowly assimilated all that he learned from his

teachers and friends. The first movement, from the First World
War until the early 30s, is a period of exclusion. Maritain rejects
Bergson's philosophy and breaks with friends such as Péguy,
who do not.[11] His first aesthetic treatise depends upon the
scholastic notion of 'connaturality': that is, he thinks of art as a
practical skill. But, by the 30s, he realizes that he has omitted to
elucidate the characteristic insight upon which art depends.[12] In
1935, he adds the supplementary essay, 'Frontiers of Poetry', to
his *Art and Scholasticism*. 'Poetry' is defined as a supra-conceptual
insight into a particular fact. Maritain appears to be drawing
upon Bergson's thought. The third stage, in which *Creative
Intuition in Art and Poetry* is composed, is the most important.
For now, without rejecting his earlier reflections, he incorporates the Bergsonian notion of intuition.[13] 'Creative intuition' is
envisaged as an emotional palpability which allows the poet to
feel his way into a thing and to be absorbed by it. The grasp of
beauty is said to be both emotional and rational. The work of
art to which such intuition gives rise expresses both an object's
interior form and the subliminal subjectivity of the poet.

Maritain's home in Paris had always been a salon for artists
and writers. Now he tries to make sense of modern art,
especially Cezanne's painting, and the poetry of Baudelaire.
Much of *Creative Intuition in Art and Poetry* consists of 'Texts
Without Comment', in which the poetry of the French Symbolists and the English Romantics predominate. He is making
good use of some features of the Romantic understanding of art
and of imagination. He says also that the New Critics have
aided his synthesis. These new elements are grafted in to a
realistic metaphysic.

Maritain could take this turn toward subjectivity because the
concrete, embodied shape of the human person was his key
perception. Emmanuel Mounier was later to write, 'Who, if not
Péguy . . . directed our bodies and souls to the sense of the
incarnation; who, if not Maritain . . . guided the fervour of our
youth away from the sin of angelism?'[14] It was in the same sense
that Maritain was to affect other younger contemporaries, such
as the Southern writers.

Maritain on the Transcendentals: Being

The beautiful, in its objectivity, is one of the grounds of the reality of the self. Maritain built a realistic metaphysics, so to defend the fulness and the limitations of human rationality. In it, he draws on the scholastic conception of the transcendental. For the scholastics, this is a universal element of being, which 'transcends' all of the categories into which being can be divided.[15] The transcendentals are causes. Maritain takes beauty to be such a transcendental property. We will propose that transcendental beauty is the ground of incarnational Christology. But it is not to stand on its own. And the question of the existence of the transcendentals must be broached, before we can discuss beauty as a transcendental.

The Degrees of Knowledge provides Maritain's most extended discussion of the transcendentals. This book reconstructs Thomas' metaphysics. It proposes an alternative to post-Cartesian philosophy. Maritain believes that Descartes' 'angelism', or his disembodiment of thought, is responsible for modern Idealism.[16] He claims that the basis of metaphysics is not the Cartesian self-thinking thought. To the contrary, the ground of metaphysics is *being*. Being rather than concepts within the mind, gives rise to thought. We cannot think without thinking about some fact. Thought has an inherent 'aboutness'. This is not simply to argue that consciousness is intrinsically intentional. For Maritain, the aboutness of thought implies that real concepts must be 'enracinated' in being.[17] He urges that all thought is thought of something which *exists*: being flows through the mind, as it achieves consciousness, and there is no thinking without an implicit positing of an existent. Being cannot be deduced from thinking, since it is ontologically prior to it.

The being from which thought flows has its universality. Before it is a particular fact, or belongs to a kind, an object must simply be. Porcupines, pine trees and pigs have something in common, over and above their specific and generic differences. The 'is-ing' of each specific fact is one action. All objects have their part within a single being. Were it not so, it would be impossible to think systematically. For if being were not shared by all things, every object in the universe would be absolutely distinct from every other. With the scholastics, Maritain maintains that being extends across all existents: that it is a *transcendental.* We can make some generalizations about objects, for they share in the single action of being. Because of their commonalty, the transcendentals build networks amongst the objects which participate in them. To exist means to belong to the transcendental network of being, and thus to be related to all other things. All things are analogically interwoven in the objective web of being.

The commonalty of being is not purely universal or 'univocal'. As Maritain says, being is an analogical, or 'polyvalent' notion.[18] To participate in a transcendental is to be a member of a field which has an infinite scope. This field can give rise to any number of variants. Analogical relationship is intrinsically various. If all existents share a common being, this does not mean that they replicate each other. The acts of being are not mirrors one to another. Analogical similarity depends upon sameness – oneness – but also upon difference. The ways in which things share in being are diverse. Each carves out its own specific 'to be'. In sum, objects like mountains, tortoises and penknives are both individual and common. Being unifies facts and also keeps them separate, cuts them apart. As Maritain puts it,

> in the perception of the transcendentals we touch on a nature greater than itself . . . as though in opening a little shoot one let loose a bird that is greater than all the world. . . . It differs . . . from the universals . . . because it is not . . . one and the same in the mind . . . it includes an actual multiplicity; the bird of my image . . . is also a flock.[19]

The mind can comprehend being as such, as transcendental, because it can elicit common notions from things. But, although it can conceive the idea of being as a transcendental, it cannot mentally encompass it. We cannot possess it, as a concept. We can only know this notion through its analogues.

In *The Degrees of Knowledge,* Maritain selects three transcendental properties as the most valuable. The first is being. The second is truth, which provides the relation of being to the mind. The third is the good: this is being in relation to the will. It is the goal towards which love is driven.

Do the Transcendentals Exist?

It need hardly be said that modern philosophy and theology do not widely subscribe to this picture of the transcendentals. As I see it, Maritain's strongest argument for the existence of the transcendental notions is that they are our only real means of communication. For, as he says, if one could only speak about the world as it reacts upon one's own body, no true conversation could take place. Each person's words would only point to what a group of things does to themselves, rather than to something beyond their own ego.[20] If our discourse is to have an objective element, we will have to speak 'through' the common network of being, over which the transcendental notions preside. The transcendentals denominate something real in things, and something which is common to all beings as such.

We will only have a community of knowledge if our judgements refer to objects outside of us. Further, these objects must have something in common, some bonds of unity, over and above their particular existence. Otherwise people separated in time and space would not share an analogous frame of reference. Truth would be one thing for the medieval Chinese and another for the modern day Russian; being would be one thing for the Fathers of the Church and another for ourselves; beauty would be in the eye of each generation of beholders. It is obvious that societies have differed in their conceptions of each transcendental. Unless some one thing underlies these varying interpretations, the varying scenes of human action have no part in a single drama. Reductionism follows on the failure to imagine societies other than our own as engaged on a parallel quest for meaning. We begin to say that the ethics of the Old Testament consist solely in the establishment of property rights, or that Patristic theology is just 'Greek philosophy' (an interesting double relativism). This is to say that their proponents were not fully human, for we experience at least some of *our own* human acts as meaningful, or as open to transcendent goodness and truth.

As the bonds of human community, the transcendentals create a public space. They give to it those shared meanings which tie the threads of one person's speech to another's. Language is the analogical bond in which the knowledge of the transcendentals is expressed as meaning. As von Balthasar puts it in his *Theo-Drama*,

> Being reveals itself, in its transcendentals, as the Beautiful, the True and the Good, and this very fact is language, at a root level. And the fact that the finite spirit experiences the illumination and follows it through is likewise the birth of language.[21]

If the search for being, for truth, and for goodness were reflected in an open, and apprehensible space, this space would express a form of beauty. The Fugitive-Agrarians took the Southern states of America as an analogue of the human community which possessed common values. Allen Tate said that

> culture is . . . the material medium through which men receive . . . the truth of what Jacques Maritain calls the 'supra-temporal destiny' of man. . . . The end of social man is communion in time through love, which is beyond time.[22]

Without a transcendent reference to God, language will be drained of its capacity to produce symbols and judgements in which a whole community can participate. When they attain this reference, symbols become the magnetic centres of peoples who are intent on an ultimate goal which transcends the human world. The burden of what follows, in relation to both Maritain and the Southerners, will be that language can be moulded into artistic forms, which are analogues of the transcendentals. For the Southerners, the world projected by each true literary form is an analogue of reality.

Maritain's Self-Transcending Narrative Compared with Wittgenstein's Immanent One

Fergus Kerr's *Theology after Wittgenstein* could well be thought to carry Maritain's anti-Cartesian offensive into contemporary theology. It deploys the later Wittgenstein's understanding of the givenness of community, so to criticize both the Cartesian *cogito* and the experiential-expressivism which is Kant's legacy to modern theology. Kerr notes that Descartes' *res cogitans* is immured inside a body whose materiality conceals the rarefied mind which is exiled therein. His enterprise runs parallel to the 'structuralist-functionalism' which von Balthasar finds to be one feature of modern philosophy: both endeavour to regain the human relationality which Descartes mislaid.[23] One of the Anglo-Saxon guises of 'structuralism' is cultural linguistic theology. Do Kerr's arguments for the givenness of sociality provide sufficient grounds for Christology?

Kerr contends that to speak is to extend oneself, not back into the mind, but out into common discourse. If so, the apparent solitude of the self-certain mind is illusory: the effort to infer other minds from within that solitude ceases to seem necessary. In our forms of life, certain patterns of action are given bodily expression, and so are immediately recognizable by others. The Cartesian doubter withholds from himself the most basic fact of his existence: the mutuality of life within a given culture. Religious faith is also communal, on Kerr's account. It is not within the heart (or head): it has, rather, a proclivity to liturgical dramatization. As a form of practical knowledge, religious experience is manifested physically. Like thinking, 'faith . . . is often visible.'[24] It is tangible as an communal way of behaving.

Thus, Kerr has a metaphysic of sociality. His project is founded upon the pretheoretical givenness of human community. As with much of Postliberal theology, his object is the living body of faith, as it shows itself in performance.[25] Kerr comments,

It will be shown in the rest of what we do whether we have faith in God. It will not be settled by our finding that we make the same metaphysical correlation between our words and some item of metaphysical reality.[26]

This shows up the pitfall in this worthwhile theological enterprise. Kerr is so intent on the fact that faith is *done* before it is thought about that he effectively denies that the intentional acts of believers are directed to an object which is believed to stand beyond the intending self. He claims: 'Worship is not the result but the precondition of believing in God.'[27] With an epistemological bias which undercuts his anti-Kantian argument, Kerr adverts to the *evidence* for belief, namely, observance of 'ritual acts'.[28] The only warrant for the assertion is the showing; but one may inquire whether the showing is all that is there. Kerr's account of religion neglects the intention of any liturgically enacted story to imitate, or to refer to, a narrative which extends beyond the liturgy. This is to exchange the object of liturgical performance for its mediatory channels. Kerr makes the delightful suggestion that '. . . religion . . . if it has any hold on people's lives and imaginations, is "danced out"'.[29] This is so: but we need not accept the conclusion that religious acts are 'about' humanity before they refer to deity. Simply on the phenomenological level, primitive ceremonies, dances and sacred games are believed to repeat the life story of the god. This is why the actors wore masks, so to disappear behind the disguise, that the god may be made present.[30]

For Maritain, the communication of meaning is the evidence for, not the foundation of, the possibility of metaphysics. Kerr's insights about bodily expressiveness must be supplemented by Maritain's perception that both thinking and bodily expression are signs of the self-transcending dynamism of human beings: the impetus is the lure of being. It is because they have this dynamism that human beings are not Cartesian mental egos. If the human person is envisaged as a participant in the drama of being, we shall demolish the Cartesian paradigm of the mind as a static self-thinking substance. That is why Maritain not only describes human action, but gives its *why*. Having supplied the metaphysical basis, we may say, not only that religion is danced into being, but that that dance recapitulates the Theo-drama.

The affirmation of realities as true, good or beautiful requires an equipoise between the thing and the 'I' who intends it. Having laid all 'items of metaphysical reality' to one side, cultural-linguistics subsumes the self within the speaking community. It defines the self, not by its act of existing – and who is to say this is a private enclosure? – but in its recognition by others. But, our ability to rely upon the patterns of expression in another's behaviour demands that they are not, for example, schizophrenics. If there are any patterns, they are integrated by a uniform consciousness. But Kerr considers that to anchor the patterns in a consciousness is to secrete them in a concealed compartment. He asks: 'Why can't "my world" individuate me just as plausibly as the putatative "real ego"?'[31] It cannot do so because, if the 'I' is purely a social construct, no specific consciousness is constructing language. Language loses its moorings in intentional acts and becomes a quasi-platonic ideal, floating like the lid of a cheese-dish over all individual selves. The 'I' is then ontologically dependent upon a generalized norm, which, as such, cannot properly individuate. And, as von Balthasar notes, the shifting perspectives of culture cannot provide continuity of self: 'If', he says,

> self-identity depends on social processes . . . we are faced with the question of the historical changes in these expectations . . .; the individual who has submerged himself in a role must lose his identity . . . if the expectations change.[32]

Maritain distinguished the 'ego', as the carrier of this one nervous-system, from the 'self', which is the person in his or her existential reach into the realm of being. If we distinguish – the 'ego', as immanent within the body, from selfhood, as it extends into reality – we may unite: the person becomes a self by shared participation in being.

If a religion is to have a transcendent basis, its philosophical theologians must also show how it is related to reality: this will require explanation, in addition to description. Having provided this, we could say that the drama of public action is the ultimate analogue of the real being which transcends those who speak about it. Unless it refers to such a transcendent reality, the culture has nowhere to point except back at itself. Unless the stories which the community tells are embedded in reality, they cannot attain even the status of immanent myth. They are stories about stories, within the closed circle of the tribe, and its comparative mythologies are emptied of all self-transcending reality. And, as Alasdair MacIntyre argues, to eliminate the identity of the self is to displace one's means of constructing a continuous narrative.[33]

Experience the Key to a Thomistic Understanding of Transcendence

MacIntyre goes on to say that modern Thomists have fallen victim to 'epistemologizing'. He implicates Maritain in this process.[34] For many of Maritain's disciples joined issue with post-Cartesian philosophy upon its theory of knowledge. Believing that modern philosophy has been misled by an erroneous conception of the knowing process, they thought to regain the lost territory of realism with anatomical diagrams of the epistemic apparatus as depicted by St Thomas. Their enthusiasm for this latter was so great that they swallowed it whole. Their attachment to such artifacts as the 'passive' and 'active' intellects was deeper than that to the basic experience of the being which alone lends credibility to the edifice. 'Epistemologized' Thomism was soon replaced by the full-blown assimilation of Kantianism in the transcendental Thomisms of Rahner and Lonergan.

When von Balthasar writes appreciatively of Aquinas, one word recurs: experience. St Thomas' work is said to draw on an original 'experience of being'.[35] The works of his modern followers do not always give the impression of having this source, perhaps because they do not. Von Balthasar reaches behind Aquinas's literal apportioning of the sensing, affective and cognitive faculties to their various tasks: he claims that Aquinas understood better than most that it is not any one faculty, but the 'whole person' who is open to facts, other people, and to God, that is to 'Being as a whole'. For Aquinas,

> Such attunement to Being . . . is . . . prior to the distinc-
> tion between active and passive experience: in the reci-
> procity which is founded on openness to reality there is
> contained both the receptivity to extraneous im-pression
> and the ex-pressing of the self onto the extraneous.[36]

In 'experiential contact' with reality, being touched by things
and responding to them occur together. Von Balthasar considers that Aquinas recognized that the one first touches things
pre-rationally. The 'touch' issues from the 'primal feeling'
which attends the response of a human consciousness to
reality. He may have read his *Summa* in the light of the work
of Max Scheler, which also contains such an insight.[37] Maritain
perhaps took Aquinas more literally than did von Balthasar. But
his works do not transcribe St Thomas' thought as a predigested
system. It may be that Bergson drew him because he spoke of
something by which Maritain had already had been touched:
the primeval world of beauty to which symbolist poetry
responds. This perhaps was Maritain's first meeting with the
self-communication of being. We turn to his study of one
iridescent aspect of being, namely, the beautiful.

Maritain on the Transcendentals: The Beautiful

Maritain describes beauty as the 'radiance of all the transcendentals united'.[38] This means that beauty is an objective
property of being. If it is a transcendental – and thus coex-
tensive with being – beauty is an element of *everything* that exists.
It is not only present in lovely or majestic things such as sea-
horses or the Acropolis. Part of what it means to be, is to be
beautiful. Beauty is not superadded to things: it is one of the
springs of their reality. It is not that which effects a luscious
response in perceivers; it is the interior geometry of things,
making them perceptible as forms. A test for the objectivity of
the beauty of the work of art, such as the musical composition,
is: can we endlessly return to it?[39] The counterpart of empirical
inexhaustibility is the metaphysical attribute of transcendentality, which includes infinitude.

Beauty has the same many-sidedness as being. All things are analogously beautiful because they are engendered by the one 'super-analogue' of beauty: God. Thus, for Maritain, only God may be said to be beautiful in the fullest sense of the term:

> Analogous concepts are properly predicable only of God, in whom the perfection they describe exists . . . in a pure and infinite state. God is their 'sovereign analogue', and they are to be found in things only as a . . . prismatised reflection of the face of God. So beauty is one of the divine attributes.[40]

Beauty in Works of Art

Following scholastic tradition, Maritain claims that the properties of beauty are proportion, integrity and radiance.[41] I will explain what these are by showing where they are found in literary works.

Proportion – Also Known as Consonance

The 'proportion' of an artistic work is expressed by its 'number or harmonic structure'. When sentences coalesce to form significant clusters, such as fictional characters, places and events, represented meanings emerge. In literary works, proportion is the extended shape into which the separate representations are built. It is the expansion of the represented objects, in their inner relation. When the different represented objects pull away from one another in their various directions, they create a mobile 'space'. This is the work's 'harmonic structure'. Maritain explains that the poetic space

> results from the . . . expansion of the various parts of the work in their mutual concurrence . . . so that it is . . . always filled with significative meanings . . . tensions and pressures (silences, voids . . . blanks reserved for the unexpressed).[42]

Integrity – Also Called Unity

The unity of the work's many parts makes it a form in its own
right. Such integrity resides in its telling 'one' story. This is why
Aristotle gave priority to the 'fable or plot' of tragic drama.[43]
The unitive energy of the story binds together the work's diverse
representations. It turns them around and brings them back
again after 'number' has sent them moving in different directions. The immanent action of the work underlies its integrity.[44]
The work's action is what it does, its own unique expressive
movement. The literary work is coiled around the action which
carries its agents. Its unitary base is the narration of one action,
such as the downfall of Oedipus.

Some of Caroline Gordon's and William Lynch's comments
help to illustrate what Maritain's conception of literary 'integrity' means. Caroline Gordon argues that a work's integrity
is conveyed by its unfolding in time. She says that *Oedipus the King*
is realistic because Sophocles has made his work,

> by so ordering his imitation of life that it corresponds to a
> picture implicit in the human imagination. In life things
> . . . are led up to by other events. Everything that happens
> in this play is prepared for in a way that life prepares its
> effects . . . [It] is related to everything that has happened
> and foreshadows what is going to happen. Every incident
> . . . has a threefold existence: in the past, the present and
> the future.[45]

If the artistic work is the fruit of poetic intuition's insight into
real being, the interplay of its proportion and integrity will be a
symbolic form. Symbolic forms are analogues of reality. Lynch
says that *Oedipus the King* demonstrates the nature of analogy
because it holds different actions together in a unifying causal
bond. Analogy in literature is created by a dramatic action; or
by a movement in which every aspect of the plot, and each
character, can be seen to interlock. Each character's actions
rebounds upon the others. Each scene circles around an
integrating centre, which synthesizes and gives form to the
whole. As Lynch claims,

one vision reinforces another. . . . A truly analogical idea
crackles with light and makes other things crackle with the
same and yet their own light. Bring the ironic self-knowledge of Jocasta back to Oedipus and his own insight will
burn more terribly still. Bring these forms to the children
and they will crackle with the immeasurable terror of a
child.[46]

The play represents one element of the reciprocal causation
within being itself. It represents reality, but not by describing
real occurrences. Rather, it produces very specific images of
persons and things, and makes them traverse a carefully
delimited and contracted space or time. The well-formed
action reflects the causal network of being itself.

Such dramatic action is not only an analogue of the generative causality which flows through all being. It not only
imitates the given, but also the humanly chosen. For the story
radiates from moral decision. As Maritain says, few works can
be 'an image of the relationship between the transcendent
creative eternity of God and the free creatures who are both
acting in liberty and firmly embraced by his purpose.'[47] Insofar
as the work is dramatic, its characters have a certain freedom.
They are not locked into a closed network of signs.

Radiance – Also Called Clarity and Splendour

The radiance of a beautiful object is the light of intelligibility
which flows through its form and illuminates it. The form
stretches the object out sideways, giving it extension. Radiance
holds the form up vertically.[48] In so doing it moves it out,
toward its audience. Radiance is the escalator which translates
the artistic object's form into aesthetic experience. It is a
perceptible light which shines from within the artistic object's
world, drawing the observer in. It transmits the work's meaning.
Radiance is the expression of reality as form. Just as the mind is
sent out into reality by being, so the beautiful object is filled by a
radiance which makes its form self-transcending.

Radiance has not the glare of the Cartesian clear and distinct

55555555555555555555 5 5

idea. The brightness of beauty overwhelms our intuitive capacities. It extends further into the depths of being than the unaided mind can venture. As Maritain states, 'The Schoolmen, when they defined beauty by the radiance of the form . . . defined it by the radiance of a mystery.'[49] It is this mystery which lends to metaphysics its dramatic character. Where the Cartesian 'idea' is a potential *essence*, radiance is the emergence, through form, of *existence*, or being in act. The theological aesthetic is no philosophical conceptualism. The beautiful form is not a 'static' idea: it is a dramatic 'doing': its radiance pulsates with the hidden energies of being. The meanings which shape its form tend upward, toward the absolute meaningfulness in which it participates, and outward, toward its audience. In the degree that the form can contain the radiance, or surplus, of being, it obtains a relation to reality. The meaning which has been tightly bound into artistic form captures the radiance of reality itself. The beautiful object presents existingness, not essences.

Beautiful Objects Are Analogical Symbols

The intuition that something in the nature of things is beautiful is at the same time a vision of God working in creation. One looks into some created thing, a cloud or a leaf, and sees that its structure goes on to infinity. It repeats itself, becomes more complex, grows in order, and becomes a thing of mystery, that is, something too intelligible to be understood by us, dazzling by its excess of formliness. This is the experience of causation, moving through reality. What is known, finally, is not only order, but the power which makes order exist. To grasp it is to know a transcendental.

Beauty is radiant because it is a reality. When one perceives the causedness and orderedness of being, its inexhaustible intelligibility shines ever more brightly. The infinite being of God is a bottomless depth of radiance. The analogical symbol reflects some element of this infinite radiance. It draws to itself a relation to all of being, created and creating. Imaginative intuition grasps something of the resonance of the complex of symbolic objects to which it is related, both below and above it, stretching up to God Himself. The analogical imagination creates images in which a deeper reference is rolled up, or compressed. For symbols represent qualities of transcendent being. Maritain states that

> The work will make present to our eyes, together with itself, something else, and still something else. . . . indefinitely, in the infinite mirrors of analogy. Through a kind of poetic ampliation, Beatrice, while remaining the woman whom Dante loved, is also, through the power of the sign, the light which illuminates him . . . Beatrice is never a symbol or an allegory for Dante. She is both herself and what she signifies. . . . he actually believes in this one and multiple identity.[50]

The beautiful symbol participates in a realm whose breadth it cannot wholly reflect, but to which it is in real relation. Poetic intuition tries to entrap some aspect of the relatedness of all things to one another, and through one another, to their Maker. Its forms have the dramatic unity of which I have spoken. Tate was affected by Maritain's conception of intuition. He describes it as the 'symbolic imagination', claiming that,

> To bring together various meanings at a single moment of action is to exercise . . . the symbolic imagination . . . The symbolic imagination conducts an action through analogy, of the human to the divine, of the low to the high, of time to eternity. . . . It is . . . the way of the poet who has got to do his work with the body of this world, whatever that body may look like to him.[51]

Once held together in its form, and carried outward by its radiance, the artistic work is a reality in its own right, an analogue of the beauty of created being, and a sign of the means through which the transcendent beauty of God is transmitted.

Christ Is Transcendental Beauty Open to the Human Mind

Artistic works make a finite aspect of beauty concrete and express it in minute portions of the 'body of this world'. If beauty is a transcendental, no artistic object can approximate to its complete wealth. Paintings, sculptures, novels, plays and symphonies draw upon transcendental beauty. But they are separated from it as the finite is from the infinite. Maritain asserts that 'No form of art, however perfect, can encompass beauty in itself as the Virgin contained her Creator.'[52] He is proposing that Christ Himself is the Form of Beauty. He is drawing on medieval tradition, for which transcendental beauty was ascribed to God the Son.[53] Christ most perfectly exemplifies the beautiful. Christ has radiance as the Word, or Idea, which illuminates the mind which contemplates Him; He has proportion because He is the fullest likeness of the Father; and He has integrity because His Form is the Father's Form.[54] For Maritain, each of the properties of beauty corresponds to a human need. It is proportionate because the mind needs order, and to see the relatedness of things; its integrity corresponds to the human person's love for being immersed in reality; its radiance reflects the need to know. This is why beauty is pleasing. The sheer objectivity of beauty gives the mind back to itself.

Transcendental and Aesthetic Beauty

Transcendental beauty and immanent, or aesthetic beauty are different. Aesthetic beauty is discovered and reproduced in forms proportioned to finitude. It is created in order to be perceived. Its Greek root *aisthanomai* means to apprehend by the senses. Maritain defines aesthetic beauty in its being simultaneously sensuous and intellectual.[55] When we grasp it, the senses are infused by the quest for knowledge, whilst the intellect 'looks through' the senses. It will be the imagination which allows them to enmesh, and thus to focus upon a concrete form. Moreover, aesthetic beauty is turned toward human acts of perception. It directly faces the finite human mind. This does not mean that it has no mystery. For the symbol is an analogue, which Maritain has distinguished from the univocal concept. If the symbol were a univocal statement, it might automatically be assimilated by us, as the equation can. The analogue is more like an aquarium; many strange creatures may be gliding in its undergrowth. The symbol alludes to transcendence, rather than mirroring it exactly, as the universal concept does. This is why it belongs to immanent rather than to transcendent being. Immanent and transcendent beauty are related analogically, not univocally. Maritain has not the Romantic Idealists' tendency to identify finite and infinite being. And yet, aesthetic and transcendental beauty are not wholly discrete. Maritain asserts that aesthetic beauty strives towards transcendental beauty. This is a 'token . . . of its spirituality'.[56] But aesthetic beauty delights an imagination which is earthed in this world. Its impulse toward transcendence comes from beyond itself.

Makers of form want apparently different things. On the one hand, the maker wants the form to be perfect. On the other, only that form which has been 'broken' is open to reality. The break, or the flaw, is the sign that it has been pierced by a larger force, which it cannot control.[57] Pure aesthetic perfection shuts reality out. This goes a little way towards explaining how, in the face of the brokenness of all human lives, we may yet claim that beauty is present in all things. As von Balthasar puts it,

> The hideous form [*Ungestalt*] is part of the world's form [*Gestalt*], and so it must be included . . . amongst the themes of artistic creation. . . . This is made clear by Expressionism . . . but equally by the presence of Iago in Othello. What is at stake is the ultimate, form-imparting word, which can be put together from 'non-words'.[58]

That 'ultimate' Word contains in itself a space for the 'other'.

Myth is the story in which the reciprocity of divine and human action is disclosed, in an image which expresses the depth, and the polyphony of values within this world. If so, then myth is the primary expression of the immanent aesthetic. Myth and revelation are related to one another as immanent to transcendent beauty. Greek drama and the Christian liturgy are two examples of aesthetic and transcendental beauty. For, as Louis Bouyer argued, the action of the Eucharistic liturgy may be understand as carrying forward the 'same' action as that found, for example, in Oedipus Rex.[59] Greek drama grew from the rites of the mystery religions, especially those of Dionysius' cult. The Greek purgation of the city by the ritual death of a scapegoat, or *pharmakos*, is formulated in the *Oedipus* of Sophocles.[60] In the drama, the human response to the skeletal pattern of the universe is acted out. The liturgy exposes a pattern which comes from beyond the human spirit's perception of meanings within this world. Maritain says that the liturgy is 'the transcendent, super-eminent type of Christian art-forms'.[61] Such reference to transcendent types is not widely popular. For Joseph O'Leary, such theological language lacks 'phenomenological roots in the experience of faith' and so 'testifies to a lack of engagement with the texture of experience.'[62] Lynch responds to such outworkings of the Kantian dismissal of mediatory form in theology by wishing that

> in the fever for the dehellenization of Christianity . . . theologians . . . would stop their obsessive reduction of all Greek thought to 'essentialism' and would discover the intense and universal dramatic genius of the Greeks.[63]

Lynch proposes that 'dramatic' form answers the modern question without succumbing to its subjective bias. It searches out the shape of the person within reality itself, rather than probing for self-evidence within subjectivity. In a sense, the myth which Greek drama plays out gives a true statement about the world. But, instead of speaking in propositions, the beautiful myth is laid open to transcendence by making reality to shine in an image of the actions of persons. Its beauty is as closely tied to reality as is metaphysical truth: it responds to being. But it is known by focusing on a different type of object, and with a specific mode of knowledge.

Art Is a Skill or 'Practical Knowledge'

Maritain takes up the Aristotelian and scholastic distinction between speculative and practical knowledge.[64] The speculative way of knowing contemplates its objects without altering them. Such knowledge does not depend upon willed choices. If it did, its object would be a human fabrication. Practical knowing, on the other hand, is a creative engagement with an object. This is a knowing which comes about only when one acts. It is closed to the detached spectator.

The scholastics also distinguish two ways of knowing by practising: the ethical and the artistic. Both are crafts; in each, it is only by doing something that one can see the good or the beautiful. The difference is that where moral action perfects the *actor*, in goodness, artistic making perfects the *thing* being made, in beauty. This is why those who are interested, not in the conscience of the artist, but for example, in the Upper Church at Assisi, will not consider that art as such is undermined by Giotto's money-lending – even at 120 per cent.[65]

But does this, as Frank Burch Brown claims, divorce artistic making both from theory and from that knowledge of the good which leads to right action?[66] No, because, for Maritain human beings have but one mind. This one mind operates in different ways when, for example, we behave charitably, or water-ski, or paint. He says that he is distinguishing 'two different ways in which the same power of the soul – the reason – exercises its activity.'[67]

In addition, the artist's ability to see and reproduce the beautiful is that *through which* the work manifests the good: think of the trite moralisms inflicted upon us by lacklustre novels; think of the rendition of forgiveness in *King Lear*.

Hence, the will must be congruent to the beautiful, if it is to direct its energy toward it. Both contemplative and practical knowledge assimilate the self to the inner form of some object. But the practical arts set the self into concordance with reality by aligning both mind and will into a shape which, as yet, is absent: the shape of a thing to be done.[68] It is desire for beauty which enables us to envisage and to recreate it.

Practical knowledge is knowledge by 'connaturality'. This is literally co-naturality: the whole personality of the artist is involved in, and takes its shape from, the form with which she works. As Merleau-Ponty said, someone learning to type incorporates a keyboard shaped space into their way of living; dress-makers are known both to design clothes for their own body, and to develop a sense of that body's potential from the clothes which they make. One becomes connatural to an object when one moves with it. The artist does not theorize about beauty: she lives through one of its forms. Connaturality informs any imaginative interplay between self and world: it means acting in time with the rhythms of the world.

If art is to be ingrained in its practitioner, it must become habitual. Habits are implanted and nurtured in the soil of our earthy nature through imitation and repetition. They are the subterranean deposit of each person's affective history, not just ingrained behavioural impulses. To have the habit of art is as much a way of being anchored in the transcendent as is speculative knowledge.[69] Maritain distinguishes 'operative' and 'customary' habits. Customary habits allow us to repose in our physical subjectivity. Operative habits extend us into the world. They are means of transcending biological immanence and moving into things. These accomplish works of art.[70]

Since artistic production relies upon practical knowing, it incorporates the fullness of experience. Artistic acts require an embodied imagination, which repeats itself in the things which they create.[71] The mind is at work in bodily actions: self transcendence is discovered not only in immaterial mental acts, but also in the interplay between corporeal gestures and their objects. Bodily knowledge here becomes the magnetic needle through which the self gravitates toward God. Maritain considers this to be the highest way of knowing. For metaphysical analysis must be superseded by mystical vision, which, he thinks, is a form of knowledge by connaturality. The second half of his *Degrees of Knowledge* is about St John of the Cross, whose writings, Maritain says, express 'practical knowledge' of God: they tell us what to *do* on the journey toward God, rather than *explaining* His Being. Although art and mysticism must not be identified, the two are more akin to each other than to metaphysics.[72] Both are based in practical experience. Each is acquired through connaturality rather than in the speculative formation of judgements. It is the whole self which must be proportioned to the transcendent beauty of Christ.

The Christian artist must, in Lonergan's phrase, have 'fallen in love with God'.[73] What a person can create depends upon the depth of their personality. This, in turn, depends upon its conscious direction, and thus upon what, and who, one loves. It is love which infuses the artist's sympathizing will with the energy which is shaped by beauty. As Maritain writes,

> if the beauty of the work is Christian, it is because the appetite of the artist is rectified in regard to such beauty, and because Christ is present in the artist by love. The quality of the work in such a case is an effusion of the love from which it proceeds . . . the work will be Christian in proportion as that love is alive.[74]

There is no Christian art without the love of God. The vision of beauty and the ways toward the good in the end converge.

Von Balthasar also envisages Christian experience as a practical engagement with God. In *The Glory of the Lord*, the formation of the self by the apprehended image of Christ is explained by analogy with artistic making. The *Theo-Drama* speaks of the practical experience of the good. The skills of actresses and actors are said to be unique, in that their own selves are the material to be transformed.[75] Such are the analogues of the Christian's performance of his or her role.

Poetic Intuition

For Maritain, poetic intuition is the intentional transformation of the self into the 'stuff' of things and the self-giving of things within the poet. An intentional unity with the object allows it to come alive within the poet's consciousness. The transformation is intentional rather than material. It is a spiritual, not a physical becoming. Otherwise, one would be saying, for example, that the poet literally turned into a daffodil, which seems unlikely.

Poetic intuition creates an affective bond between the self and the fact which it explores.[76] It brings about poetic knowledge. There is, Maritain argues, not only cognitive knowledge, but also one which is rooted in affectivity. Poetic intuition is a knowing of facts through emotion. Conceptual knowledge is given its shape by the rational tending with which the mind reaches into things. Poetic intuition is, he says, an 'emotion as form . . . which is intentional.'[77] This is not to subjectivize the notion of intuition, although hostile critics have read Maritain's later work in this way.[78] It is to propose that emotion can carry us so deeply into things that we perceive their inner analogies with other forms. Poetic intuition knows that the adulterous passion of Paulo and Francesca 'is' a restless wind: the image is 'there', inside the thing, but it is perceived supra-conceptually.

When the import of the convergence between person and fact is recreated in art, it is the work's poetic sense. This objectifies the poet's intuition by carrying her exploration of reality into the poem's structure. The poetic sense conducts its audience toward the object which it frames: it is making visible, or audible or palpable through feeling.

Maritain's way of thinking diverges in one respect from that of von Balthasar and the Southerners: he has little interest in human historicality. So intent was he upon the objectivity of being, truth and beauty, that he neglected the traditional contexts in which they are recognized. Unlike MacIntyre, he does not notice that practical knowledge requires both a teacher, from whom skills are inherited, and a community in which they are judged. Maritain thus has a tinge of what Lonergan calls the 'classicist' perspective. For Lonergan, 'classical culture' is built on the paradigmatic value of the universal, whilst 'empirical culture', which he says governs the modern world, is based upon that of the experiential and the historical.[79]

I have stated that Bergson's method was somewhat like Husserl's: both set out to delineate the web of relations in between consciousness and its objects. Husserlian phenomenology is guaranteed by a direct insight, or intuition.[80] Its insight grasps the necessary connections which bind substance kinds together. For Husserl, the paradigmatic sciences are those which are purely theoretical. The sciences of contingent, empirical fact rest upon those which define universals.[81] Bergson takes the opposite view: the conscious relation to the individual fact is the typical, most highly valued case of understanding.

Maritain's aesthetic follows suit. Poetic intuition does not engage with facts in their uniform or conceptualizable level. It touches the concrete particular. Poetic intuition is a quixotic animal. It gives us real knowledge of external things, just as philosophical knowledge does. But it is not directed to generalities. It is the seeing of meaning within one unique fact. It finds out the necessary connections within some contingent detail of the natural world. In his 'Frontiers of Poetry', Maritain claims that poetry is the

> divination of the spiritual in the things of sense . . .
> Metaphysics . . . pursues the spiritual, but . . . Whereas
> it keeps to . . . knowledge . . . of truth, poetry keeps to the
> line of making . . . one snatches at the spiritual in the idea
> . . . the other glimpses it in the flesh . . . Metaphysics
> pursues definitions, poetry every form glittering by the
> way . . . The one isolates mystery in order to know it, the
> other makes use of mystery like an unknown force.[82]

'Poetry' leads through the qualitative density of particular things into transcendence. It points to the aspect of things which exceeds conceptual definition. Because it is not harnessed by a concept, such knowledge is open to the infinite.[83]

Maritain's aesthetic gives experiential knowledge its status. And, as he conceives it, poetic intuition impels the mind toward particular realities. It is by circling upon the unique fact that the poetic mind captures a nexus of certainties. Poetic intuition provides the basis of a 'particularizing metaphysic'. It sees and creates objects which convey the surplus of being which pulses through simple facts – as in Van Gogh's chair, and especially for Maritain, in Cezanne's paintings. 'Poetic intuition' is intended to explain a contemporary, not an historical, fact. But it is an analogue of the grasp of meaning in historical fact which Christianity requires.

In his *Creative Intuition in Art and Poetry*, Maritain describes the development of Western art. He selects four phases as its pivots. Poetic intuition is said to evolve from being overwhelmed by the presence of things, to representing the exterior world through the medium of poetic self-awareness. This history was made possible by the doctrine of the Trinity, which ascribed person-hood to God. In Byzantine and Romanesque art, the human self annihilates itself before the spectacle of the kingship of Christ.[84] In the second, Gothic phase, 'the human soul gleams everywhere through the barred windows of the objective world.'[85] In the art of the Renaissance, which succeeds this, the objective world is recreated in the crucible of the painter's imagination. The fourth phase begins with the Romantics, and is still with us. The poet now shows both the givenness of beauty, and how it resounds in the self. She imparts to her work both the illumination of the thing and the play of colours which the thing throws upon the self.

Where Maritain speaks of the emergence of the poetic 'I', von Balthasar claims that Dante inaugurates the existential period of theological aesthetics. From here on, instead of understanding God's glory through the cosmos, one knows that glory in the unique person.[86] As the two authors see it, the ancient and the modern poetic intuition are both realistic. The 'classical' intuition, Maritain suggests, was filtered through an arch of concepts. The typically modern insight aims simply to repro-duce the poet's 'flash of reality', in its infinite extension. This requires a more intensive and 'affective' bond between the poet and her world. In classical poetry, the complex web of con-ceptual designation holds the individual words apart. The modern poem is more 'impacted'. It is held together by a fluid, and yet cohesive emotion. This is why the poetry of Tate and of Hopkins is somewhat 'hermetic': the words inhere tightly in one another, as if trying to become a single meaning.[87]

Some modern art has lost the balance between a world known through the self, and a world transmuted into the self. It forgets that the knowing through emotion in which poetic knowledge consists is an intentional relation. Maritain urges that it is only when the poet identifies reality with his self – as in one side of Rimbaud – that his words become a self-sufficient kingdom. Having engorged the world, the poet can spin from his self a web of magical words, weaving a world wholly within his control. The fictional world thus created has no relation to being as the 'other'. Maritain calls this project 'narcissistic' and 'Promethean'. It has excised intuition from making.[88] It is not the *necessary* outcome of the methods of modern art.

Conclusion

Maritain's aesthetic Thomism draws upon both the shape of the subject and the particularity of the facts to which it looks. The transcendental Thomists, such as Lonergan, delineate the former with lucidity. But, because he is preoccupied with universal *truth*, the dynamism of Lonergan's work moves away from the single, beautiful fact of which myth and revelation speak. The cultural-linguists, such as Kerr and Lindbeck, can say why faith is bound to a story sequence. But, although their critique of modernist subjectivism is well placed, they treat the self as an epiphenomenon of the social narrative. If we begin in the wonder of being, beyond narrative and self, we can include both.

Both the restoration of the shape of biblical narrative, to which postliberal theology sets its hand, and the quest for the forms of experience, to which Lonergan aspired, are necessary for Christology. The restatement of Maritain's perspective will go further. By pointing to the dialogical character of being it draws out the relational character of experience. It can show where being touches the subject – without embroiling itself in epistemology. Thus will it liberate philosophy from its post-Kantian *pudeur* in the face of real being.

The beauty of being emerges through proportion and integrity, taken together as form, and through radiance. The facts in which these properties coinhere are analogical symbols: Maritain claims that the analogical forms of artistic works bear witness to the unity of being. His idea of intuition suggests how imagination grasps the abundance of existence within particular facts. The person faces a finitude like their own; but that otherness is infinite.

I have treated Maritain's 'poetic intuition' as equivalent to what some of the other writers in this study call realistic imagination. This is not accurate. It is only the combination of art and poetic intuition which creates that fully embodied relation to the world which allows the self to feel its way into individual facts. 'Art' and 'poetry' conjoin to effect concrete knowledge. Like goodness, beauty is known as much by practical engagement as in theories. In the chapters about the Southerners, the imagination will be put to work as a means of perceiving beauty. With Lynch, the image becomes a guide to human action. Finally, von Balthasar will supply the Christological application of the notion of human connaturality with the transcendentals. These writers create a metaphysic for an empirical culture.

They regard imaginative knowledge as a practical engagement in being. It is not a special aesthetic perception, but a *rapprochement* with reality which is informative in the degree that it is direct. If it involves us in the given, it sheds the light of contemplative intuition on the transcendental which is known through theory: that is, on truth.

The propensity of human beings to create independent, meaningful forms is a paradigm for the theological aesthetic: thus is the relation of God to the world. And if, as Newman said, Christianity is a 'supernatural tale', which 'tells us who the Author is by saying what he had done', the two poles of heaven and earth are not immobile.[89] Both have a part in a drama. In response to that drama, human beings create language, the primary dialogue with being. The ability to speak meaningfully is discovered within a given society. The true proposition would be so whether or not there were a community to understand it. But it has its evidential force within a community. Community is thus a concrete presentation of the transcendentals. Lacking such analogues, the transcendentals fall upon deaf ears. Christ is the ground of the forms of beauty, of the communicability of truth, and of the real presentation of being. The 'one and multiple' identity of the sign flows ultimately from Christ the Word. If our imagination fails in realism, we may be blind to Him also.

NOTES

1 Such as that of Louis Buchner and Karl Vogt. Vogt claimed that brains, presumably including his own, produce thought in the same way that the liver secretes bile. Harald Hoffdung, *A History of Modern Philosophy: A Sketch of the History of Philosophy from the Close of the Renaissance to our Own Day*, Volume II, pp. 499–504.

2 Edmund Husserl, 'Prologomena to Pure Logic', in *Logical Investigations*, Vol. I, pp. 53–247. Herbert Spiegelberg notes the kinship in *The Phenomenological Movement: A Historical Introduction*, Vol. I, p. 119.

3 Bergson says that consciousness is 'the direction of a movement' in his *An Introduction to Metaphysics*, p. 77.

4 Ibid. p. 20.

5 Ibid. p. 6.

6 D. Newton Smith, 'Jacques Maritain's Aesthetics: to Distinguish, to Unite', in O. B. Hardison Jr (ed.), *The Quest for Imagination: Essays in Twentieth Century Aesthetic Criticism*, p. 130.

7 Kevin Kerrane, 'Nineteenth Century Backgrounds of Modern Aesthetic Criticism', in ibid. p. 19–20.

8 Bergson, *An Introduction to Metaphysics*, pp. 16 and 58.

9 Maritain said later 'I was crazy with Baudelaire'. *Carnets* 24, quoted in *Mounier and Maritain: A French Catholic Understanding of the Modern World*, by Joseph Amato, p. 32; see also pp. 35 and 47 and Raissa Maritain, *We Have Been Friends Together: Memoirs*, pp. 79 and 83–98.

10 Maritain broke with Bergson on deciding that we need not respond to one form of 'conceptualism' by rejecting propositional truth as such: Maritain, *Bergsonian Philosophy and Thomism* [1914], pp. 16–17.

11 Raissa Maritain, *Friends*, pp. 192–197; Daniel Halévy, *Péguy and Les Cahiers de la Quinzaine*, pp. 134–135.

12 Newton Smith, 'Maritain's Aesthetics', p. 138.

13 Wellek says that this book can 'be interpreted as deserting Thomism for an almost Bergsonian intuitionism which . . . exalts French symbolism.': 'Philosophy and Post-War American Criticism', in *Concepts of Criticism*, p. 322.

14 Emmanuel Mounier, cited by Amato, *A French Catholic*, p. 97.

15 Appendix 2: The Scholastic use of the Term Transcendental, pp. 195–197.

16 Maritain, *The Dream of Descartes* pp. 29–30, 38 and 156.

17 Maritain, *The Degrees of Knowledge* [1932], p. 84.

18 Ibid. p. 261.

19 Ibid. pp. 260–261.

20 Maritain *Art*, pp. 32–33.

21 von Balthasar, *Theo-Drama: II*, p. 25.

22 Allen Tate, 'The Man of Letters in the Modern World', in *The Man of Letters in the Modern World: Selected Essays 1928–1955*, p. 22.

23 Hans Urs von Balthasar, *Theo-Drama: Theological Dramatic Theory: Volume I: Prologomena*, p. 43.

24 Fergus Kerr, *Theology After Wittgenstein*, p. 149.

25 Lindbeck, *Doctrine*, p. 121.

26 Kerr, *After Wittgenstein*, p. 153.

27 Ibid. p. 183.

28 Ibid. p. 150.

29 Ibid. p. 184.

30 van der Leeuw, *Religion in Essence*, p. 216.

31 Kerr, *After Wittgenstein*, p. 75 and 96.

32 Von Balthasar, *Theo-Drama: I*, p. 535.

33 Alasdair MacIntyre, *Three Rival Versions of Moral Enquiry: Encyclopedia, Genealogy, and Tradition* pp. 54–55.

34 Ibid. pp. 72–76.

35 For example, von Balthasar, *Glory: V*, pp. 9–10.

36 Von Balthasar, *Glory: I*, p. 243.

37 Francis Dunlop, *Max Scheler* p. 47–48.

38 Maritain, *Intuition*, p. 162.

39 Paul Matthews pointed this correlation out to me.

40 Maritain, *Art*, p. 30.

41 See the Appendix on Patristic and Scholastic Theories of Beauty, on pp. 189–194.

42 Maritain, *Intuition*, p. 365.

43 Aristotle, *Poetics*, B, Chapter 6, II, 1450a 16–20 and Chapter 8, 1451a 30–35.

44 Maritain speaks about 'immanent' action in order to make it clear that he does not refer to the work's effect on its readers.

45 Gordon, *How to Read a Novel*, p. 48.

46 Lynch, *Christ and Apollo*, p. 156.

47 Maritain, *Intuition*, p. 138.

48 This extension is spatial for pictorial/sculptural works and temporal for musical works. For Suzanne Langer, such extension belongs to the 'virtual space' of a painting, and to the 'virtual time' of music: *Feeling and Form*, pp. 69–76 and 109–112.

49 Maritain, *Intuition*, p. 162.

50 Ibid. pp. 128 and 371.

51 'The Symbolic Imagination: The Mirrors of Dante', in Allen Tate, *The Man of Letters*, pp. 93–112, p. 96.

52 Maritain, *Art*, p. 46.

53 Appendix on Patristic and Scholastic Theories of Beauty, on pp. 189–194.

54 Maritain, *Art*, p. 32.

55 Maritain, *Intuition*, p. 164.

56 Ibid. p. 165.

57 Gordon, *How to Read a Novel*, pp. 120–131 and 144.

58 Von Balthasar, *Theo-Drama: II*, pp. 27–28.

59 Louis Bouyer, *Life and Liturgy*, pp. 87 and 101.

60 Martin Hengel, *The Atonement: A Study in the Origins of the Doctrine in the New Testament* pp. 1–32.

61 Maritain, *Art*, p. 71.

62 O'Leary, *Questioning Back*, pp. 85 and 94.

63 William Lynch, *Christ and Prometheus: A New Image of the Secular*, p. 58.

64 Aristotle, *Nichomachean Ethics*, Bk. VI, Ch. 2, 1139a, 29–32.

65 Jean Gimpel, *Against Art and Artists* pp. 14–22.

66 Burch Brown, *Religious Aesthetics*, p. 28.

67 Maritain, *Intuition*, p. 46.

68 Ibid. p. 47.

69 Maritain, *Art*, p. 34.

70 On the distinction, see Maritain, *Art*, pp. 9–11.

71 For an illuminating description of the interplay between 'imaginative body' and work of art, see Marion Milner, *On Not Being Able to Paint*, p. 36.

72 Maritain, *Degrees*, pp. 347, 388, 390, 400–404, 406–408.

73 Bernard Lonergan, *Method in Theology*, pp. 105–109.

74 Maritain, *Art*, pp. 70–71.

75 Von Balthasar, *Glory: I*, pp. 220–242; *Theo-Drama: I*, p. 287.

76 Maritain, *Intuition*, p. 118.

77 Ibid. pp. 119–120.

78 Harold Weatherby, *The Keen Delight: The Christian Poet in the Modern World*, Chapter 6.

79 Lonergan, *Method in Theology*, pp. 301–303 and 'The Transition from a Classical World-View to 'Historical Mindedness', in *A Second Collection: Papers by Bernard Lonergan*, edited by W. F. J. Ryan and Bernard J. Tyrell pp. 5–6.

80 Spiegelberg, *Phenomenological Movement*, Vol. I, p. 117.

81 Husserl, *Logical Investigations*, Vol. 1, pp. 225–231. This is said not to be a judgement of value.

82 Maritain, *Art*, p. 96–97.

83 Newton Smith, 'Maritain's Aesthetics', p. 141.

84 Compare Aidan Nichols on the Iconophilic theology of this period, in *The Art of God Incarnate*, pp. 57–58.

85 Maritain, *Intuition*, p. 22.

86 Von Balthasar, *The Glory of the Lord: A Theological Aesthetics: Volume III: Studies in Theological Styles: Lay Styles*, edited by John Riches, pp. 24 and 29–34.

87 Maritain, *Intuition*, pp. 261, 312, and 318.

88 Ibid p. 79.

89 Von Balthasar, *Theo-Drama: II*, p. 11, quoting from J. H. Newman, 'The Tamworth Reading Room', in *Discussions and Arguments on Various Subjects* (1872), p. 296.

Chapter 4

'Reality Means Simply Inexhaustible Quality.' The Literary Imagination in the Writings of the Fugitive Agrarians

This chapter describes the Southern writers' conception of the image. Maritain was a close associate of these poets and novelists, in late years.[1] Some of their ideas stem from his work. William Lynch was also a friend of Allen Tate, and they owe each other a mutual debt. Tate's criticism and fiction, the philosophy of Maritain, and Lynch's Christology are interdependent. For Maritain, the Southerners, Lynch, and von Balthasar, the *image* is the guarantor of an objective reality which the various idealisms seem to them to deny. Maritain's later aesthetic includes the creative self in a realistic metaphysics. Von Balthasar delineates the structures of religious experience in order to graft them into the self-expression of God. The philosophical, poetic and theological aspects of this study each propose that objective form creates a pattern for perception. For the theologians, Christ is the transcendent Form which synthesizes human knowledge. To give such a Christology a base in human understanding, I explain why the Southerners treat imagination as the source of unified experience.

The Vanderbilt Fugitives

These writers were born in the Southern States of America, in the farming communities of Kentucky and Tennessee.[2] The group gathered at Vanderbilt University, in Nashville, Tennessee. John Crowe Ransom was the oldest, teacher and mentor to the others. He graduated from Vanderbilt in 1909. He went from there to Oxford, where F. H. Bradley was his tutor. Bradley enlarged Ransom's knowledge of Kant's philosophy.[3] He returned to Vanderbilt in 1914. Allen Tate (1899–1984) entered Vanderbilt in 1918. He attended Ransom's lectures. In reply to the pompous suggestion that Ransom had taught his students the 'knowledge of good and evil', Tate observed that Ransom trained them in 'Kantian aesthetics' and imbued them with a 'dualism' based in the *Nichomachean Ethics*.[4]

By the early 1920s, Ransom, Donald Davidson, Tate and Robert Penn Warren were meeting to read their poetry out loud. A journal grew from these meetings. They named it *The Fugitive*. It was published from April 1922 until 1925.[5] Its arrival did not create much excitement. There was one exception. A journalist from the *Chattanooga News* wrote the headline 'U.S. Best Poets Here in Tennessee'. This was Caroline Gordon. She and Tate married in 1924. Since it would have been impossible to discuss the Southern literary renaissance in its entirety, I have restricted myself to the work of John Crowe Ransom, Allen Tate and Caroline Gordon.

The Historical Imagination

C. S. Lewis observed that the medieval imagination was sheltered by a cosmos redolent with mythical meanings. Von Balthasar says that the loss of this image stripped the analogy of being of its 'perspicuity'.[6] The historical culture of the South had to some extent remained a social theatre. Its myth did not reach up into a heaven filled with the concentric spheres of Ptolemaic astronomy. It stretched back to the Roman civilization which the South believed itself to recreate. Its myth was historical, not cosmological. It was for that reason humanly accessible. The Fugitives' first analogue of the transcendentals was the history of the South. Their education in a historically conscious society led them to devise an imaginative defence of tradition. Historical facts are spread out in time and in space: they are known in an act which is likewise extensional.

The Social Quest for the Transcendentals

When the Fugitives first began to meet, they were not consciously attached to the Christianity of their upbringing. It was not until the Scopes trial in 1925 that they found themselves, to their surprise, on the side of the biblicists as against the evolutionists. They recognized that, despite the biblicists' anti-intellectualism, their acceptance of Scripture as binding sheltered a sense of mystery. They now began to envisage themselves as Southern writers, acknowledging the effects of Southern traditions upon their own sensibilities.[7] They were more attached to an ideal of the South than to that of the inerrancy of Scripture.

They saw the Scopes trial as an incursion of the North upon the South. The 'North' became these poets' symbol of Platonism coupled with scientific progress. They linked 'Northerness' with the industrializing forces which were changing the face of the as yet agricultural South. The 'earth' of the South was again being attacked by protagonists whose spiritual ideals incorporated no bodily image of the spiritual nature of man. The Fugitives became apologists for the farming basis of the Southern economy. The first fruit of this defence was *I'll Take My Stand*. Published in 1928, this volume of essays champions the 'contemplative' rural life, as against an ever-moving industrial volition. It led its authors to find the centre of their vision: 'the symbol of the land.'[8] The history of the 'earth' of the South became the archetypal image through which the Fugitives perceived the transcendentals. This earth acts on its inhabitants as a concrete given: a fence, and a boundary for the imagination, as well as a means of transcendence. To imagine it is to be drawn into a dense, singular fact.

The Poetic Quest

Tate was the evangelist of literary modernism to the group. The youthful Tate translated some of Baudelaire's poems, such as the 'Correspondences'.[9] Baudelaire's poem begins

> La Nature est un temple où de vivants piliers
> Laissent parfois sortir des confuses paroles;
> L'homme y passe à travers des forêts de symboles
> Oui l'observent avec des regards familiers.

which Tate translates as

> All nature is a temple where the alive
> Pillars breathe often a tremor of mixed words
> Man wanders in a forest of accords
> That peer familiarly from each ogive.

It concludes

> Qui chantent les transports de l'esprit et des sens

which Tate renders as

> To transports of the spirit and the sense!

Tate's translations of Baudelaire's poetry were the beginning of his quest for the drawing together of the world into a 'temple', a space set apart, as a single, sacred whole, which encapsulates the holy within itself. If the cosmos is a single whole, it will have the cohesion which Maritain's notion of the analogy of being envisages. Caroline Gordon says of 'Correspondences' that it,

> resolves itself . . . into its component parts of Complication and Resolution. The Complication is man's effort to find out what the pillars are saying to him. Baudelaire resolves the complication by means of a series of similes which . . . combine to form the metaphor which will transport us to the level of symbolic action. . . . the 'familiar looks' are . . . the things by which we are surrounded every day [and] . . . 'they sing the transports of the spirit and the senses' – that is, they are able to lift us

from the natural level to the supernatural level.[10]

The writings of the French symbolists were Tate's means of rediscovering the corporeal interrelation of all the world, and of the poet to that world. The essays which he published in *The Fugitive* defend their worth. Tate told Davidson that he admired 'late nineteenth century French poetry because that poetry represented an integration of sensibility.'[11] Tate's quest is marked at its outset by a desire for the 'unity of being.'[12] His first concern was for the consequences of the 'unity of being' for the self, in the 'integration of sensibility'. He was not to discover the 'unity of being' through philosophical concepts but in the tangible data to which poetic intuition is directed. Poetic insight does not achieve its synthesis through abstraction; it makes sensible images unfold into one another. Maritain says that in Baudelaire's poetry,

> the poem has been transformed into a single missile conveying a single . . . intuition. . . . all its parts . . . are joined together only by the fire of the poetic intuition, because the logical sense has been burned away . . . and is now only a channel for this fire.[13]

Poetic intuition springs directly on the thing which it desires to know, and grasps it supra-conceptually. Tate believed that poetry must fuse a 'subject' with a 'vision'. He needed to find how to make the self transparent to external things, and to find a way of imagining facts in which they illuminate his own experience. He required a metaphysics which presented the interrelation of 'world' and cosmos. He would unearth it through the channels of poetic intuition. His grasp of the 'unity of being' will depend on connaturality, rather than on rational explication.

The Realistic Imagination

Ransom claims that 'reality means simply inexhaustible quality' in a letter to Tate of 1927.[14] It becomes so when it is known as an image. For Ransom, an 'image' is

marvellous in its assemblage of many properties . . .
science can manage the image . . . only by equating it
to one property . . . It is . . . by abstraction that science
destroys the image . . . It is thus that we lose the power of
the imagination . . . by which we are able to contemplate
things in their rich and contingent materiality. But our
dreams reproach us, for in dreams they come alive again.
Likewise, our memory; which recall[s] the images in their
panoply of circumstance . . . It is the dream, the recollection, which compels us to poetry and to aesthetic
experience.[15]

These are Ransom and his pupils' recurrent themes. 'Science' is
pictured as a methodology which is divorced from experience,
and as a way of thought which breaks the natural and social
worlds into pieces. Ransom's 'science' is similar to what Lynch
will call the 'univocal mind'. The univocal mind disregards the
distinction between things in order to transpose them into a
single logical pattern. It requires universal connection, not
specific fact. Conversely, by virtue of its relation to the past,
'imagination' recaptures the fullness of experience. It enables
one to block out 'scenic meanings'. Such an aesthetic perception
is said to be nearer to real experience than an analytic
concourse with the world. Likewise, for Tate, 'the imaginative
wholeness . . . of vision . . . yields . . . the quality of experience.'[16] Imagination manifests human experience in the round:
the univocal work of 'science' only affords a partial glimpse.[17]

Ransom: The Ironic Imagination

Ransom's conception of imagination is a partially Kantian
one. The voracious discipline which he calls 'science' is not
unlike the construction which Kant's followers placed on the
faculty he called 'understanding'. Ransom found the opposite
principle of the synthetic imagination in both Kant and
Coleridge. A true rendition of experience is found, not in
the logical order of the Kantian or Coleridgean 'understanding', but in the image.[18] Bergson's writings also mediated these

attitudes to Ransom.[19] Bergson prefers intuition to analysis: he claims that the scientific attitude is manipulative, where intuition allows its object to repose in itself.[20] Bergson goes beyond the Kantian aesthetic, in arguing that Kant's method stretches experience upon the Procrustean bed of concepts. In their deep surplus of the 'concrete', images are more like to things than to concepts. Ransom echoes these themes. He adds that imagination is to be found in the common life of a traditional society. For Ransom, imagination is active when we stand back, and let objects be singular things. This allows their many facets and contours to be seen. Where the mind whose frame is generalized by utilitarian purpose seizes the object in its universality, the object which is played upon by the imagination manifests its uniqueness.

Artistic manufacture interposes a form between maker and object.[21] Because it is responsive to this form, the aesthetic approach to an object is marked by a certain piety. The scientist's approach to his object is under no such restriction. It wrings from things their uniform and predictable properties. But to imagine is to come up against resilient and autonomous facts, which do not exist only in relation to practical need. Imaginative apprehension knows the world in that form in which it is the least assimilable by the mind: that is, as the repository of bottomless and refractory *things*. It allows them to rest in their manifold singularity. As *things*, they are somewhat impassible to intellectual translation into universal concepts. Thus, imagination can concede that the world is other than we would make of it. As Ransom wrote to Tate,

> The poet . . . will . . . refer concept to image with the intention . . . of showing how the concept, the poor thin thing, is drowned in the image . . . and how, ultimately, this world can be neither understood nor possessed. In the poet's art we will . . . see . . . a religious . . . attitude to which we will come perforce after the conceited Subjectivism into which we have been persuaded by the practical and the scientific life alike . . . In the degree that poetry approaches this plane, it approaches tragedy . . . In tragedy we admit to the . . . failure of our effort to grasp

and dominate the world. But in tragedy we also return to [the] . . . very healing attitude . . . of respect.[22]

Ransom is taking part in the resurgence of philosophical realism which took place at the turn of the century. Its proponents deflated the idealistic metanarratives of an earlier era. G. E. Moore and Franz Brentano contended that the philosophies of their predecessors are inadequate to the data given by consciousness.[23] Bergson's thought belongs here. He held that his 'intuitive metaphysics' transcends both realism and idealism, by depicting the rich 'duration' of consciousness, as a whole, and not as the fragments into which the psychologists of his day had dissected it.[24] We begin to recover the unity of being through the phenomenological examination of experience.

The imaginative contemplation of contingent particulars reveals their boundless resources of aspects and attributes. Maritain drew on Ransom in order to argue that the poetic image captures something of the obdurate concreteness which is lacking in ideas.[25] Ransom underlines the point that the *thingliness* of an imaged object surpasses the capacity of the intellect to grasp it.[26] For both, specific things open into a ridged and differentiated depth. Both define the poet's task as the revelation of the many-layeredness within particular things. Ransom shares Maritain's belief that imaginative knowledge embodies some truth about reality. He states that,

> imagination is an organ of knowledge whose technique is images . . . The image presented by the imagination ordinarily means to be true in the commonest sense of true: verifiable, based on observation.[27]

Literary works contain significant information about reality. To deny that is to believe that images are projections which obscure or distort the simple facts over which they lie. This is to have an eviscerated notion of what 'information' can be like. The question is that of the depth of real being: on how many levels can the mind rightly relate to it? That of sense alone can neither do justice to nor account for the concordance with reality which imaginative works transcribe.

Ransom's belief that literature is stimulated by an ironic

perception is integral to his own poetic realism. Perhaps the
apprisal of the otherness of reality which he mentions to Tate is
ironic rather than tragic. The contrast between desire and the
world to which it must be accommodated is always present to
Ransom's mind: tragedy attends primarily to the external
pattern. Ransom's advocacy of irony is an important source
of a realistic understanding of the imagination.

It is not our first immersion in things that creates a realistic
image. It is, rather, the recreation of that initial contact, after we
have grasped the tension between how things are and how we
wish them to be.[28] In a letter to Tate, Ransom describes the
content of the 'three moments' of experience. In the first, we
meet things in their material individuality. There follows the
'second moment' of classification, in which our scientific interests predominate. Now the particular thing disappears into the
'pure memory', says Ransom, quoting Bergson.[29] The 'third
moment' is, at once, an attempt to return to the spontaneity of
original perception and an acceptance that this is no longer
possible. It is ironic because it admits to the plurality of
experience. It is ironic because giving up the romantic, direct
engagement with nature is

> so unwilling . . . that the fruit of it is wisdom and not
> bitterness . . . Irony is the rarest of the states of mind,
> because it is the most inclusive; the whole mind has been
> active in arriving at it . . . both poetry and science.[30]

Aesthetic activity is the product of a mind which has gone
through all of the phases of experience: Ransom is no primi-
tivist. As a work of the third moment, poetry contains both
abstract concepts and tangible images. It relates, if it does not
reconcile, image and generalization. It extends further into
reality than the mind of science can reach: it represents the
world on the level of form. 'Primitivism' gives us the image as it
reacts upon our senses. The ironist, utilizing both concepts and
images, imagines simple facts on the level in which they have
their own basis in reality.

As Ransom sees it the Romantics, such as Wordsworth,
attempt to create poetry simply by expressing emotion.[31] Such
is their dislike of 'science' that they eject it from composition.

The result is a formless poetry, whose descriptive potency is minimal. Ransom upholds the principle that Maritain represented, and that von Balthasar and Lynch will maintain: the mind has to transverse form on the way to a deeper meaning. For Ransom, such meaning does not seem to be referred to any transcendental being. It reflects, rather, the brute factuality of this world. But, Ransom's statements recall Maritain's suggestion that it is preferable not to imagine God's relation to the world in universal and abstract terms.

In his *Images of Faith*, Lynch argues that the theological imagination develops from a wholly receptive attitude to one which has a sense of irony about its beliefs, shedding the innocence which demands immediate perfection. In order thus to grow, it confronts those things which are contrary to itself. Lynch treats this absorption of otherness as the principle of drama. A dramatic representation of the world is realistic. It presents an imaginative knowledge of the world by showing many levels and types in one concrete form. Such imaginative irony perceives the bonds of being even within the very specific facts of which Ransom speaks. As Lynch puts it,

> We have often abstracted from the actual existence of things and called it God. So we may say that God is not heavy like iron. But supposing I say that he is even more actual than iron, meaning that if you think iron is really there, that is the direction to take to imagine, that God is there.[32]

Because they love the expanse and the variety of the world's forms, both Ransom and Lynch depict the engagement with reality as a comic movement. Ransom envisages the imagination as descrying an almost bottomless amplitude within facts. This depth will only reveal itself to us if, in the abatement of practical appetite, we allow it to do so.

Allen Tate: The Historical Imagination

The hand of his teacher is apparent in Tate's contention that the literary imagination is a channel of a rounded perception of reality. Having absorbed Ransom's belief that literary works are to be construed as *forms*, Tate will proceed to look for the transcendent form which upholds the aesthetic synthesis of perception. Tate found in the literary imagination the representation of human actions as significant forms. The imaginative representation of things is its 'own goal':[33] it is an end in itself. Those analogues upon which it touches are not absolutes outside and above the shapes of our lives. Rather, for Tate, they are narratives which flow through and guide our experience. Maritain thought that the literary work's integrity carries its action. Tate's conception of the literary work as a 'synthetic whole' and as a 'dramatic image' are interrelated. Both bring the literary form within our grasp. If the capacity to know or to express dramatic form is lost,

> we fail to see any great portions of our experience as wholes: I use the verb see to mean actual vision, which . . . reduce[s] the chief human passions to a perceptible scale . . . To represent as action, and as a whole, any human experience, one must make a fable, and when the fable is typical of one kind of action it becomes a myth, which conveys its meanings dramatically. When we read poetry we bring to it the pseudo-scientific habit of mind; we are used to joining things up in . . . disconnected processes in terms that are abstract and thin and so our sensuous enjoyment is confined to our immediate field of sensation.[34]

Tate's poetry sought out the dramatic form which illuminates and unifies the texture of experience. His pursuit of an image which combines 'subject and vision' is initiated in the early twenties, when he lost his confidence in the ability of science to provide such a full description of reality (if ever he had it). But he was still seeking an escape from the solipsism which he held to be attendant upon the 'failure' of which he speaks above ('*confined to our immediate field of sensation.*'). Tate looked first to history for the light which was to unify experience. All of the Fugitives' search for the unity of being were rooted in their relation to the history of the South. Tate had an especially historical imagination. But he had a less literal attachment to the idea that the manners and morals of the Old South could be made to survive into the modern world than had most of his Fugitive colleagues.[35] And, as Robert Dupree argues, it was the vividness of Tate's historical re-creations which led him to find that history cannot give the ultimate version of reality.[36] He set out in the 1920s with the image of the Old South. But this culture alone could not take the weight which he laid upon it. Tate looked behind the specific forms of the South toward what he took it to symbolize: it meant the contemplative society. He then asked 'what would uphold such a social world?' He moved past the South towards symbols which would be simultaneously historical and religious. His reflections on historical myth made it evident that the self disintegrates without a relation to the history of its society. The relation to history is the poet's paradigm of all the other bonds between self and world. And yet, the historical myth will be found to rely upon a myth which is broader still: that provided by religious belief. Tate had learned from Ransom that the more concrete a symbol, the richer its analogy to reality. Moving beyond Ransom's semi-Kantian and naturalistic synthesis of experience, he tried to imagine symbols which thread consciousness into the world, and yet exist beyond it: he wanted symbols which are both definite and transcendent.

Tate found that imagination and the historical sense are interwoven. For historical apprehension requires an image which can assume the horizontality of time and space.[37] In his essay 'Religion and the Old South', Tate criticizes what he calls the 'Long View' of history, such as was held by Hegel: it converts the historical image into an abstract concept. Conversely, he praises the 'Short View' for its narrow and specific vision of historical events. The 'Short View' was typical of the mentality of the Old South. Its members, Tate claims, loved to dwell upon the figures of the past, treating them as moral exemplars, and as aesthetic 'wholes'. This particularistic exemplarism gave the Southern imagination a mythic quality.[38] Poetic intuition – the concentration of imagination in particular things – now becomes historical. If history is regarded in its specifitude, it becomes an aesthetic object which attaches imagination to the world.

In his 'Religion and the Old South', Tate gives two examples of aesthetic objects: horses, and the figures of history. He praises the society which, he says, allowed both objects to retain a certain 'inviolable' individuality. That is, with respect to the horse: the society was not exclusively interested in those of its aspects which it holds in common with other horses, in which it is a commodity, or a repository of power. On the part of the historical figures: it took the 'Short View', and did not translate them into abstract ideas.

This is the imagination which delights in the intricacies of historical facts, and makes them flower in meaning. In words which Lynch echoes in his comparison of an infinite, faceless Apollo with the finite and historical Christ, Tate claims that,

> The Southerners . . . were virtually incapable of abstract-ing from the horse his horse power, or from history its historicity . . . There is . . . from the viewpoint of abstract history, not much difference between a centaur, since we speak of horses, and a Christ, since we speak of history. Both are mythical figments reducible in one set of proper-ties to the abstract man-ness. But the Short view . . . is incorrigibly selective, and has been known to prefer Christ to the man-horse.[39]

Both the beasts which the Southerner kept on his farm and the history which he studied at home (so to emulate its characters) had an autonomous value. They were not only objects to be utilized in some pragmatic or idealist system. They were comprehended as images. Images contain more aspects than the mind can put into, or abstract from them. They can be perceived aesthetically: that is, as self-sufficient wholes.

Tate believed that the Southerner's reserve with regard to such objects grew from a religious conscience, in that 'Religion undertakes to place before us the whole horse as he is in himself . . . the modern mind sees only half of the horse – that half which may become a dynamo or an automobile.'[40] Both concrete history and religion give a certain wholeness of experience, in centering it upon a solid image. The mind which is moulded by such forms can rest. It no longer has to brutalize reality, in order to create a model universe. It has found what it needs in an image which is deeper than itself.

The Southerners were marked by an aversion to that abstracted vision which Tate would call the 'angelic intellect'. To be grounded in one's past is to be adjoined to the earth. The 'Short View' of history is earthier and more specific than the 'Long View', which elongates the details of historical character and event in order to render them fit pointers within a preconstructed pattern which becomes all pattern and no fact. The communion with the past which the 'Short View' supplies is one way out of solipsism – the entrapment of the individual in the present, and within the island of its own sensations. It is a way of conversing with the dead. Tate binds himself to the past by making an image of the dead, who are now buried inside the earth.

It is within the soil, or the land, which is the veridical image for the Fugitive-Agrarians, that both history and an imaginative grasp of one's complete – bodily and spiritual – self is to be found. In his poem 'Emblems', Tate writes

> Maryland, Virginia, Caroline
> Pent Images in sleep
> Clay valleys rocky hills old fields of pine
> Unspeakable and deep
>
> Out of that source of time my farthest blood
> Runs strangely to this day
> Unkempt the fathers waste in solitude
> Under the hills of clay . . .
>
> When it is all over and the blood
> Runs out, do not bury this man
> By the far river (where never stood
> His fathers) flowing to the West,
> But take him to the East where life began.
> . . .
> Men cannot live forever
> But they must die forever
> So take this body at sunset
> To the great stream where the pulses start
> In the blue hills . . .

By the great river the forefathers to beguile
Them, being inconceivably young, carved out
Deep hollows of memory on a river isle
Now lost – their murmur the ghost of a shout

In the hollows where the forefathers
Without beards, their faces bright and long
Lay down at sunset by the cool river
In the tall willows amid birdsong . . .

The dead ancestors are encased in 'hills of clay'. Their concavities within the soil are pockets of value and remembrance.
The speaker asks to be united with them in death, and so to be
drawn into the chain of history; indeed, to be properly at rest
because lying alongside those spaces of meaning which the
'forefathers' create. The river by which the narrator wishes to lie
flows to the east. Eden was in the east. The prelapsarian
Paradise is the broadest image which is intuited by the aesthetic
imagination. Maritain suggested that the place in which the
artist forms his images is a kind of mythical Eden.[41] As an object
of contemplation, the eastern flowing river – opposed to the
western moving river – may intend the cessation of the
unceasing drive of the scientific intellect. Tate claimed that
the poetic imagination provides 'a focus of repose for the will
driven intellect'[42] The speaker asks to be buried in a hard place:
'Clay valleys rocky hills old fields of pine'. This is not a typically
lush, Edenic scene. The poem shows a still image of the river
isle, as a burial place. But it also presents the pioneer settlers,
building their homesteads by a river. Not only the masculine
forefathers are here, but also the feminine. The feminine is seen
in the place names, 'Maryland, Virginia, Caroline', (and is thus,
again, an historical image), and in the 'Deep hollows of
memory', excavated by the fathers. The 'fathers' go about
their tasks, but in order to die, or to cease to act, they must
give themselves up to the feminine earth.

In such modern poetry, the poet discovers a meaning within
reality which corresponds to his subjective forms of imagination.
The speaker wishes to be instilled in a soil containing the
historically formed patterns of a life-giving meaning – the
bodies impressing their shape upon the earth. The soil has

been implanted with those bodily forms which, because 'Out of that source . . . my farthest blood runs', give back to the narrator that restful image of death which he requires. Death is lent significance by its connection to a particular place, and to the specific bodies of Tate's dead ancestors. These are the 'emblems' through which he may journey towards death. While curled asleep in the earth, the 'forefathers' are reconciled to the intractable land, in acknowledgement of their own finitude and mortality. The place becomes an image.

But we do not pass from death to resurrection. If meaning is dug from the earth, it finishes there: the poem concludes:

> They've slept full and long, till now the air
> Waits twilit for their echo; and the burning shiver
> Of August strikes like a hawk the crouching hare.

At this juncture, the window opens into nature alone: no path is to be discerned through the sensible into the supernatural.

Tate's first images are external. This is a limiting directive. The history of the self must also be given imaginative shape. Once it has aesthetic form, the self is an analogue of transcendence. We pass through three inclusive analogues of the transcendentals: the land, history and the self.

Conclusion

The literary work conveys knowledge precisely as an intentional *form*: as a form, it is a set of structured meanings; as intentional, it is directed outward. As Maritain said, literary works reflect the intelligibility of reality, by recreating it as a form. This is what the Southerners mean when they say that imagining gives us 'knowledge'. If the imaginative work shows the intelligibility of being, it expresses a truth. For Tate, the truth of the image is its power to show how selves are related to reality: this action carries its audience into that same world.

An incarnational theology must give account both of the otherness of the world, and of its openness. Maritain's view of transcendental beauty extended our initial proposal that beauty is self-communicative. He argues that symbolical forms are entwined in the created analogy of being. They can be a moving stairway into the fullness of reality, and that as representations of the world of particular facts. The literary imagination is a way to knowledge, which must be a way to truth. But truth is given, here, by the self-communicative form which lures the mind into a particular fact. It is known through the beautiful which, as Maritain said, allows all of the transcendentals to shine together.

The Southern writers expand further on the expressiveness of beauty. Utilizing the resources of Romanticism, they defend a traditional culture. The literary imagination preserves intact the fragile individuality of the world. It does this by creating autonomous forms, whose variety of actions imitate the real world, in which brute matter and enlightening shapes are so curiously juxtaposed. The 'realisms' of Ransom and Tate restate the doctrine of analogy in poetic terms. The analogue is the particular image. The notion of the literary analogue as a particular form may derive from Kant.[43] As with Bergson, such forms are seen directly, or intuited within unique events.

The Southerners took part in the return to realism which marked the turn of the century. One of Tate's earliest essays draws on G. E. Moore, Russell, and Whitehead in order to show that poetry forms an image of the 'pattern of perception' by capturing and unifying the convexities and concavities of experience. Here his later comments upon the 'Long View' of history are paralleled by a note about Hegel's aesthetics:

> Romantic German aesthetics, through Hegel, . . . identi-fied poetry with the absolute, but in the conception of the absolute as substance (noumenon), poetry became un-thinkably abstract, substance being absolute only in abstraction and vanishing utterly in concrete experi-ence.[44]

Tate goes beyond Ransom, in thinking that imagining intuits symbolic forms in which the many layers of reality – from the physical to the spiritual – are compacted. Ransom retains the tension between form and sensuous image: this implies some fracture between intelligence and sense. Tate tries harder to close this gap, perhaps because he experienced more keenly the danger of being at the mercy of sense impressions alone. The symbolic form provides a means of self transcendence by enclosing sense within an objective form. It can, he says, only be known by a human 'intelligence'.[45] Intellect is not subordinated to sense or imagination, for, as Tate argues, 'good poetry is a unity of all the meanings, from the furthest extremes of intension and extension . . . our recognition of this unified meaning is the gift . . . of our total human powers.'[46] As with Ransom, 'intension' stands for the concrete object of the sensibility, and 'extension' for that generality which is perceived by the intellect. To bypass either is to lose the true form, and so the meaning, of poetry.[47]

These writers' recovery of realism showed them that the realistic imagination has a tragic aspect. Christian faith must include tragedy because its first, limiting image is the suffering person of the crucified Christ. Christ brings imagination up against something which is infinitely more extensive than itself: this fact compacts into the narrowest intension the most extended of meanings, and holds them together. This paradox is the basis of von Balthasar's and Lynch's theology. It is the ground for the Southerners' belief that simple objects can rightly be imagined in depth and complexity.

NOTES

1 Squires, *Literary Biography*, pp. 152 and 189–192.
2 Louis Rubin, *The Wary Fugitives: Four Poets and the South*, p. 65.
3 F. P. Jarvis, 'F. H. Bradley's Appearance and Reality and the Critical Theory of John Crowe Ransom', in Thomas Daniel Young (ed), *John Crowe Ransom: Critical Essays and a Bibliography*, pp. 206–209.
4 Allen Tate, 'A Southern Mode of the Imagination', in *Collected Essays*, pp. 554–568 (pp. 556–557).
5 Most of Ransom's poetry was written during the 1920s, whilst the contact amongst the Fugitives was closest. Some of his best work appeared in *The Fugitive*: 'Bells for John Whiteside's Daughter' in February, 1924, and 'The Equilibrists' in September, 1925. His essay, 'Thoughts on the Poetic Discontent' was published in the March, 1925 issue. On the effect of the group on his criticism: Thomas Daniel Young, *Gentleman in a Dustcoat: A Biography of John Crowe Ransom*, pp. 126, 147–148, 157–158 and 185–186.
6 C. S. Lewis, *The Discarded Image*; von Balthasar, *Glory: III*, p. 105ff.
7 After the Scopes trial, Tate told Davidson 'I agree with Sanborn [their

philosophy teacher] that science has little to say for itself . . . he used to emphasise that view but I scoffed . . . science . . . as we inherit it as Mechanism from the 17th century has nothing . . . to say about reality: if the Church or a fishmonger asserts that reality is . . . cheese . . . Science . . . has no right to deny it.' Dated 3rd March, 1926, in *The Literary Correspondence of Donald Davidson and Allen Tate*, edited by John Tyree and Thomas Daniel Young, p. 158. Davidson and Ransom agreed: Rubin, *Wary Fugitives* p. 55; Donald Davidson, *Southern Writers in the Modern World*, pp. 40–41.

8 Louise Cowan, *The Southern Critics*, p. 16. See also Louis Rubin's Introduction to the new edition of of *I'll Take My Stand*, p. xi-xv and xvii.

9 *The Fugitive*, December, 1924; Tate's *Collected Poems: 1919–1976*.

10 Gordon, *How to Read a Novel*, pp. 165–166.

11 Dated 23 June 1925, in Tate and Davidson, *Correspondence*, p. 140.

12 R. K. Meiners, *The Last Alternatives: A Study of the Works of Allen Tate*, p. 15.

13 Maritain, *Intuition*, pp. 262–263.

14 John Crowe Ransom, 'Art as Adventure in Form: Letters of John Crowe Ransom to Allen Tate', edited by Thomas Daniel Young and George Core, *Southern Review*, Volume 12 (Autumn, 1976), p. 796.

15 John Crowe Ransom, 'Poetry: A Note on Ontology', in *The World's Body*, pp. 115–116.

16 'Three Types of Poetry', in Tate, *Essays*, p. 92.

17 William J. Handy, *Kant and the Southern New Critics*, pp. 10 and 43–44.

18 Coleridge draws the distinction between reason and understanding from Kant: Basil Willey *Samuel Taylor Coleridge*, pp. 89–90; Lovejoy notes the influence of Jacobi and Schelling: *Essays in the History of Ideas*, p. 254. For Kant, reason and understanding-serve purely epistemic purposes. For Coleridge, the distinction symbolizes the failures of the mind of his time. He blamed an exclusive reliance on understanding for the mechanistic science, the utilitarian ethics, and the literalistic biblical exegesis of the modern age. His distinction is meant to show that thought is both assimilative (through understanding) and visionary (on the part of reason). Understanding focuses on means, whereas reason looks for ends and causes: Coleridge, *On the Constitution of Church and State: According to the Idea of Each*, edited by John Colmer, pp. 58–59. Understanding should treat reason as a higher authority: *Aids to Reflection: On the Several Grounds of Prudence, Morality and Religion*, edited by Edward Howell pp. 189 & 198ff. Understanding creates a neat mosaic of information: reason seizes the inner 'necessity' of this structure (ibid). Understanding is 'discursive', where reason is 'contemplative' (ibid). Understanding is passive, whereas reason creatively grasps the essence, and actively transmits its comprehension: *The Friend*, edited by Barbara Rooke, Vol. I, 'The Landing Place', Essay 5, pp. 155–157. Reason raises consciousness above material determination. It is thus for Coleridge the source of moral freedom: Lovejoy, *Essays*, p. 255. Reason and Understanding correspond, in Coleridge's view, to Imagination and Fancy. Coleridge calls the Scriptur-

al imagination 'that reconciling and mediatory power, which incorporating the reason in images of the sense, and organizing . . . the flux of the senses by the . . . self-encircling energies of the reason, give[ing] birth to a system of symbols: 'The Statesman's Manual: A Lay Sermon, in Samuel Taylor Coleridge, *Lay Sermons*, edited by R. J. White, p. 29.

19 Handy, *Kant* pp. 13–15; Young, *Gentleman*, p. 151 and René Wellek, 'Philosophy and Post-war American Criticism', in *Concepts of Criticism*, p. 339.

20 Bergson, *An Introduction to Metaphysics*, pp. 14, 16, 34–35, 57 and 73.

21 Ransom, 'Forms and Citizens', in *World's Body*, pp. 29–54.

22 Dated 20th February, 1927, in Ransom, 'Adventure in Form', p. 795.

23 G. E. Moore, 'The Refutation of Idealism', *Mind*, Vol. 12 (October, 1903), 433–453, and Franz Brentano, 'The Distinction between Mental and Physical Phenomena', translated by D. B. Terrell, in *Realism and the Background of Phenomenology*, edited by Roderick Chisholm.

24 Bergson, *An Introduction to Metaphysics*, pp. 22–27 and 48.

25 Maritain, *Intuition*, p. 325–333.

26 John Crowe Ransom, *Beating the Bushes: Selected Essays 1941–1970*, p. 11.

27 Ransom, 'A Psychologist Looks at Poetry', in *World's Body*, p. 156.

28 In 1927, Ransom wrote a book about this, planning to call it *The Third Moment*. The publishers rejected it; he then burned it: Thomas Daniel Young, *Gentleman*, p. 174. It resurfaces in articles such as 'An Address to Kenneth Burke', in *Beating*, pp. 45–47.

29 Letter to Tate, dated 5th September, 1926, in Ransom, 'Adventure in Form', p. 791.

30 'Thoughts on the Poetic Discontent', *The Fugitive*, June, 1925, cited in Louise Cowan, *The Fugitive Group: A Literary History*, p. 200.

31 Ransom, 'Wanted: An Ontological Critic', *Beating*, pp. 21–22.

32 William Lynch, *Images of Faith: An Exploration of the Ironic Imagination* p. 63.

33 Tate, 'Three Types of Poetry' in *Essays*, p. 106.

34 Tate, 'A Note on Milton', in *The New Republic*, 61:112, December, 1929, quoted in R. K. Meiners, *Alternatives*, p. 18.

35 Rubin, *Wary Fugitives*, pp. 207–220.

36 Dupree, *Augustinian Imagination*, p. 130.

37 Tate, 'A Southern Mode of the Imagination', in *Essays*, pp. 563–567.

38 'Religion and the Old South', in ibid, p. 317.

39 Ibid, pp. 306–307.

40 Ibid.

41 As noted above, p. 20.

42 'Three Types of Poetry', in Tate, *Essays*, p. 113.

43 Kevin Kerrane, 'Nineteenth Century Backgrounds of Modern Aesthetic Criticism', in O. B. Hardison, Jr., (ed.) *The Quest for Imagination*, p. 7.

44 Tate, 'Poetry and the Absolute', *Sewanee Review*, 35 (1927), p. 52).

45 Tate, 'Preface to Reactionary Essays on Poetry and Ideas', in *Essays*, p. xv.

46 Tate, 'Tension in Poetry', in Ibid, p. 82.

47 Ibid, pp. 83–84.

Chapter 5

'Myths' of the Christian Image in the Southerners' Writings

The Theatre of the World

There is a relation of analogy between the aesthetic beauty of myth and the reiteration of the acts of Christ, the transcendentally beautiful, in the liturgy. Elaborating on Maritain's idea that pre-Christian art is 'Christian in hope', Caroline Gordon proposed that a 'primal plot' of story is 'the Christian scheme of redemption.'[1] As the beautiful image of the quest for the good, the mythic story gives its characters their right relation to reality. It gives its hero his form.

The Southerners contrast such a mythic imagination to what they take to be the solipsistic tendency of Romantic poetry. Such solipsism derives from the inability to perceive the world as a cosmos: that is, as a system of parts so built as to form a whole, which is outside of us. During the nineteenth century, both the externality of the world and the spatial and temporal coherence of human experience were eroded, and that because the good, the true, and the beautiful were set apart from the movements of particular facts, and thus from the dynamism of human action. For Shelley, the beauty of 'poetry' is the opposite of a temporal narrative, for it expresses the eternal archetypes within the human mind.[2] The Southerners disparage this aspect of Romanticism. Ransom finds little 'determinate' meaning in Wordsworth, whilst Tate considers that the elevatory heights of Shelley's poetry refer to no specific object.[3] The Southerners say

88

that the poet's first task is to create a verbal net of analogical images. The form is dramatic: its parts may well move across the sequence of a narrative.

The unbounded absolute which poets such as Shelley sought was an abstract moral ideal. The Southerners did not banish the good from art. But they knew that no transcendental can be known unless it is woven into form. This is the difficult task of an imagination which is embedded in the physical world: such an imagination utilizes both 'poetic intuition' and 'art'. A moralized notion of literature neglects to locate its absolutes within a limited form: this is the necessity of art.

Moreover, the fecundity of the moral sense stems from its rootedness in an imaginatively conceived cosmos. Von Balthasar describes Dante's effect upon Beatrice like this: 'Just one look at her was enough for him to perceive in his heart the moral discernment that regulates, in a Christian way, situations on earth.'[4] He notes that, with the passing of the medieval world, aesthetics and ethics have been divorced.[5] One principle which will emerge from the Southerners' 'myths' is that moral action becomes impossible when it is conceived as rigid adherence to an absolute pattern, instead of emerging from the interplay of a person with their world. To be related to the good is not to subscribe to abstract regulations, but to act, with a practical and earthy imagination, on the demands which this world makes.

In his *Theo-Drama*, von Balthasar points to the moral demand of the beautiful, drawing on Rilke's 'Archaic Torso of Apollo':

> There is no place in it which does not see you
> You must change your life.

So to be called is to be given the 'outlines' of one's prospective self: it is *you* who must change.[6] Once the good becomes an issue, we must speak of how the self gains its integrity. Unity of persona across an extended narrative is a prerequisite of the ascription of moral responsibility.

For the Southerners, imagination is a means of centring perception in a particular image, so to relate a self to an apprehensible world. Ransom calls upon the poetic 'miraculist' to create a unified cosmos. The miraculist captures the shape of human experience in narrative form: that is, as myth.

The structured cosmos can become a 'theatre of reality', from which ethical action emerges. The world becomes a stage which enfolds the story of human action. The miraculist displays the transcendentals on a mythic level, as informing and elevating a culture. This supplies the immanent ground within which the theological aesthetic can play. It is also the foundation of the reality of the self. For it provides the imaginative space for what von Balthasar calls the 'theo-drama': the theological notion of divine and human action in relation to the good.

I will present those of the Southerners' writings which lay out the 'mythological' forms of Christianity. Only the imagination which has a concrete presentation before it can act. This form, moreover, is able to enter formlessness without being dissolved by it.

John Crowe Ransom: The Psychological Element

The assembled narrators of Ransom's 'Antique Harvesters' find the prospect of harvest wearisome

> Declension looks from our land, it is old.

The land is unresponsively dry, as are those who should harvest the 'spindling ears' of corn which it reluctantly yields. Their task is lacklustre, their speech repetitive. But, whilst energy fails, and conversation circles, an image begins to grow

> And talk meets talk, as echoes from the horn
> Of the hunter – echoes are the old men's arts,
> Ample are the chambers of their hearts.

The scene which had been flat and colourless yields its secret resources: out of that 'ample' the land's own amplitude emerges:

> Here come the hunters, keepers of a rite;
> The horn, the hounds, the lank mares coursing by
> Straddled with archetypes of chivalry . . .

The mythic attitude perceives the forms which extend within the given because it does not will directly to seize them.

Ransom's *God Without Thunder* (1930) contrasts a 'new' and an 'old' religion. The God of the new religion undergirds the scientific exploration of the universe. Its 'ethic' is purely pragmatic. Lynch calls this 'Prometheanism'. Maritain says that it results from servitude to voluntaristic philosophies. The new religion is the pragmatism of the American post-Kantian idealists, for whom thought itself is a form of action.[7]

On the other hand, in Ransom's schema, there is the 'old religion', in which the will is abeyant in the face of the real. The 'old religion' corporately worships the mysterious being of God. It is characterized by its use of what Ransom calls 'myth'. Its adherents uncover the consequence of concrete individuals, in all of their magnetic power to attract the human mind into themselves. Ransom's myth is not superimposed on a set of facts which, like the cake, are ignorant of their icing. It is an explication of a fact which goes beyond the naturalistic. In his sense, 'mythologizing' is that exercise of the comic imagination which multiples the given beyond the neat categories in which the logical mind would prefer to contain it. There is more in nature and in history, he suggests, than can be ascertained by quantitative judgements alone: 'The myth of an object is its proper name . . . unique, untranslatable, overflowing, of a demonic energy that cannot be reduced to the poverty of a class concept.'[8] Such mythologizing could be a form of phantasizing. But Ransom limits the use of myth: he says that 'old' religions instinctively bind themselves to one myth, which becomes a dogma.

Ransom goes on to claim that the one who makes use of myth, 'has a memory. He . . . would compel us to perform the critical act of recollection, to restore the individual image.'[9] The 'links' of human time can be forged into a chain which is known by imaginative recollection as a significant form.

Ransom's position is close to the subject: it is rooted in the humanly imaginable shapes which are reduced or abolished by the positivist. His book is subtitled 'An Unorthodox Defence of Orthodoxy'. His 'Unorthodoxy' is that 'myth' is no transcendent revelation, but rather, a 'psychic necessity'.[10] This is to give the religious imagination a suggestive, but insufficient base. He assaults the humanistic reduction of Christianity. But he examines and defends myth as an innate quality of the human spirit.[11] Yet, on the other hand, just because the faith which it proposes rests in subjective requirements, *God Without Thunder* may be taken as a defence of the humanity within faith. Without this, objectivity has nothing to which it can attach itself.

The aesthetic attitude finds in God a presence too specific to be constrained within the generalizations of 'science'. The idea of God, Ransom says, performs two functions:

> First, to represent its indefiniteness in extent . . . [second] the universe might be defined in terms of its natural history, and yet no item in it was ever fully explained by natural history. . . . These are two Gods, an extensive and an intensive. Sometimes they merge, in the thought of the expert myth-maker, into the one very great God.[12]

Ransom's God combines infinite form with complete particularity.

The Inclusive Myth as 'Miracle'

Ransom's aesthetic approach allows for the existence of religions as objective, overarching forms, just because it is mythological. The essay 'Poetry: A Note on Ontology' lays out Ransom's doctrine of 'miraculism'. The poet performs the miracle by aligning diverse aspects of experience in a single image. Miracles weld distinct things together, whilst enabling each to retain its own specifitude. This juxtaposition of disparate realities is an expression of the same energies which religions employ to 'create' the immediate presence of supernatural realities. It is the poet's intuition which embodies religion:

> the poet . . . gives . . . a nature and a form, faculties and a history, to the God, most comprehensive of all terms, which, if there were no poetic impulse to actualise and 'find' him, would remain the driest and deadest among Platonic ideas, with all intension sacrificed to infinite extension . . . miraculism . . . leaves us looking, marvelling and revelling in the

thick *dinglich* substance that has just received its strange representation.[13]

Now, the poet does not literally 'give' the living God anything. But one can take Ransom to mean that it is the aesthetic imagination which defends faith against the naturalist's 'separatist' and literalistic conception of experience. To make visible the latent concordances within reality is the task of the poetic 'miraculist'. He discovers those relations between facts of which the scientific mind is unseeing or oblivious.

Ransom says that the loss of the synthetic 'theatre' of reality was brought about by the forces of abstraction, under the guise of puritanism. The act which had once held together all of the diverse, and yet interpenetrating, branches of human activity stemmed from a religious understanding:

> The religious impulse used to . . . hold together . . . all of the forms of human experience . . . But Puritanism . . . separated religion from its partners . . . the most important of these separations was that which lopped off from religion the aesthetic properties which simple minded devotees and loving artists had given it. The aesthetic properties constituted the myth . . . Theology . . . is purer than ever before, but . . . it . . . cannot . . . assemble all of those who once delighted in the moral precepts, the music and the pomp, the social communion, and the concrete Godhead, of the synthetic institution which was called religion.[14]

Ransom's turn toward the subject entails that what metaphysicians call the unity of being is also a unity of human activities. The diverse 'forms of experience' are linked to one another. This is a concrete unity, known in poetic intuition.

Without such knowledge, Christianity lost a qualitative richness which philosophy by itself could not protect. It then ceased to appeal to the complete, sensuous and spiritual person. It called upon reason, artistic will, and ethical drives in abstraction from one another. The perceptive channels for the different transcendentals – as the true, the beautiful and the good – were cut apart. The imagination was thus stripped of its theatre of common action. Consequently, as Ransom claims, it ceased to project that supreme analogate which could retain in relation all of the lesser analogues of Divinity. The expressions of the myth which I shall now present are 'types' of the relation of the self to reality, with or without that larger analogue.

Allen Tate's The Fathers: A Myth of Disintegration

The Fathers is about the tragic 'fall' of a classical society. Tate considered that 'naturalism' portrays history as a 'logical series'.[15] The perception of history as tragedy, on the other hand, uncovers the human quest for meaning, albeit upon its ruins. The novel is narrated by Lacy Buchan. It is set at what was once his family 'place', 'Pleasant Hill'. The events which he recounts take place at the outset of the Civil War.

The Buchans are destroyed by George Posey, who marries Lacy's sister, Susan. The society which is despoiled was like a miniature universe, complete unto itself. George cannot belong in such an ordered world. He is unwilling to attend his mother-in-law's funeral. Having arrived with the intention of enduring the ordeal, he suddenly rides away again:

> My new brother George had needed intensely to . . .
> escape from the forms of death which were, to us, only the
> completion of life, and in which there could be nothing
> personal, but in which what we were deep inside found a
> sufficient expression.[16]

The Buchans can act their roles in the funeral ceremonies; George Posey cannot. But the Buchans' lives are too well ordered. They cannot recognize that their own way of life came into being at one time, and may sometime disappear. This flaw leaves them without protection against the irrational.

As a symbol, the traditional society – which 'Pleasant Hill' reflects – engages its members in reality. But its prescriptions for conduct leave the utile as unimaginable, because beneath consideration. There is an absence of imagination on the part of both Poseys and Buchans, and so a failure to make contact with concrete facts. For the Poseys, it is the fantasy life effected by their lack of ties to their material surroundings, through work, tradition, or manners. For the Buchans it consists in the adherence, at all costs, to the romantic notion of the gentleman.

It is not the Buchans' play-acting which Tate blames for the fragility of their way of life. He thinks that their impersonal code of conduct enables them to make of life a drama. The Buchan's way of life is undergirded by a chivalric myth. Without such myths, Tate says, 'men . . . are no longer capable of . . . forming a dramatic conception of human nature.'[17] To live within a dramatic image is to have a broader horizon than one's sole ego. It is to Major Buchan's credit that he knows how to act a part, whilst it is a fault in George Posey that he can only be his own sincere self. When the self steps out on to the stage of the public human drama, appropriately masked and costumed, it rises above its egoistic material needs and becomes a person. If it cannot participate in common human experience, and is separated from cultural communication, it remains a mere, quantitative individual.

The atmosphere of the Poseys' house is reminiscent of Edgar Allen Poe. Lacy says that George's uncle, Mr Jarman, is like Roderick Usher. He lives on the top floor of the house, where he writes poems – or their first lines. For Tate, Poe exemplifies the 'angelic imagination', which surges toward essences without touching upon the matter in which they are enclosed. Tate learned from Maritain's *The Dream of Descartes* that this is what angels, but not humans are supposed to do. For Tate, St Augustine embodies an 'outward gaze', whilst Poe is an image of 'narcissism'.[18] Following Aquinas, Maritain proposed that it is impossible for an embodied human being to make judgements which are not based upon an image.[19] This is how both philosophers implanted the genesis of thought in the real world. Tate's essay 'The Angelic Imagination' is subtitled 'Poe as God'. Poe's disembodied mind is said to parallel that of the Cartesian dualism. Poe's imagination is an absolute: it flies directly up into beauty, without crossing the material world.[20] Tate claims,

The reach of our imaginative enlargement is no longer than the ladder of analogy, at the top of which we may see all . . . that we have brought up with us from the bottom where lies the sensible world. If we take nothing with us to the top but our emptied, angelic intellects, we shall see nothing when we get there. Poe as God sits silent in darkness. Here the movement of tragedy is reversed: there is no action.'[21]

The Poseys are angelists. They excel in the projection of vivid phantasies, because they have no bearings on physical things, which the imagination has presented to the mind. Mr Jarman magnifies and complexifies everything which he perceives, adding to it an extraneous glamour. He cannot take it in when Lacy comes upstairs to tell him that Aunt Jane Anne Posey is dead; and fails: 'Death couldn't be an old lady, his sister-in-law, downstairs; death was the sunderer, or time, or our enemy.'[22]

The Poseys lead a life of complete inaction in order to avoid suffering. They cannot make the descent, out of the tops of their heads, into the 'body of this world'. They cannot endure anything which is an obstacle to their will – as pure spirit. Lynch claims that this movement instigates an ascent into insight, through a 'crucifixion' of the human mind and will upon a particular fact. Tate says that, having relinquished imagination's dependence on physical facts, Poe 'surround[s] us with Eliot's 'wilderness of mirrors,' in which we see a subliminal self endlessly repeated or turning, a new posture of the same figure.'[23] Poe's 'angelic' imagining ends in solipsism.

George Posey's limitless energy is untrammelled until he meets Lacy's brother, Semmes, and takes up the 'Confederate Cause'. Against the Southern pretence that the Civil War was fought by gallant defenders of States Rights, the figure of George suggests that the South was tragically compromised in its own defenders, as by slavery. The good which the South wrought, in the traditional society which the Buchans inhabited, was destroyed along with the evil.[24] It was torn apart because it had no whole, practically embodied conception of the good.

Maritain saw Beatrice as the exemplary figure of beauty. The radiance which shines through this feminine figure gives its beholder a sense of reality, but only when the witness binds themselves to this one, single form. George Posey's mind springs away from simple things, into a world of fantasy adventure. Susan cannot attach him to reality, for he would prefer endlessly to juggle with various hypotheses, rather than to allow one to determine the actual for him. George is never with Susan, as the story reaches its climax; he is travelling around, buying and selling arms for the Confederate army. And Susan goes mad.

The disaster to which the action leads is Semmes' shooting of Yellow Jim, George's negro half-brother, and George's reciprocal murder of Semmes. Lacy flees toward home, and, in a state of delirium, meets his dead grandfather:

> He didn't mean to do it, I said to my grandfather and he said: No . . . your brother-in-law . . . does evil because he has not the will to do good. The only expectancy he shares with humanity is the pursuing grave, and the thought of extinction overwhelms him because he is entirely alone . . . my son . . . you have read . . . the pathetic tale of Jason and Medea and the Golden Fleece. Jason was a handsome young blade of royal descent. . . . nothing ordinary interested him; and he called together a great party of heroes and went after the wool of a remarkable ram . . . the king of the country where lived the golden ram commanded him to subdue a certain number of savage bulls, a feat that he . . . accomplished with the aid of the king's daughter, Medea, a high-spirited girl who came from a more primitive society than that from which the arrogant Jason came . . . It was Jason's misfortune to care only for . . . impossible things, while getting himself involved with the humanity of others . . . which it was . . . his very nature to betray. For he came to love another woman . . . he was . . . repudiating . . . the very meaning of human loyalties . . . If the Fleece had been all-sufficing, would he have taken Medea with him back to Greece? My son, I do not think so.[25]

Jason has the destructiveness of those who love an impossible, rather than a real, beauty.

Major Buchan is not innocent of his son's death. It was he who drove Semmes to the Poseys'. His traditional code was an ethical idealism, leaving him unable to deal with the grit of factual events, which the outset of the Civil War placed before him. The Buchans fail in the art of practical action because of they are without realistic imagination. Tate has constructed a dramatic universe, and then shown the dissolution of a form which is not sufficiently embedded in imaginative action.

Allen Tate: Myths of the Reintegration of Light and Form

We find Tate's 'Sonnet to Beauty' (1928), in the 'Texts Without Comment' in Maritain's *Creative Intuition*. In this aesthetic, it is light, or radiance, which translates the perception of the viewer into the form of the artistic object. Light mediates between the artistic object and its subject, and unites the two in consciousness. Tate's poems present incoherence of experience through images of darkness, damage to the eyes, or blindness. He uses 'blindness' as a symbol both of the corrosion of sensibility, as a kind of optical involutedness, and of the inability to respond to, or properly to see a supernatural reality. 'Sonnet to Beauty' begins

The wonder of light is your familiar tale

This was so, at least, until

Mr Rimbaud the Frenchman's apostasy

Beauty is made bloodless when it is drained of light. Light thickens and reifies the object through which it flows. Rimbaud's 'apostasy' is the relativization of the values of art to those emotions which produce subjective excitement, but which are insufficiently attached to the object upon which they are directed. With this, beauty becomes a 'Lithe Corpse'. Having moved beyond the reach of the light which actualizes form

Broken, our twilit visions fail.

The first lines of the next stanza suggest that the sensuousness

and the objectivity of art are based upon the physical embodiment of verbal, and 'all-sufficing', meaning in the flesh of a man,

> Beauty, the doctrine of the incorporate
> Word Conceives your fame; how else should you subsist?

Tate is thinking, not of the 'incarnate' but of the 'incorporate'
Christ. Christ's extensional revelation of light within human
flesh, shining through tangible matter, grounds the reality of
beauty, or is identical with it. The poem goes on to speak of the
light which traverses the stained-glass windows in a church
building. The beams

> . . . twist and untwist
> The mortal youth of Christ astride an ass.

It is the bodily nature of Jesus which matters here. But when, in
the window's picture, this man is brought together with the ass
upon which he rides, there is a hint of the proximity of spirit and
matter. Here the two are merely laid alongside one another,
whereas in the sunbeams which take their colour from the
window, the two are one in motion.

Tate's later poems sometimes venture upon an ascent toward
a female figure who enables the narrator to transcend his self.
He is looking for someone who will assist in the rehabilitation of
experience. He is seeking a vehicle through which to incorporate imaginative insight within the bodily senses. The vision of
the supernatural cannot be engrafted upon a broken and
'closed' human nature. Yet the help comes at last from beyond
the natural world. Tate looks for the unification of experience in
the gravitational pull of forms external to human psychology.

His 'Seasons of the Soul' was published in 1944. Its narrator
is led through the various levels of the self, searching for
transcendence. 'Summer' is the season of the flesh. The
flourishing body and the unconditioned intellect struggle for
mastery. The field of the body cannot hold its own against the
cold, tractor-like intellect:

> If now while the body is fresh
> You take it, shall we give
> The heart, lest heart endure

> The mind's tattering
> Blow of greedy claws?
> Shall mind itself still live
> If like a hunting king
> It falls to the lion's jaws?

The mind, in turn, is hunted by a force stronger than itself: it cannot come to terms with temporality:

> Then, like a primal cause
> It had its timeless day
> Before it kept the season
> Of time's engaging jaws.

The narrator comes next upon the centaurs whom Dante and Virgil saw in hell: the man-beasts join a mechanical reason with a bestial animality.[26]

'Autumn' finds him 'down a well' and in an 'empty hall', recurrent symbols of solipsism for the poet.[27] He is in an unfurnished corridor. Nothing stands out against which he can orient his gaze. He might as well be in one place as another, an utterly detached observer. There are no markers through which he could return to the same spot, if he moved. He is trapped:

> The round ceiling was high
> And the gray light like shale
> Thin, crumbling, and dry:
> Nor any carved detail
> To which the eye could glide
> I counted along the wall
> Door after closed door
> Through which a shade might glide
> To the cold and empty hall.

He attempts to leave, but, as in a nightmare, the door will not open.[28] His father, looking at him with an 'unseeing glint', and mother walk past without recognizing him. He cannot communicate with his immediate past: as Donald Davidson put it, 'it is a vision of the dead whom you cannot reach; and you question them and get no answer, as both Vergil & Dante

were able to.'[29] It is the distortion of his sight which has pinned
him here, he

> . . . whose vision froze
> Him into the empty hall.

Neither the regression to the level of pure intellect, in 'Summer',
nor that to childhood, in 'Autumn' produces a consonant
relation to the world. Reason alone becomes a weapon of
destruction, whilst childhood's passivity to sense entails self-
enclosure. In 'Winter', the narrator goes further back into
himself, coming upon a

> Goddess, sea-born and bright,

Venus. He tries to make his way out through the erotic centre of
the self. But it is impossible to return to the worship of the gods
of nature. In this place, a shark will 'pace' beside the dove. The
narrator says that

> All the sea-gods are dead.

Spring finds him inside a cave, trapped there by his 'burning
arrogance'. But this time, rescue is at hand:

> Come, old woman, save
> Your sons who have gone down
> Into the burning cave:
> Come, mother, and lean
> At the window with your son
> And gaze through its light frame
> . . . Then, mother of silences
> Regard us, while the eye
> Discerns whether by sight or guess,
> Whether, as sheep foregather
> Upon their crooked knees,
> We have begun to die
> Whether your kindness, mother
> Is mother of silences.

Tate often returns to the image of the 'burning cave'. Plato's
'cave' is the realm into which those who are enthralled to sense
impressions are thrust. If these latter are taken to ground the

relation between the person and reality, consciousness remains immanent to itself, trapped in the cave of sensible 'states' and 'processes' of which Tate spoke in his essay on Milton. The cave is 'burning' because it is a tormenting place to be. Tate has said that

> As I look back on my own verse . . . I see . . . that its . . . theme is man's suffering from unbelief; and I cannot suppose that this man is some other than myself . . . in my own writing there is a habitual rejection of certain naturalistic dogmas . . .; yet I tend to depict man as overwhelmed by them . . . his disasters are the result of his failure to possess and to be possessed by a controlling sense of redemptive powers in his experience.[30]

The 'mother of silences' has been identified with St Monica.[31] St Augustine conversed with his mother before a window. The dialogue gave place to silence, as mother and son shared in a vision which surpassed both.[32] The speaker in the poem asks to be placed within the beneficent, and perhaps salvific 'regard' of the woman: this is the purification of sight. He hopes that, if his eye is healed, he will gaze unhindered upon the light which pours through the window. An escape from introspection is glimpsed in the life-giving figure of the woman. The woman in 'Seasons of the Soul' is at once St Monica, an image of the larger feminine figure who lies behind her, that is, the Virgin, and a realization of the poet's imagination, giving the material and affective relation between the poet and his vision.

In the poem, St Monica is the healing presence which assures a relation to light. Monica is historical; her son's theology rests on contemplation: he is one of von Balthasar's 'theological aestheticians'. For Augustine, as for von Balthasar and Tate, the beautiful is, first of all, that which is to be *seen*. It is often mirrored by a feminine figure, who educes the material relation of form to historical reminiscence. The *Confessions* is a search for a God who cannot literally be identified with any concrete image. But the self who pursues such disembodied illumination is himself pursued, by the demands of recollection in the shape of Monica. The quest for transcendent insight is consummated in Augustine's dialogue with his mother, shortly before her death: his discussion of memory immediately follows.[33] Tate says that St Augustine knew

> that memory is like a woman. The Latin *memoria* is properly a feminine noun for women never forget; and likewise the soul is the *anima*, even in man . . . the custodian of memory, the image of woman that all men pursue and flee. The imaginative writer is the archeologist of memory, dedicated to . . . definite things – *prima sacramenti memoria*.[34]

The memory which the woman embodies lends harmony to experience, and binds it to transcendence. When it returns upon itself, the Augustinian self finds, not privacy, but healing light.

Tate's early essays spoke of the recurrent 'patterns of experience' to be found in poetry. In the 1940s and 50s he wrote a series of pieces, such as 'The Symbolic Imagination', 'The Angelic Imagination', and 'Our Cousin Mr Poe, in which his attention turns to the power of physical form to make present a spiritual reality, and to the expression of that reality through light. As he says in 'The Symbolic Imagination', 'Light *is* Beatrice.' He describes the guiding image of *The Divine Comedy* as a mirrored analogy: Dante, the narrator, looks into Beatrice's eyes and sees what she sees.[35] The vision is 'reversed': it comes from beyond his own eye. The objective figure guides his vision, and becomes his perspective. This is Tate's second 'reversal': in addition to the 'pattern of experience', there is a form which both renders it incarnate and aligns it to a reality.

Tate makes his own Maritain's belief that it is humanly necessary for form and light to be materially incarnate. Von Balthasar might concur with the conclusion of 'The Symbolic Imagination'. Tate has said that when the narrator of the *Divine Comedy* sees God, he does not grasp His essence:

> the light imagery is . . . what permits us to see the body, of the poem. The rash suggestion that *The Divine Comedy* has a tragic mode I shall . . . be made to regret . . . the symbolic imagination is tragic . . . in the degree of its development. Its every gain . . . imposes so great a strain upon any

actuality of form as to set the ultimate limit of the gain as a defeat. The high order of the poetic insight is that the final insight must elude us, is dramatic in the sense that its fullest image is an action in the shapes of this world . . . It never begins at the top; it carries the bottom along with it, however high it may climb.[36]

The tragic vision seeks an absolute assurance of the objectivity of form. Perhaps it is first attentive to *light* because of its existential objectivity and depth. The form approximates itself to this light. This is the case for both Tate and von Balthasar.

A Myth of the Imagination: Caroline Gordon

According to Caroline Gordon, heroism entails combat with the inhuman: she says that 'heroes . . . confront the powers of darkness. For that has always been the task of the hero, the confrontation of the supernatural in one or other of those forms which men of every age have labelled "monstrous".'[37] In her novel *The Glory of Hera*, Heracles' father Zeus has him 'in mind . . . for the redemption of mankind'.[38] Zeus has become the 'Father of Gods and Men', by overcoming his father, Cronus and his grandmother, Gaia. The novel tells of Heracles' defeat in combat of their multiple progeny. His twelve labours are a sequence of forays against those subterranean powers which the Olympian gods have subdued, but which lie in wait, resentful of their current subordination and eager to recapture their ancient prerogatives. Some of the ugly and amorphous beasts which he captures, plunders, and kills live in underground caves; the three-headed dog of Lerna resides in Hades; Antaeus takes his strength from the earth; many are just serpentine. Heracles ventures into the depths of earth and sea to wrestle with the powers of formlessness. In this comic action, the human is raised up, and the reality of objects is not problematic. The comedian plunges into the solid weight of the earth, in order to unleash its radiance.

In comedy, elevation is not equivalent to spiritualization. It will lift as much of the corporeal as it can. If the comic moment is to break through, the facticity of both spirit and of the concrete thing which incorporates it must be affirmed. Zeus' high designs are furthered by metamorphoses which 'frequently caused him to cut a ludicrous figure'.[39] In comedy, there is a concordance between quality and quantity: if something is good, it must be enormous – and growing! In it, the numinous is multiplied as by a natural force.[40] The humour of the *The Glory of Hera* is not that of incongruity, which wars against the symbolical imagination. It is that of excess. Too much is being pressed into a very small space.

Light countermands the impulsive lure of the earth. Heracles recognizes the presence of the gods by a brightness in the air, as when Athena and Aphrodite visit him on Mount Cithaeron.[41] It is Hera who, having obstructed each of his labours, raises him to Mount Olympus and proclaims him as her 'glory'. The reward for Heracles' ingenuity is the elevation of this most physical hero. This is the culmination of the novel's comic action. Heracles has the innocence, and the superabundant energy of the typical comic hero.[42] His hunting skills flow uninhibitedly out of the force with which he exists and into the world. The demons are repelled, not by intellectual devisings, but by a man whose essence it is to act.

Comic villains are invited to return to the society to which they have laid waste. If comedy intends to raise up – not to crush – and to assimilate, rather than to isolate, then Heracles' defeat of the gods of the earth is not their annihilation. He has not to destroy the primitive religion, but to redirect its meaning. Bainard Cowan describes the development of one such action:

> Heracles enters . . . wearing the head of the Nemean lion which he has killed . . . Heracles wearing the lion's head is a sign of liberation; he retains the sign of the chthonic while detaching it from the monstrous form which had imprisoned it. . . . he both conquers and recovers the power of the earth.[43]

This hero is a mythical image of Christ, in His descent into the depths of hell, so to defeat death. Caroline Gordon takes the plot of the Christian scheme of redemption to underlie all good stories. Our imaginings of the heroic instinctively take that shape. The heroes themselves need not grasp their deeds as little myths. Heracles once sees a picture of one of his labours, the slaying of the lion of Mount Helicon:

> A brooch of beaten gold lay beside the cloak . . . a goldsmith had wrought upon it the likeness of a man wrestling with a lion. The lion, erect on his hind legs, offering his throat to the master's grasp, looked more like a large dog rehearsing some trick than a monstrous beast engaged in a struggle to the death, Heracles thought. He concluded that the goldsmith . . . had had to depend upon his imagination to know what the monster looked like. 'Yet I, who fought him, could never have imagined what he was like!' he told himself.[44]

And yet, he has made the goldsmith's artistry possible. Heracles' action has made the story imaginable.

The Glory of Hera completes the train of thought which Ransom's *God Without Thunder* set in motion. It is a myth, but a highly sophisticated one. Its author knows that the artist's task is not to recover an immediate and literal rapprochement with reality. Further, in an dramatic emblem, the novel shows the pattern of human action as a microcosm of the divine. Form enters its opposite – the hero grapples with death – and emerges triumphant. This is a myth which lifts earth up to heaven. And yet the tale is comical because the telling is so matter of fact.

Conclusion

Ransom depicted 'Orthodoxy' as a rich, mythological religion. It is created by poets who give shape to the forms latent in their memories. Ransom's myth-maker is a 'miraculist': one who imitates the Creator's unification of the diverse rhythms of life into a single, aesthetic cosmos. This cosmos is a mythical reflection of the metaphysical analogy of being, in which all forms are bound together in analogous imitation of God. It is mythical not because it is more colourful and 'thingly' than the metaphysical cosmos, but because it emerges from the shape of human action. Yet both pictures provide a shared theatre of communication and action. The mythic image corresponds to a metaphysical truth, or reality.

This myth shows the dynamics of the imagination. We examined three mythic themes. The first occurs during the absence or disintegration of the theatre. In *The Fathers*, the outcome is the loss of imaginative connaturality with the world: it is replaced by an ethical or aesthetic dream-world. Neither the good nor the beautiful can be grasped in practical or imaginative ways. Moral action is not channelled through concrete realities; beauty is lifted above simple facts. The destruction of the 'theatre' severs the ties of the self to the world and to the community which embodies human meaning. The second theme is the quest for vision by one who is now submerged in his own interiority. The light of reality is recovered through a single person. The third theme emerged from *The Glory of Hera*: it is the imagination incarnate in practical action.

These myths map the shape of human desires, and of the world which, if properly imagined, yields an answer. The relation between the two takes shape when the self models itself upon a fixed and personal form. For this, the self must belong to a human community whose pillars are belief in the transcendentals. The transcendental perfections – as the self-givenness of being, the openness of truth, and the good as the motivation to bold action – are apprehended through a beautiful form.

Our myths reflect the way in which Lynch and von Balthasar conceive Christ's revelation of Form. They run parallel to the root principle of von Balthasar's theological aesthetic, as encapsulated in his statement that 'Christianity becomes the aesthetic religion par excellence' because it rests on the giveness of absolute meaning within form, in the transfusion of a specific corporeal being with transcendent light.[45]

NOTES

1 Caroline Gordon, 'Some Readings and Misreadings', *Sewanee Review*, 61 (Summer, 1953), p. 385 (on Maritain, 384).
2 Percy Bysshe Shelley, 'A Defence of Poetry', (1840), in *Shelley's Poetry and*

Prose, selected and edited by D. H. Reiman and S. H. Powers p. 485.

3 Ransom, *Beating*, pp. 21–22; Tate, 'Three Types of Poetry', in *Essays*, esp. p. 92.

4 Von Balthasar, *Glory: III*, p. 51.

5 Ibid. p. 13

6 Von Balthasar, *Theo-Drama: II*, p. 24.

7 Maritain, *Moral Philosophy*, pp. 103 and 162–163; Royce, *Lectures in Modern Idealism*, pp. 2 and 85–86.

8 Ransom, *God Without Thunder: An Unorthodox Defence of Orthodoxy*, p. 65.

9 Ibid. p. 66.

10 Ibid. p. 81

11 Ibid. pp. 188–189.

12 Ibid. pp. 67–68.

13 'Poetry: A Note on Ontology', in Ransom, *World's Body*, pp. 140–142.

14 Ransom, 'Poets Without Laurels', in *World's Body*, p. 64.

15 'Humanism and Naturalism', in Tate, *Memories and Essays: Old and New*, pp. 180–181; Squires, *Literary Biography*, p. 20.

16 Allen Tate, *The Fathers* pp. 22–23. This edition represents the book as it was first published. Tate later altered the book's ending. The revised edition is published by Louisiana State University Press, 1977, as *The Fathers and Other Fiction*.

17 'What is a Traditional Society', in Tate, *Essays*, p. 301.

18 Dupree, *Augustinian Imagination*, p. 14.

19 St Thomas Aquinas, *Summa Theologiae*, Ia, Q. 75, Art. 7, ad3; Q. 76, Art. 4, resp.; Q. 84, Art. 7, resp.

20 Frank Lentricchia cites Poe's 'Letter to B-': "'think of poetry, and then think of – Dr Samuel Johnson! Think of all that is . . . fairy like, and think of all that is . . . unwieldly; think of his huge bulk – the Elephant! – and then of . . . the Midsummer Night's Dream . . ." For Poe, it takes a "wild effort to reach the beauty above."' Lentricchia, 'Four Types of Nineteenth Century Poetic', *Journal of Aesthetics and Art Criticism*, Vol. 26, No 3 (Spring 1968) pp. 360 and 361.

21 'The Angelic Imagination: Poe as God,' in Tate, *Essays*, p. 454.

22 Tate, *The Fathers*, p. 235.

23 'Our Cousin, Mr Poe', in Tate, *Essays*, pp. 457–458.

24 Tate describes Stonewall Jackson in this way: 'Tom Jackson had no physical objects, no possessions whatsoever. Without possessions a man did not morally exist . . . In the South the man as he appeared in public was the man.' *Stonewall Jackson: The Good Soldier. A Narrative*, p. 12.

25 Tate, *The Fathers*, pp. 267–269.

26 Dante, *The Divine Comedy: Hell*, Canto XII, Line 75, translated by Dorothy Sayers p. 144.

27 Alan Williamson, 'Allen Tate and the Personal Epic', *The Southern Review*, 12, (Autumn, 1976), p. 722.

28 Tate describes the recurrent dream from which such aspects of the poem were drawn in a letter to John Peale Bishop, quoted in Squires, *Literary Biography*, pp. 169–170.

29 Dated 21 March, 1944, in Tate and Davidson, *Correspondence*, p. 340.
30 Tate's contribution to 'Religion and the Intellectuals', a symposium in *Partisan Review*, 17 (1950), pp. 251–252.
31 The first in print was Vivienne Koch, 'The Poetry of Allen Tate', which is reprinted in Radcliffe Squires, (ed.), *Allen Tate and his Work: Critical Evaluations*, pp. 253–264.
32 St Augustine, *The Confessions*, Book IX, Chapter 10.
33 Ibid. Book X, Chapter 8 ff.
34 'A Lost Traveller's Dream', in Tate, *Memories and Essays: Old and New*, p. 12.
35 Allen Tate, 'The Symbolic Imagination: The Mirrors of Dante', in *The Man of Letters*, pp. 93, 101 and 108).
36 Ibid. p. 112.
37 Caroline Gordon, 'Cock-Crow,' *The Southern Review*, n.s. 1 (July, 1965), p. 562.
38 Caroline Gordon, *The Glory of Hera*, p. 117.
39 Ibid. p. 35.
40 M. M. Bakhtin, 'Forms of Time and of the Chronotope', in *The Dialogic Imagination*, pp. 167–206.
41 Gordon, *The Glory of Hera*, pp. 159–160.
42 Gordon praises Fielding's Tom Jones as a 'blundering hero', *How to Read a Novel*, p. 178. Bainard Cowan comments on the similarity between Tom Jones and Heracles in 'The Serpent's Coils: How to Read Caroline Gordon's Later Fiction', *The Southern Review*, n.s. 16, (II) (1980), p. 287.
43 Cowan, 'The Serpent's Coils', pp. 291–292.
44 Gordon, *The Glory of Hera*, p. 209.
45 Von Balthasar, *Glory I*, p. 216.

Chapter 6

William Lynch: Christ as the Image of Reality

The Realistic Imagination

I spoke at the beginning of the objective and subjective presuppositions of Christology. I then set out the philosophical and the poetic dimensions of the realistic imagination. We can now examine the theologies of Lynch and of von Balthasar insofar as they exhibit such presuppositions. The acting principle of their thought is the revealed beauty of Christ. Lynch believes that the analogizing imagination, which Maritain, Ransom, Tate and Caroline Gordon explored, emerges from the Image of Christ.

Human beings search for transcendent absolutes; yet they are always surrounded by objects which are insistently contingent. This given world is inescapable. Lynch rejects what he sees as the 'romantic' manoeuvre of transcending the 'evidence' for faith, in Kierkegaard and Karl Barth.[1] Lynch believes that, by cutting the causal link between the act of moving into the world and its culmination in knowledge of God, such presentations of faith eliminate its element of drama. The search for absolutes is not solved by the revelation of Christ. The imagination integrates the 'I' with exteriority by embracing specific things, and finding the meaning which it seeks in them. Christ is the creative energy Who encircles and defines such imaginative acts.

According to Lynch, it is only by grounding our lives upon

Christ, the 'lord of the imagination', that we will be able to keep interiority in touch with that which faces it from the outside.[2] If the two are separated, we retreat into fantasy: the real world is experienced as a hostile force. Lynch attempts to rebuild an energetic and vital relation of self to external things. This requires an image of the world as being neither an alien, inhumanly self-sufficient mass nor an infinity of ungovernable things. The image should accept the finitude and contingency of facts, but mark them with a human figure.

Lynch's friendship with Allen Tate enriched his view of the imagination. The theologian and the poet helped one another to consider how a realistic imagination binds the mind to limits. The mutual influence is evident in Lynch's *Christ and Apollo*. Tate's 'Religion and the Old South' contains an incipient statement of his distinction between a 'Christ' who presides over clearly demarcated form and an 'Apollo' who rules so variously and so universally that he makes no specific patch of earth his own. Here Tate compares the 'Short' and the 'Long' conceptions of history. He argues that, for the 'Long' View,

> since the Christian myth is a vegetation rite, varying only in some details from countless other vegetation myths, there is no reason to prefer Christ to Adonis. Varying only in some details: this assumes that there is nothing but a quantitative difference between a horse and a dog, both being vertebrates, mammals, quadrupeds. But the Short View holds that the whole Christ and the whole Adonis are sufficiently differentiated in their respective qualities (details), and that our tradition compels us to choose more than that half of Christ which is Adonis and to take the whole, separate, and unique Christ.[3]

Lynch's 'Apollo' personifies the 'anonymous mind', which is supra-territorial, and the 'chameleon imagination', which declines to adhere to some fixed and definite form. Christ, on the other hand, is the model of realistic imagining. Whether realistic or not, imagining is a way of being related to external circumstance. Christ and Apollo are two ways of being imaginatively turned toward the world: the way which will attune us to the finite, and the way which will not.

Tate's essay 'The Unliteral Imagination, or, I too, Dislike It' criticizes that modern poetry which does not render objects precisely. He comments that his thesis is stated with greater complexity in *Christ and Apollo*. The essay proposes that the modern 'dissociation of sensibility' is not precisely Eliot's separation of feeling from thought but, rather, a cutting asunder of the inner world from the external. Tate claims that

> modern poetry begins at the moment poets lost control of the literal significance of their metaphors. Poets have always done this . . . yet . . . at present . . . it has become almost impossible for a poet to find literal images that will not merely point to a paraphraseable meaning, but will actually contain the meaning. I suggest that what was dissociated . . . was the external world which by analogy could become the interior world of the mind.[4]

This dissociated imagination soars upward toward the empty heaven of unformed emotion and shapeless intellectuality. In the realistic image, the extended fact and the interior world are related. The image is not 'extended', within the mind. Rather, the ways in which it can be drawn out, in fact and in imagination, are related 'by analogy'; that is, in an image which can be stretched into different modes, and yet remain itself.

The imagination can be realistic only by learning to propel the human energy which yearns for the absolute into the actual world. The realistic imagination is the analogizing imagination: its images enter the self-shaping movement of concrete facts and of persons. Once it can engage with things, the imagination becomes analogical.

Just as the Southerners had adversely contrasted 'science' and imagination, so Lynch differentiates the univocal and the analogical imagination. The analogical image, he says, allows the diverse presence of the real to emerge, whereas the univocal pattern is a grid which is externally imposed upon facts. Both the analogical and the univocal mind intend to bring about unity. But the univocal mind orders things logically, 'on paper', by selecting from its objects one point of connection, and disregarding everything which distinguishes them. Analogizing thinking, conversely, creates harmony through an act which allows each separate object to remain its own, diverse self.

The analogizing imagination therefore enables contraries to co-exist in one act. The analogical image sets in motion the 'co-illuminative' potential of different things. Unlike the univocal intellect, the analogical mind sets itself in relation to concrete facts. Delving into reality, it will find all of the significance which the 'Long View' had looked for above the world, and the univocal, outside of it. It finds its basis in the historical acts of Christ, which, Lynch says, brought opposites together into such close juxtaposition that their capacity to participate in the same act of being was revealed.

Imagining Human History

The analogical imagination turns the self and its objects toward each other. Such imagining joins itself to the interior movement of its objects, and follows that movement, so to re-mould the world of things and to give it a humanly apprehensible shape. It is a way of knowing other than that of a detached observer *confronting* a neutral reality. Lynch claims that we are

> made not only to have a place but to make places, not out of whole cloth, not in terms of an isolated and sterile imagination, but in terms of an imagination that is in . . . creative relationship with the world. It is on this state of mutuality that even the simplest facts depend, and out of which they emerge.[5]

The realistic imagination incorporates the temporality of human life. Just as dramatic meaning emerges through the stages of the narrative, so imagination recreates human temporality as a gradual concretion of significance. One does not achieve instantaneous elevation into a beautifully timeless noumenal realm. For one begins in limitation, in the 'literal level' of plot.[6] Through the plot, the image emerges through a series of acts. It generates understanding through temporal progression. In the same way, images of human life can be held in creative tension by the time which separates and unites them. The realistic imagination does not fear the contingencies of time through which the human image makes its way.

The first object of imagination is the course of human life. Imagining is a continuous movement into the world, which displays the path of the human image, as it passes through its own opposites toward the reaffirmation of its own identity. Such imagining is dramatic. It unfolds meaning by slowly traversing different situations, each of which must be imaged in all of its natural facticity, and then related to the others. It creates images of the self, as it moves, act by act, from dependent beginnings to a helpless end. Since the image is dramatic, it presents these facts as a unified whole, in which each part is causatively entwined with the others. These images guide us into reality, if we can experience the world through them. In some sense, the image is the reality, for it captures it at the moment in which it gains a significant shape.

When it does this, the Christian imagination is informed by the narrative of Christ's life. The imagination imitates the expressive figures which Christ's actions carve. Christ performs exemplary actions, as did the heroes of myth. He does so with a degree of precision and invariability known to history alone. Lynch dwells on two of these: the mobile image of His death, as a descent into the 'earth' of finitude, and His resurrection, as the elevation into unbounded intelligibility which the descent effects. These are the grounds of the drama of the imagination's own search for meaning.

Christian faith imagines within an enclosed space, or stage: the theme of the action which is played thereupon is the life of Christ. Its forms are invented by the human imagination; it also reflects, as it images, the life of Christ. The imagination is the form of the self. Faith requires a life of imagining, which comprehends otherness and limitation within figures. Faith transforms the reality which we experience into perceptible shapes. The experience *is* the figure which we make of it:

> the Hebraic-Christian faith . . . is a paradigm within which we experience or imagine the world . . . It is a moving paradigm which will not be understood until it has moved through all the stages of the life of man, and in the same act, all the stages of the life of Christ.[7]

The life of faith is not a floating, up out of the burden of creaturely existence into a supra-sensuous realm lying above it. Closeness to God is achieved by tunnelling through all the orders of created being, and of the space and time which bind it. These are the only things which can mediate God to us. As Lynch says,

> time . . . is a kind of ontological prayer. There is no other form of union with God . . . the most orthodox form of prayer . . . is not rest but motion; a coursing . . . through the mysteries – that is, the stages, of the life of Christ.[8]

We will see the same belief in the innate temporality of human existence in St Irenaeus, who is von Balthasar's first 'theological aesthetician'. Lynch shares Irenaeus' belief that humanity is saved in and through its historicality. Both regard the univocal as the anti-historical. As Gustaf Wingren describes Irenaeus' view of Christ's defeat of death and the evil: 'the defeat of the enemy is . . . accomplished in conflict – victory ensues in a series of events, and not timelessly as a logical consequence of the fact that the invading power is stronger than . . . the enemy.'[9] As Irenaeus reads it, Christ's work required an imagination which was willing deftly to make sense of reality by enduring it, not by looking at it or transcending it. For Irenaeus, Christ's work is to draw all of created nature up into Himself. He calls this unification of the diverse aspects of the world *anakephalaiosis*. One of Lynch's early articles describes Irenaeus' idea of *anakephalaiosis*: it concludes by stating that

> Christ . . . is the Sun, but the course of this sun is through man . . . The entry into man and into the historical human patterns is the entry into God. We miss the point if we only say that Christ is the gate and do not . . . add that man is the gate. It is the great mystery of man and God in the one act.[10]

The Ground of Analogy

The task of the theological imagination is to perceive this mystery. It comprehends in one action both the form of the human search for meaning, and what movement Christ's life carries out. Both actions are dramatic. Their initial steps are tragic. They pass through a tragic drama, in which the imagination encloses itself in the grave of finitude, and dies there. If the quest for transcendence has the shape of tragic drama, the image of death is at its centre. When death is accepted, it no longer just happens to us: it becomes a 'weapon' of creative understanding.[11] Lynch takes the death of Father Zossima in Dostoievsky's *The Brothers Karamazov* as an image of the discovery of meaning in the acceptance of finitude. Father Zossima's religious discourses may have gone up too high.[12] Alyosha's grasp of Zossima's death brings him back down into the reality of the earth. He must now make a new image of the world which includes the fact that one's loved ones die and lie stinking. This entails an act of imaginative empathy. Lynch writes that,

> Dostoievsky explores the passage into the exact structure of a fact by . . . the realistic imagination as opposed to the 'fantastic' imagination . . . the monk whom Alyosha loved, is . . . dead. . . . his body is already decaying. Nor the air is filled with fantasy, with lies and Alyosha's imagination must travel through it all, give shape to it, and find a way. . . . Alyosha reaches it: the simple fact is that he whom I loved is dead. That is all that is there. At this stage, the achieved fantasy is no fantasy at all, but a sense of vision . . . that is effected by a perfect contact with some part of the human reality . . . We are faced with a constriction and it is no constriction at all.[13]

The image of death is completed by experiencing the journey of life into death in terms of Christ's first performance. Christ's death is His fullest acceptance of the finite and historical human condition. It is thus His own instrument of resurrection. The human tragedy is guided by that of the God-Man, without losing any of its simplicity or hard reality.

The two actions have the following scenes. Christ's 'plunge down' into the earth in the Incarnation is the ground of the human self-launching into real being.[14] His crucifixion and death brings with it the possibility of 'insight' on the natural level, and 'resurrection' on the supernatural level. Both are generated by the precipitation into the real. That is, they are *brought about* by it, just as in the dramatic image of literature, a passage into time moves through suffering to self-knowledge. Insight is created by the dramatic image which binds events together by making them to circle around a unifying centre. Like that image, the crucifixion of Christ moves natures into one another's field of force. Lynch says that

> As a good artist . . . he . . . knew what he was talking about when he said: If I be lifted up upon the cross (in complete isolation and differentiated uniqueness, without anonymity, without friends), I shall draw all things to me (in sameness, in love, in a universal Church) . . . In that place and hour was brought about a wedding of the altogether unique and different Thing . . . and the ultimate society of the Church . . . this, their common mystery of identity, stands as the model for every analogical act of the imagination . . . Philosophy can only speculate about things already done. Theology and Christ can act, and thus give us the ground for all later analogizing.[15]

Lynch places the image of the crucifixion of Christ at the base of his theology. He believes that the search for complete images of reality demands the descent into finitude. This is a death for the human spirit. It is an acceptance that the mind lives within the externally imposed necessity of finding its sustenance within certain boundaries and conditions. Every truly imaginative act transverses the image of death; every such act is brought up against those things which constrict the mind. It is the acknowledgement that existence contains the form of tragedy which converts us to comprehending our lives through the paradigm of the life of Christ. The acted image of Christ's dying underlies every creative effort to enter limitation, in the acceptance that a multitude of strange and resistant objects lie in wait for it. The ascent into fulfilled meaning, or resurrection, is the fruit.

The concordance of properly variegated things in the realistic image is an analogue of another type of unity: that between the self and the objective world. The question of whether objectivity is simply otherness, a world of cold mechanical fact, which is to be transcended by the mind of faith, has been with us since the seventeenth century. Lynch's Christic imagination creates a convergence between the two worlds.

In so doing, Lynch relies upon the truth of the metaphysics of analogy. But he extends it. For if human reality and its conditions are truly to be integrated, we must be able to give a shape to history. This had also become an obstruction to faith. Lynch holds, to the contrary, that the borders of time contain a boundless expanse. He sets human intentions into a story-form, or a drama. Now the passage of time can communicate a value. History becomes expressive. It is open to us.

When we engage in the forms of time, we find that Christ has already done so. He has not added any extraneous significance to time and the story, but has progressed through them in the most resourceful manner. This action allows history to yield the shape for which it is looking: the image of the human person.

A Comic Theology

We can ascertain how a theologian apprehends the world, not only by his or her explicit statements – although these are not lightly to be disregarded – but also by noticing the direction in which their imagination naturally tends. For Lynch, even the movement down towards death becomes an upward motion, in so far as it explores the texture and the contours of the concrete fact. His analysis of death leads him up, toward an expansion of created being. It draws us up into that fulfilment of the human imaginative drive which is the comic mode of experience. This places his imagination under the sign of comedy.

Lynch's Christology is imagined 'from below'. His vision of God is telescoped through finite humanity. He suggests that, 'the order of belief called Christology is a belief in the capacity of the human actual, if we imagine and live through it, to lead somewhere.'[16] Lynch's Christ does not descend into human nature from on high, but, rather, pushes up into it, through its roots. The comprehension of who and what Christ is flows from our ability imaginatively to grasp what human nature is – not least our own – and in that grasp to know the human as valuable. Lynch's thinking is comic. The comic images of Caroline Gordon and John Crowe Ransom waited upon an amplitude within reality which carries the self upwards. Such elevation occurs when the imagination becomes capable, not of rising above the world, but of lifting it up, by finding a pattern of meaning within it. The image of elevation which the comic theme shows confirms human nature, and so validates the whole world of simple natural fact. Only that elevation is real which occurs because the imagination has struggled to uplift a real fact. The human reality often appears to resist such a comic resolution. The analogizing of being results in such manyness that we shrink back from it. There is also a heaviness in the world: the stolid, humourless weight of evil. For Michael Edwards, the comic 'glimpsing of a marvellous language' reveals the boundless elasticity and depth of reality. And yet, as he takes it, the 'basic plot of comedy is a plot against the fallen condition.'[17] But, it is only if the imagination plots, not against, but with the world that it can lift that which is given as human up. To thread oneself toward the good amidst a fallen world one needs innocent worldliness, not innocence of the world.

What we discover in comedy, and what it does to us when we imitate it, has been described by Anthony Burgess as having, 'a meaning in terms not of contents but of effects, elation, acceptance of the world, of the fundamental disparateness of all the elements of the world.'[18] For Lynch, the theological imagination takes its shape from definite, historical events, which took place once for all in a specific place. Opposites converge in this sacred history. The alignment of apparently foreign forms is a sign that the comic spirit is at work. In *God Without Thunder*, Ransom has it that 'Humor is more privileged than poetry and religion . . . The grotesque effects in which it indulges are miraculous.'[19]

Comedy mixes high minded things with corporeal ones. It uncovers the supernatural in an unlikely receptacle. Comedy shows the natural, finite object as base, and as a marvel. It makes present in a single action the mundaneity and the dignity of the contingent human world.[20]

Comedy's roots in the concrete image embarrass that mentality which Tate termed 'the angelic mind': it recalls it to its physicality. In the 1950s, the 'angelic intellect' became Tate's metaphor for the mind which has misplaced its body. He says that it

> has intellect and will without feeling; and feeling . . . is our tie with the world of sense . . . Imagination in an angel is . . . inconceivable, for the angelic mind transcends the mediation of both image and discourse. I call that human imagination angelic which tries to . . . circumvent the image in the illusory pursuit of essence. When human beings undertake this . . . program, divine love becomes so rarified that it loses its human paradigm.[21]

The comic imagination shows the light of existence shining through the grossness and the paucity of corporeal things. It recalls us to our bodily weight.

The angelic mind cannot imagine the revelation of God in the particularity and contingency of historical events. It abhors the localization of significance in time and space. Such is the mind of the Enlightenment, with its refusal of the Judaeo-Christian history's containment of God's revelation in a tiny space of the world's geography, through His covenant with a minute portion of humanity – the tribe of Israel. In the nineteenth century, Hegel and Strauss took the specifitude of the gospel story as a mark of what they called its 'mythic' character. The particularity of the image will be transcended in the movement of Spirit towards universal conceptions.[22] Turning the tables upon Strauss and his twentieth-century followers such as Bultmann, Hans Frei argued that the gnostic 'saviour myth' is characterized by its 'universality'. As such, it is the product of 'the unconscious poetizing of a folk-consciousness'. With this Frei contrasts the 'storied figure' of Christ, who bodies forth the 'unsubstitutable' uniqueness of His identity in the resurrection.[23] It is in His particularity that Christ reveals himself to human touch and vision. But, modern Christology has been cramped by its enduring tendency to oppose generality and particularity. We need to recover, not only the unique fact, but also the fusion of its 'extension' and 'intension'. Ransom discerned that synthetic images lie at the roots of religious faith. For Lynch, the construction of such images involves the comic, and especially the ironic imagination. An inhuman angelism can turned back upon the concrete by that ironic imagination which, as Ransom believed, conjoins concepts and particularities. Once welded together by the comic touch, the image is the vehicle through which the world can be known as the congruence of narrow fact and broad universality. Lynch's *Images of Faith* argues that the ironic imagination holds together both endless potentiality and those smaller things which are humanly graspable. He writes here that

> Christ himself in his particularity is the final model for the successful relationship of the smaller and the greater line. Against the background of enormous space time, at a completely specific and free moment in the millions of light years, with a body that occupies a few feet of all our universes, he seizes upon and declares importance and seriousness, his own. This is ironic, that this should happen at an infinitely small point in an infinitely large space time.[24]

The comic imagination dwells on the insignificance and arbitrariness of the material and the finite: this brings into focus its glory. If irony holds contraries together, then nothing is more ironic than the act of an infinite God in becoming incarnate in an ordinary human nature. It is no surprise that the gospel of the radiance of the Word made flesh (John 1.14) has been found to be a gospel of multiple ironies.[25] In this comedy of errors, the Pharisees inquire 'Are we blind?' (John 9.40); Lazarus, as Martha pointedly and with more perspicacity, comments, 'stinketh' (11.39); Christ is glorified *because* he is nailed to the upright cross. For its audience, the evidential force of John's gospel derives from the understated mis-positioning of the literal and the spiritual: the disciples see at once that Christ must have been brought some refreshment, if, as He says, 'I have meat to eat that you know not of'; Mary Magdalene takes the risen Christ for the gardener (4.32; 20.15).

Ironic Faith

Christ and Apollo finds comedy standing guard against those types of faith which negate the human in order to make way for the absolute. Comedy respects the boundaries of the secular. It will not deprive natural facts of their proper character and autonomy. If the comic drama is inclusive, it will not ignore the empirical realities which matter to the post-Enlightenment mind. As Lynch sees it, a theological problem emerges once people recognize that the secular field has its own rights, and that it must be studied with its own particular method, which is to be a critical way. This poses two questions for the religious imagination: firstly, the question of its attitude to the evidence, and secondly, that of the freedom and self-identity which it must render to the secular world.

Austen van Harvey's *The Historian and the Believer* describes how the attitude of faith and that of criticism went their separate ways. The key moral value of the Enlightenment was intellectual autonomy: this value was enunciated by Kant. It follows that historians who investigate the biblical history must stand back from their faith; they must not be merely spokesman for their church; they must detach themselves from the pressures of religious commitment. To do otherwise is to be false to the historian's vocation.[26] Kant and the Enlightenment add an ethical note to Descartes' method of doubt: they consider that full humanity is achieved in autonomy and in the moral freedom which accrues to it. The outcome, as van Harvey notes, is that theologians as various as Barth and Bultmann, otherwise embattled in their conceptions of Christianity, cannot simultaneously be men of faith and biblical historians.[27]

The culture of criticism and of faith have seemed to be at war since the eighteenth century. Each became an absolute: one chooses isolation or immersion. For Lynch, the latter is a form of romanticism. He calls it 'Dionysius'. Dionysius rules over the primal, pre-rational faith which indiscriminately acknowledges any and every possible object as religiously compelling. The Dionysian attitude refuses to part with the childlike condition of pure receptivity. It believes that the 'real I' is the untouched self with which one is born. It could have all manner of experience, acquire numerous habits, or be inculcated into the mores of a community. None of it will matter to the 'real I': it cannot learn from them. Its history is superimposed upon the true self, who lies, a naked aborigine, under stultifying layers of facts. It will try to rediscover itself by abstracting from the shape of its experiences. Where imagining is described as an escape from the carapace of experience – returning to the 'literal' perceptions of the child – religious faith will entail discarding the veil of worldly sophistication. It is hoped that a genuine self lies underneath. If we rely on faith alone, we absolutize just one level of experience. We become entrapped in simple receptivity, which allows no exit into a world which transcends the senses.

The attitude which removes itself from its objects in order to get a better look at them cannot help us either. Imagining must take part in the movement of being, if it is to know any thing. Newman took a step away from the purely sceptical paradigm when he wrote that 'I would rather have to maintain that we ought to begin by believing everything which is offered to our acceptance, than that it is our duty to doubt of everything. The former, indeed, seems the true way of learning.'[28] Lesslie Newbigin has lately reiterated the case: 'Doubt . . . is essential but secondary in the enterprise of knowing how things are. What is primary is the act of attending and receiving, and this is an action of faith.'[29] Or as Lynch says, 'without faith the mind cannot enter into existence at all.'[30] Belief underlies the operations of an aesthetically stated faith. In his *Images of Faith*, Lynch notes that Christian faith has its Dionysian aspect. Religious belief is synthetic, not analytic. It is not produced by assembling the separate pieces of evidence. It is total, accepting the reality of its object as a whole, from the beginning, and only subsequently embarking upon an investigation of the distinct facets of the synthesis. Or, as Clifford Geertz argues, religion entails 'committment', not 'detachment'. Geertz says, 'Religious belief involves not a Baconian induction from everyday experience but . . . a prior acceptance of authority which transforms that experience.'[31] For Geertz, religion commits one to a 'system of symbols', going together to make a story which imaginatively encloses the believer's world.

The story system has the characters and actions which its synthesis requires. Those inside the Christian story perceive sin and redemption in the comings and goings of men and women.[32] We can, however, make excursions 'outside the book' into the world of 'common sense'. One might ask: how does the world of the everyday get into the world of absolute meaning? Lynch might say that the two spheres interpenetrate through irony. Irony opens a door which lets some unintellibility into the perfect world of faith. Faith dragoons every fact as evidence for itself. But irony carefully sorts through experience, in order to find what is valuable. Faith requires the counterbalance of scepticism. Lynch says that (Dionysian) faith and (Christian) irony need one another: 'a very usual circular rhythm in life is this: Faith goes blindly and independently about until it discovers the guide of irony. Irony (or mockery) breaks out into autonomy and needs the guide of faith.'[33] Like Ransom, Lynch rejects the romantic effort to retain one's Dionysian faith whatever one's experience. Because it needs to learn, Christian faith goes on to be tutored by irony. It becomes less credulous and less demanding of perfect certainty. Lynch claims that death is a second infancy, but one for which we must work: 'Birth and death have faith carved into them. But in between is the need for the development . . . of what I am calling irony.'[34] The Dionysian attitude differs from the Christian in that the latter grows and changes through experience. But, as Newman perceived, it should be our *first* relation to the world.

Faith interprets the world. It both creates and reveals the evidence for itself. Faith implies that we can expect that reality will not brutalize our wishes. Ironic faith depends upon the promises of a God who pulls those whom He calls through the sieve of history. Whilst retaining this expectancy, it also includes something which, coming to us from ahead of our imaginings, redirects our hopes. It holds at bay the satirical impulse. It remains firm both to security, and to ignorance:

> A promise made to faith leads one to expect. God enters into a covenant with Abraham, telling him the great things he shall expect . . . The other element of educated faith is the element of the unexpected. You must slay

> Isaac, your only son . . . It is only by keeping the
> expected and the unexpected together in an irony of a
> definite character that faith is able to compose and
> recompose evidence . . . To learn to recompose is the
> heart of its education . . . The coming of Christ is
> expected by the imagination . . . But . . . The ironies
> of Christ had not been expected.[35]

Faith differs from that rationalism which, having invested all of
its hopes in patterns which follow single, uniform lines, must
reject anything which expands the pattern into the unknown.

The univocal mind refuses the ironic gesture which accepts
both the indeterminacy of history and the many levels and
differences within faith itself. It knows no analogical 'poly-
valence' of fact and experience. When Lynch takes comedy
as 'the great enemy of the univocal mind'[36] he will use it to
integrate what univocal thinking had divorced: faith and doubt,
and the ordinary with the novel.

The Image of the Person

In his *Christ and Prometheus*, Lynch considers how the religious
imagination can find new ways of assimilating a world which,
since the Enlightenment, has laid claim to its own 'unconditionality'.[37] This book follows the pattern of Aeschylus' dramas,
in which, he says,

> every . . . story begins with a plunge into action . . . the
> action meets reality . . . and passes through a suffering
> history; through the suffering the action reaches a new
> insight or point of reconciliation. These three words
> summarize all: drama, pathos, mathos.[38]

The book uses this exemplar, yet also makes full use of the comic
insight that contingency is not meaninglessness.

When the Enlightenment defended the self-identity of the
secular world, it rejected what Lynch calls the 'cosmological'
imagination. This is the imagination of the great medieval
syntheses, which gave each natural object meaning by locating

it within a hierarchy, whose transcendent term is God. Without its scale on the ladder, the thing has no sense. The modern claim is that the fields of human inquiry are defined from within, without reference to the cosmological schema. As the scientific description of nature expands, the religious image diminishes. The religious imagination must accept the justice of the secular claim to explain its own objects. It must defend the emergent activities of the 'Prometheus' in human nature. This is not simple. For the growth of human autonomy has a phantasmagoric shadow side, which projects an image of conquest. It asserts itself against an inflated 'cosmological' world which seems to it to crush human self-designation. This shadow image is the energy which Lynch calls 'Prometheanism'. He says that 'Prometheanism is a project of the will separated from the imagination and from reality; separated from most of the human.'[39]

Romanticism had two strains. One saw the artist as the channel of divine creativity. The other imagined the artist as a 'Promethean' figure, who is fated to wrestle with God, nature and human society.[40] For Lynch, the latter typifies Romanticism. He regards the Prometheus figures of Shelley and of Goethe as products of an imagination whose sole thought is defiance of the objective order.[41] Lynch's 'Prometheanism' touches the facet of the Romantic mind which gave up the effort to unite the person and the world, and turned instead to projecting reality from the will. 'Prometheanism' lacks imagination, and so cannot come to terms with externality. It can only either fight against reality, or ignore it, and create its own subjective replacement.

This is why outwardness becomes a 'cosmological' threat to human inwardness. Nor does the colossal energy of Prometheanism stop there. It spawns its own inhuman 'cosmology' of oversized things, which, in their turn, threaten to dominate the human. It also creates a new 'objectivity': the objectivity of mechanized science and reductionistic psychology. Lynch considers that Bultmann envisages biblical 'myth', in its 'externality', as the objectivity pictured by the voluntaristic, Promethean mind. This evacuates human self-identity, and so must be side-stepped.

The first step of the resolution is to allow the secular world to be itself. But secularity must then be transformed into a shape governed by human concerns. The image of faith will thus be 'anthropological'. Its centre will be the human image. It finds a place for finite humanity beside the true infinity of God and the fantasy infinities created by Prometheanism. Prometheanism must part with its will to power, and make a place for the smaller sphere of the human.

As Lynch recalls, the hero of Aeschylus' *Prometheus* is tormented by Zeus for the crime of giving humanity the implements of culture: this is an image of the combat between the cosmological and the human. A second model for his book is the *Oresteia*. Each act of *Christ and Prometheus* follows the plot of the *Oresteia*. In the latter, the action is initiated by the apparently unstoppable reaction of crime against crime, as one member of the house of Atreus assassinates another. Clytemnestra has killed Agamemnon; Orestes, with the same axe, has murdered his mother; he is now pursued by the Furies. It seems that there is no end to this tribal justice. The next stage finds Orestes in the newly constructed court of the Areopagus, tried for the murder of Clytemnestra. This is the 'pathetic' stage, in which a new 'hypothesis', different from that of the Furies, but including its demands, has yet to be found. There is no majority, in the vote, either for or against Orestes. But Athena, standing for the upsurgence of the human imagination,

> casts a deciding vote on the side of an ending; she declares him released. But nowhere does the goddess declare that he has not committed a crime . . . Nor does she . . . reject the Furies; . . . she declares that the new city of man . . . shall never be able to do without the . . . terror of justice. She welcomes the Furies into the city . . . We are at last in the presence of a new justice . . . not a justice destroyed but a justice transformed and humanized.[42]

Von Balthasar assesses Athena's triumph in the same way. He considers that Aeschylus has achieved the first task of the analogizing imagination: in leaving nothing out, Aeschylus has reconciled the chthonic and the Olympian religions.[43] Just as in *The Glory of Hera*, the monsters with whom Heracles wrestles to the death are recovered and transformed, so here the cosmological is given a new birth, in the heart of the human image.

Lynch's image of faith is dramatic. It moves through its own opposites, in order to rediscover its own identity. So, in *Christ and Prometheus* the human imagination is seen as Prometheus, travelling through a tragic drama. The text is set out in three acts. The first is the 'Search for Man'. Here the autonomy of the world emerges. This reality impinges on the will; the religious imagination is estranged when it discovers that it can no longer superimpose itself upon the secular world. The second act is 'The Search for Light'; an attempt to generate a new image after the failure of the old. This is the stage of painful discovery. It learns that the world is no mechanical engine, but the sphere of moral combat. Autonomous humanity is capable of terrible things. The final act, called 'The Search for Innocence', incorporates the old image within the new. Now the insight is yielded up, after the acceptance of death. It is a vision of Christ as the one who generates the unconditionality of the natural world. He gives the human imagination its finite scope, and so makes possible a creative movement between inner and outer worlds. These can be themselves, whilst held together by His recapitulative movement. And, as von Balthasar says, recapitulation, or *anakephalaiosis*, means, 'the active power of the fulfiller to give every emergent thing scope within itself, in order, by assimilating it to himself, to bring it to its own fulness.'[44]

Conclusion

As Lynch conceives it, the movement of the Christian imagination is like the action of myth: it creates the coincidence of the absolute with the limited. As such, it issues in a vision of transcendence which is related to the finite human person. It is a dramatic way of engaging with reality: the imagination springs forward because it has uncovered the evidence which allows it to do so. For Lynch, the power of the dramatic image comes from Christ. The objectivity of Christ is imagined as a force which moves through, and grapples with, the very limitations into which the human imagination is set. As the form which reconciles finitude with the unlimited, He expresses and creates the realistic imagination. We find, again, that the problem of externality is solved neither by insisting upon a blind and anaesthetized interiority nor by taking one's stand upon objectivity alone. Rather, we look to a kind of 'double-sidedness'. This time, it belongs to the Form of God Himself.

Lynch lays out the form of the Christian imagination with reference to tragic and to comic drama. The tragic theme is very much present. There is no insight without suffering the implacable otherness within the world, nor without accepting the possibility of error and evil within our own enterprises. Perhaps it was when it forgot this that the Romantic imagination lost touch with the transcendence of nature from the self, and of God from the world.[45] But Lynch's paradigm of faith is comic. He does not seek absolute certainty. The image emerges from a slow exploration of concrete history. Theological vision is turned around so that it can recover the forgotten material detail. Analogy does not give way to naturalism, but the literalness of fact does not become an absolute. Above all, Lynch aims to lift the human image up.

NOTES

1 Lynch, *Images of Faith*, pp. 51–52 and Lynch's 'The Imagination and the Finite', *Thought*, Vol. 33, No. 129, (Summer, 1958), pp. 217–219).

2 Lynch, *Christ and Apollo*, p. 157.

3 Tate, 'Religion and the Old South', in *Essays*, p. 311.

4 Allen Tate, 'The Unliteral Imagination, or, I, too, Dislike It', *The Southern Review*, n.s. I (Summer, 1965), pp. 536–541).

5 Lynch, *Images of Hope*, p. 193.

6 Lynch, *Christ and Apollo*, p. 154.

7 Lynch, *Images of Faith*, p. 14.

8 Lynch, *Christ and Apollo*, p. 50.

9 Gustaf Wingren, *Man and the Incarnation. A Study of the Biblical Theology of Irenaeus*, p. 82.

10 Lynch, 'Theology and the Imagination', *Thought*, Vol. 29, No 112, (Spring 1954) p. 73.

11 Lynch, *Christ and Apollo*, p. 66.

12 Ibid. p. 22–24.

130 *Christ the Form of Beauty*

13 Lynch, *Images of Hope*, pp. 200–201.
14 Lynch, *Christ and Apollo*, p. 12.
15 Ibid. pp. 157–158.
16 Lynch, 'Theology and the Imagination II: The Evocative Symbol', *Thought*, Vol. 29, No. 115 (Winter, 1954–1955), p. 546.
17 Edwards, *Christian Poetics*, pp. 69 and 47.
18 Quoted in Robert Heilman, *The Ways of the World: Comedy and Society*, p. 47.
19 Ransom, *God Without Thunder*, pp. 66–67.
20 Lynch distinguishes the tragic and the comic respectively, as the diminishment of the finite in the face of the infinite, and the enlargment of the finite: 'Theology and the Imagination III: The Problem of Comedy'. *Thought*, Vol. 30. No. 116, (Spring 1955), 18–36 (20), and *Christ and Apollo*, pp. 100–109.
21 'The Symbolic Imagination: The Mirrors of Dante', in Tate *The Man of Letters*, p. 97.
22 Gunton, *Enlightenment and Alienation*, pp. 115–125.
23 Frei, *The Identity of Jesus Christ*, pp. 136 and 139.
24 Lynch, *Images of Faith*, pp. 95–96.
25 Paul Duke, *Irony in the Fourth Gospel*.
26 Austen van Harvey, *The Historian and the Believer: The Morality of Christian Knowledge and Belief*, pp. 39, 42 and 47.
27 Ibid. p. 164.
28 J. H. Newman, *An Essay in Aid of a Grammar of Assent* (1870), p. 294.
29 Lesslie Newbigin, *The Other Side of 1984: Questions for the Churches*, p. 20.
30 Lynch, *Images of Faith*, p. 60.
31 Clifford Geertz, 'Religion as a Cultural System', in *The Interpretation of Cultures: Selected Essays*, pp. 112 and 109.
32 Ibid. pp. 90, 98, 119, 124.
33 Lynch, *Images of Faith*, p. 102.
34 Ibid. p. 175.
35 Ibid. pp. 126–127.
36 Lynch, *Christ and Apollo*, p. 107.
37 Lynch, *Christ and Prometheus*, p. 117.
38 Ibid. p. 24.
39 Ibid. p. 63.
40 Monroe Beardsley, *Aesthetics From Classical Greece to the Present*, p. 262.
41 Lynch, *Christ and Prometheus*, pp. 63 and 105–106.
42 Ibid. p. 91.
43 Ibid. p. 92.
44 Von Balthasar, *The Glory of the Lord: A Theological Aesthetics. II: Studies in Theological Style: Clerical Styles*, edited by John Riches, p. 52.
45 Erich Heller, 'Goethe and the Avoidance of Tragedy', in *The Disinherited Mind*, pp. 37–63.

Chapter 7

Christ the Expression of God in the Theology of Hans Urs von Balthasar

The Story So Far

In *The Glory of the Lord*, von Balthasar affirms that the crucified Christ is the expression of transcendental beauty. The beautiful is to be perceived. The historical form of Christ makes it perceptible. The good is an action which rebounds between free persons. The *Theo-Drama* is founded in the ontological dialogue between the persons of the Trinity. In it, Christ plays the exemplary role.

Maritain gave a modern exposition of St Thomas' idea of beauty as *species* and *lumen* (form and light). Returning to the original source, von Balthasar takes this up.[1] Maritain's 'integrity and proportion' and his 'radiance' are depicted by von Balthasar as form and splendour. In Caroline Gordon's *The Glory of Hera*, Heracles descends into the abyss and is then borne up to Mount Olympus. His heroic adventure is a myth of the symbolizing imagination, in its imaging forth of the net of analogy between heaven and earth. Heracles' journey is that of form into an underworld. This is the work of Christ, as von Balthasar transcribes it. But here, where the theatrical model is tragic, Christ ventures forth, not only against death, as did the heroes of myth, but also against sin. Lynch underlined the specific boundaries of the figure of Christ; von Balthasar's

131

theology turns upon His form. Lynch's fable of Christ's plunge down into finitude in order to rise up in the resurrection of meaning renders von Balthasar's principle that form and splendour move one another into being. Von Balthasar's theology includes the metaphysics of analogy which Maritain illustrated and the Southerners imagined. The Southerners argued that 'a-cosmic' interiority issues in a fissure within beauty – as between meaning and fact – and in the good – between self and role. The Christological confirmation of myth will push the idea and the fact together. The locus of von Balthasar's concern is the transcendent beauty of Christ. Yet he believes that reality is *intrinsically* aesthetic, and analogical.[2] The aesthetic moment occurs when someone hears a rhythm within reality and responds to it. This concordance has its source in a transcendent Form which is found inside the patterns of being and thus of experience. The rhythm is the analogy of being.

Of the twelve 'theological aestheticians' presented in volumes II and III of *The Glory*, those most important to its author are Irenaeus, Pseudo-Dionysius, Augustine, Bonaventure, Anselm, Pascal and Hopkins. Von Balthasar interweaves poets of earthly things with those enchanted by light: his heart is with the latter. The outlines of his theology appear when one sketches the themes which he shares with Dionysius. First, there is 'symmetry': God gives to creatures the degree of being which their own shape and nature can express. God's communication of being to persons, and their response has a 'missionary character'.[3] Imagine, Dionysius says, a 'shining chain hanging downward from the heights of heaven to the world below. We grab hold . . . [But] it is already there . . . and we are being lifted upward to that brilliance above.'[4] Dionyius' 'procession and return' of being figures as von Balthasar's 'descent and ascent' of God and creatures. The divine-human engagement is imagined as an 'encircling'.[5] This is not an extrinsic metaphor. It has for von Balthasar deep, and somewhat deleterious, implications. It is also linked to his interpretation of the theological symbol: this is both affirmed in God's descent, and negated in the human ascent. Thus, finally, for Dionysius God is 'supraconceptual' because beyond created being.

For all of the writers of whom I have spoken, beauty is espied

by the symbolic imagination. Yet they have little adulation for
the Romantics, from whom they inherited these themes.
Ransom spoke of the 'conceited subjectivism' of the Romantic
project; Lynch called it 'Promethean'. Von Balthasar's disserta-
tion, of 1928, was called 'The Eschatological Problem in
German Literature': that is, its deflection into 'Titanism'.[6]
The 'problem' is laid out in the fourth and fifth volumes of
The Glory of the Lord. Von Balthasar claims here that

> 'Glory' stands and falls with the unsurpassability of the
> *analogia entis*, the ever- greater dissimilarity to God no matter how
> great the similarity to Him . . . In so far as German Idealism
> begins with the *identitas entis*, the way back to Christianity is
> blocked.[7]

The non-Christian hero of these volumes is Plotinus; their chief
adversary is Schelling, whom the author regards as the leading
proponent of aesthetic 'Titanism'.[8] This is the point at which a
Barthian resonance enters von Balthasar's tones.[9] He designates
Barth's greatness as the regaining of the transcendent glory of
God, drowned in the Idealist's univocalism – the *identitas entis*.[10]
Natural beauty depends on the supernatural beauty, that is, the
glory, of Christ. But, if metaphysical and poetic beauty were not
real, von Balthasar's theological aesthetic would be sheer
paradox. This he does not intend it to be. He does not follow
Barth in taking Christ's descending Form as the sole analogue
between God and the world.[11] We will not know beauty as
revelation unless we have loved the beauty of this world.[12]

In the final, Old and New Covenant volumes of *The Glory*, the
good becomes discernible.[13] The *Theo-Drama* draws out the
theme. Franz Rosenzweig's *The Star of Redemption* (1921) is
present here. That book had two targets: the impersonal
immanentism of Idealism, and the 'a-cosmism' which the
author called 'pantheism in reverse'.[14] Rosenzweig throws
the glove down with his first premise: the All does not die:
the solitary self does. For the Idealists and their postmodern
successors, the self is generated by a whole too general to found
the 'I's uniqueness. For von Balthasar, Christ's free entrance
into death creates a space in which human persons are given an
irreplaceable form. Antiquity discerned the analogy of being in

the cosmos: modernity draws upon the personal 'analogy of freedom'. The image of this analogy is the self moving in response to a call.

A Contextual Key

Von Balthasar studied philosophy in Vienna in the late 1920s.[15] He was taught by a Plotinus scholar, Hans Eibl. He was also affected by the ideas which flowed from the Austrian phenomenologist Franz Brentano. Brentano was the fountain-head of a stream of philosophers and psychologists who analysed their objects in terms of the relations of parts within a whole. Brentano studied the relations of part to whole within consciousness: his pupils applied his conceptual tools to external facts.[16] His influence had two 'loci': one stems from Prague and the other from Göttingen.

Brentano had a musician among his disciples: this was Christian von Ehrenfels (1859–1932).[17] From 1897 until 1932, Ehrenfels was professor of philosophy at the University of Prague. In 1890, 1922 and 1932, Ehrenfels published three seminal essays on 'Gestalt Qualities'. He was led to re-invent the notion of the 'Gestalt' by considering the nature of melody. Realizing that musical experience does not consist in hearing a drawn-out series of chords or tones, he saw that one perceives a 'unity' within the changing sequence of sounds. Further, a melody retains its specific quality when it is transposed into a different key.[18] This must result from the Gestalt, which inheres in and shapes each melody. The inbuilt Gestalt founds and guides musical experience. A Gestalt is thus a 'type of formedness'. Ehrenfels was to infer that every object has some degree of formedness. Von Balthasar's first published essay was called 'The Development of the Musical Idea' (1925). In *The Glory* he says that Ehrenfels' Gestalt is a recovery of the scholastic conception of substantial form.[19]

One of Brentano's themes was the critique of psychological atomism. Edmund Husserl was his greatest student. In the *Logical Investigations*, Husserl argued against nominalism, and for the reality of universals.[20] He later abandoned such realism, turning toward idealism. But the *Logical Investigations* had drawn disciples to Göttingen. Here they formed a circle, led by Adolf Reinach (1883–1917). Its members included Husserl's assistant Edith Stein, Jean Héring, Roman Ingarden and Max Scheler (1874–1928). Their project was the investigation of the necessary relations within objects, and between consciousness and its objects.[21] The principle is: as is the object, so is the act which intends it. Scheler said that, if colour is recognized by sight, or danger by fear, we need not conclude that colour or danger are inventions of the senses which intuit them.[22]

In 1913, Scheler composed *On the Nature of Sympathy*. This is a study of fellow-feeling, as an intentional relation. The community between persons is said to be a *given*. In early infancy, a certain 'primal feeling' leads us to identify our own consciousness with that of others.[23] Our own consciousness is later differentiated. Sympathy directly apprehends another's emotion. It is not a reconstruction of another person's emotion within ourselves: if it were, the emotion would not be disclosed as belonging to someone else. Rather, the other's face, or body, immediately presents us with joy, or shame.[24] Physical gestures compose expressive unities. One is given a single affective meaning to grasp, not discrete actions. Sympathy is thus an immediate perception of who the other person is.

For von Balthasar, an expression is 'extroverted': the form it manifests is not behind or inside it.[25] Expressed forms are communicative because the structure which shapes the interior spreads across its surface. Such wholes are the outward foundation of sympathy, as a direct perception. He notes that Scheler grasped the meaning of 'seeing', as the sensory intuition of the meaning of a person's life within or upon their face and body.[26] Scheler's phenomenological examination of self-giving in expression is crucial for his own theology. The idea of communicative form is so pivotal for von Balthasar's work that one scholar describes it as a theological phenomenology.[27]

Scheler envisages 'cosmic' objects as cohesive forms. But he distinguishes their value from that of persons. The perception of another person is the supreme act of sympathy, for it requires a free self-disclosure. Empirical objects are simply there for us to grasp; a person has to allow himself to be known. Christianity has the gift of knowing God in personal, rather than cosmic sympathy.[28] Scheler says that Christian discipleship is a

> practical self identification with a Person, the complete putting oneself in his place and at his disposal. Such an indwelling in the substance of a person entails . . . a remaking and ingrafting of one's own self in the image . . . of the Master. It is a . . . dynamic chain of ever-fresh impressions made by the spiritual Master pattern in the material of one's own inner experience.[29]

Von Balthasar could have written that. He considers that, whilst faith transverses the natural world, its heart is the freely chosen assimilation of a natural to a supernatural Person. He thinks of religious experience as a sympathetic response to the Gestalt of Christ: it is the interplay between a formed consciousness and an informing Person, Who plays upon it.

The Music of *Ente* and *Essentia*

By the early thirties, von Balthasar was a seminarian in the Jesuit house at Pullach. Erich Przywara was here, completing his *Analogia Entis* (1932). He was to be von Balthasar's guide.[30] Przywara first 'heard' the analogy of being, in ' "music as form" . . . which I later placed as "polarity", and then "unity in tension" and finally as "analogy" at the centre of my work.'[31] For Przywara, being is analogous because it is 'measured' movement.[32] Analogy is a 'towards'. Within immanent being, it is the 'rhythm' driving created natures from potentiality to actuality. The *Analogia Entis* expands on Przywara's study of Thomas' elucidations of the difference between the Being of God, which is His essence, and that of creatures, which is not. Przywara found in Thomas' *ens* a ceaseless oscillation between created natures and the necessary 'To Be', from which it descends. He defines Thomas' *ens* as both an absolute caesura between God and creatures and as the source of their unity. He stresses the caesura. If, for Przywara, there is an kinship between Bach's *The Art of Fugue* and the analogy of being, the 'analogy of sound' culminates in an 'analogy of silence'. The analogy

between God and creatures holds sway over 'reciprocal alterities'. God's Being is incommensurable with created being.
Citing the formula of the Fourth Lateran Council, to which
von Balthasar has in part already directed us, Przywara argues
that the 'greater' the 'similitude' of the creature to God, the
'greater' is God's 'dissimilitude'.

Przywara claims that the human subject and finite being
'measure' philosophy, whilst God 'measures' theology.[33] He
says that his conception of the analogy between created and
uncreated being dates from his acquaintance with Scheler. It
was, he confesses, Scheler's *On the Eternal in Man* (1922) which
placed him 'truly face to face' with him.[34] In this book, Scheler
argues that, although their object is ultimately the same, the
metaphysical and the religious act are phenomenologically
distinct. For Scheler, as for von Balthasar, the metaphysical
act asks: why is there something rather than nothing?[35]

For von Balthasar, the first answer to the metaphysical
question is, not so much the acceptance of the givenness of
being, as the experience of being accepted by it. It is the
experience of being held in reality by another. It passes
between mother and child. Von Balthasar says that the child's

> 'I' wakens in the experience of a 'Thou' . . . The body
> which it snuggles into is a . . . kiss of love in which it can
> take shelter because it shelters there a priori . . . The fact
> that it experiences Being . . . and human existence . . . as
> the incomprehensible light of grace, is the reason why it
> engages in play.[36]

This is the delight in that which is given absolutely, and yet with
a certain lightness of touch. It is the first sense that, as a being,
one has one's Being from without. This is the experience of the
ontological difference. It leads to the metaphysical question of
the existence of God.

Scheler says that the religious act is not an inference from this
world to another: it is an intuition of a region of being absolutely
demarcated from contingent fact.[37] In the act in which it makes
itself known, absolute Being shows that it transcends created
being. The religious act perceives self-existing being. In Scheler's avowedly Augustinian schema, it does so because God

shows himself. As von Balthasar has it, 'a relation between finite and infinite freedom must include self-disclosure on the part of infinite freedom.'[38]

For von Balthasar, the theological act issues from beyond created being. It is touched by glory indefinable.[39] But he distances himself from Przywara's belief that the human and the divine 'measures' only converge in the 'rupture' of finite being. He says that Przywara's 'similarity in dissimilarity' imports an 'exaggerated' sense into the Fourth Lateran Council: his formula would be 'hazardous' if applied to Christology.[40] Incarnational theology must show how created and Uncreated Being can interlock.

Theology Sublimed – Being Unpresentable

Von Balthasar claims that, with Nicolas of Cusa, 'man . . . steps out beyond the cosmos into a realm where he is unprotected.'[41] After Dante, he says, the analogy of being lost its 'perspicuity'.[42] For the metaphysical doctrines of the schoolmen were not only intellectually convincing. They were also contained by an imaginative world-picture. Once the medieval picture of created beings as existent because porous to the light of infinite Being was lost, the self-giving meaningfulness of things ceased to be perceived. The imaginative reversal gave rise to the adjudication of the reality of objects by the measure of sense perception. Empiricists, such as Hume and Locke, then adopted the representative theory of perception. Consciousness is then envisaged as being related to internal pictures of objects, not to the objects themselves. It looks at the reality mirrored in its own representations; it does not transcend itself. This epistemological closure carefully safeguards the 'unprotected' soul against exposure to its own ontological contingency.

Coleridge challenged this imprisonment of the self in a sensing body.[43] But, as the Southerners argued, Romantic literature did not escape the solipsistic implications of mechanistic philosophy. All too often, the imagination was taken to create the world, rather than to perceive it. Some Romantics let go of a natural world which appeared fully defined by science.

Those who did not imagine nature or history as being built from real, self-transcending forms, approached God without the mediation of any perceptually graspable shape. But His action cannot be imagined without that mediation. Coleridge said that this was lost once Descartes had 'left a lifeless Mechanism whirled about by the dust of its own grinding.'[44] The quantitative science of nature undermined the belief that form is interposed between the natural universe and the infinite depths of God's light. Theology had then to choose between God's unbounded splendour or the barest of facts. Seeming no longer to move beyond itself, the world appeared as a storehouse of self-regulating machines. God was not reflected here: He dwelt unapproachable in the blinding glare of unmediated splendour.

The Romantic Sublime

The Romantics dreamed of 'transport'. In order to achieve it, they looked to the *sublime*. During the eighteenth century, Longinus' *On the Sublime* became a valued document in this quest. Tate thought that *On the Sublime* shows how skill is enmeshed with elevation.[45] He claims that Longinus' aim was to indicate the technical resources which underlie an elevatory text. Some Romantics read the text differently. Fascinated by its statements about the grand feelings which magnificent or wondrous objects induce, they leaped past the formal content of art, seeking its infinite, uplifting tension alone.[46] Unwittingly, they were led to sunder what Longinus had put together. As Wesley Trimpi notes, this leaves us with

> a mystical vision on the one hand and a natural empiricism on the other. The only communication between these two extremes will be through symbols whose external forms . . . will express little or nothing of the nature of the things they signify.[47]

Such a sublimed imagination is less and less able to see natural form. For, as Allen Tate says, 'even the physical sight may be controlled by the religious selectivity, which fixes the height and the direction of the casement framing our inspection of the world.'[48]

Kant enthrones the Romantic sublime in his *Critique of Judgement*. He claims that sublimity is brought about by 'limitless' vistas which 'outrage' the imagination.[49] Sublime conceptions are too immense to be visualized or apprehended. They have a moral value: thus to be staggered is to recognize one's inner yearning for absolutes. As Kant explains it:

> this thrusting aside of the sensible barriers gives [the imagination] a feeling of being unbounded; and this removal is thus a presentation of the infinite. As such it can never be anything more than a negative presentation – but still it expands the soul. Perhaps there is no more sublime passage in the Jewish Law than the commandment: Thou shalt not make unto thee any graven images.[50]

If the sublime does not touch a form, it exceeds human apprehension. For Kant, the tension towards the sublime has no proper object. His 'sublime' is a subjective sense of boundlessness, not a property of nature.[51] Even if it had been an objective facet of being, the form which carries the sublime could not be adequate to it. The shape is detachable. Jean-François Lyotard claims that the implications of this passage from Kant's *Critique* are realized in Postmodern art. In its eschewal of representation, he says, such art bears witness to the unpresentability of reality.[52] Lyotard might as well have commented that it bears witness to the absence of being.

Pantheism Reversed

Theology preceded art, in this instance. In the nineteenth century, it lost its sense of formed outwardness. Coleridge warned that religious thought must find a medium between the allegorical and the literal (as Trimpi's 'mystical' and 'empirical').[53] Few took note. The outcome was the disembodiment of theology: the physical texture of its object was gradually debilitated.[54] Hence, the shapely, finite fact of Christ cannot carry transcendent deity.

Bultmann was perhaps the first theological Postmodernist. He eschews the images in which God stretches Himself out into the extended, horizontal Form of the Word. He contends that faith dissolves the intuitable imagery of the life and language of religion. The idea of God's self-interposition in facts, in history, or in the 'inner life of the soul' is mythological. God is to be approached in abstraction from human perceptibility, under His aspect of infinite, figureless Light, for the 'action of God . . . is not visible or capable of objective scientific proof. The action of God is hidden from every eye except the eye of faith.'[55]

Bultmann's theology is 'a-cosmic' because his empirical reductionism is allied to an 'inverted' Neo-Kantianism.[56] Empiricism compelled the religious imagination to shrink back into itself, and no longer to find God's acts reflected in the external world: inverted Idealism then became acceptable. Defined as a categorical projection, 'myth' is inimical to the passivity of faith. From the late 1920s, Bultmann also drew upon his student, Hans Jonas', work on Gnosticism. Jonas convinced him that primitive Christianity and Gnosticism shared the recognition that religious faith must 'deworldize' its objects. Like Jonas' Gnosticism, Bultmann's Christianity prescinds from facts, as from a cosmos from which significance has been emptied. Eric Voeglin also connects the emergence of Christianity with that of Gnosticism. But he says that, if

> The area of existential consciousness . . . is over-empha-sised, the cosmos and its gods will become the 'alien earth' of the Gnostics . . . Unless the Unknown God is the undifferentiated presence in the background of the . . . intra-cosmic gods, . . . there is no process of revelation in history . . . but only the irruption of an extra-cosmic god to whose mankind he hitherto had been hidden.[57]

Bultmann decided that both Paul's letters and John's gospel drew on the Gnostic myth of the 'sending' of the divine redeemer in human 'disguise'.[58] John has stripped from his redeemer all cosmic trappings. The recognition of the glory of the 'empty fact' of revelation is a blind decision. In John's gospel, he says, 'The salvation-drama – incarnation, death, resurrection, Pentecost – is concentrated into a single event: the Revelation of God's "reality" in the earthly activity of the man Jesus.'[59] The great narrative of salvation is here telescoped into an atemporal moment. Like Lyotard's Postmodern sublime, the divine is, for Bultmann, the unpresentable. Because its existentiality is underlined at the expense of its object, faith is not conceived as an imaginative recreation and interiorization of the scenes of Christ's life. The 'inner life of the soul' is also defigured. Because this internal faith is not modelled on form, its acts will be empty and non-referential. This is not only because they will have no objective referent. It is also because the inner structure of experience demands that persons take on a form by relating themselves to one which exists beyond them. The personal form must have an intentional object, in order to transcend itself. Maritain and the Southerners uncovered myths that live within, and inform the world of facts. Lynch claimed that imagining – or forming – means engaging in reality, and including it within the self. Both he and von Balthasar contend that a unified interior experience is given shape by a transcendent and supernatural Form. Here the myth – the immanent/cosmic Gestalt of the 'gods' – coalesces with its transcendental counterpart: the beautiful Form of Christ. In his self-disclosure as aesthetic form, Christ richly makes present the reality of being.[60]

Form and Splendour

For von Balthasar, the beautiful is an infinite 'vertical' depth of splendour and a 'horizontal' extension of form. Beauty is the meeting place of finite form with infinite light. It unites a definitely shaped form, upon which the mind can come to a stop, with an endless sea of radiant being, into which the mind can move without limitation. The human mind can only grasp forms; boundless things elude it. The beautiful form makes the depths of 'vertical' splendour present. Form concretizes a transcendence which overflows it, but which is its lure. Maritain took Beatrice as the human symbol of Christ. Dante *wants* to make the ascent because she is *radiant.* Captivated by her allure, he is elevated through the heavens, toward the vision of God. The radiance of which Maritain writes is a poetic/ philosophical analogate of von Balthasar's theological notion of splendour. Splendour is the light of meaningfulness which shines through all form (created and Uncreated). By so doing, it draws us into itself. As the manifestation of the beautiful, Christ holds together in His person the infinite depths of splendour and the visible presence of form. The 'transport' which we seek must be expressed by the appropriate form. If we wish to intuit any thing at all, we must pass, not through a shapeless infinite, but through the narrowness of His revealed form. Unless we enter through that clear cut shape we will be blinded by the light of God.

Von Balthasar understands the Incarnation as the capture, by Form, of a splendour too bright to be seen. It is the act of beauty. Hopkins' poem 'The Blessed Virgin Compared to the Air We Breathe' presents one of its scenes. Here the filtering function of Form is ascribed to the Mother of God. She is a veil, without which our eyes could not bear the white-hot glow of the Sun:

> Whereas did air not make
> This bath of blue and slake
> His fire, the sun would shake,
> A blear and blinding ball
> With blackness bound, . . .
> So God was god of old:
> A mother came to mould
> Those limbs like ours which are . . .
> Whose glory bare would blind
> Or less would win man's mind
> Through her we may see him
> Made sweeter, not made dim,
> And her hand leaves his light
> Sifted to suit our sight.

The transcendental beauty of Christ is a Form (Gestalt) of a spatial and temporal width, through which an infinite depth of splendour (*Glanz*) moves. The splendour awakens a desire for more of itself than can be held. It assimilates and 'transports' us into the Form.[61] The tactile, apprehensible Form of the incarnate Christ includes a certain light. Drawing on the Christmas Preface of the Roman Rite, von Balthasar defines Christian faith as a type of seeing, albeit one which is empowered from the outside. It depends on 'a "new light" . . . which illumines this particular form, a light which . . . breaks forth from within the form itself. . . . the "new light" will . . . make seeing possible and be . . . seen along with the form.'[62] Through the scenes of the Incarnation, faith begins to depend upon touching a perspicuous Form/Gestalt. The Form radiates a Splendour which throws Him into illuminative relief.

Expression

Bultmann's experiential-expressivism errs on three counts: it misstates the nature of human experience, it loses the objectivity of faith, and its divine 'glory' has no dramatic extension. This may be countered by a thorough examination of each. Von Balthasar produced what may be called a 'revealed phenomenology'. The formed action within God gives to religious experience its characteristic shape.

When human behaviours are taken as a meaningful structure, they are understood as a drama. Such actions are reflected in the human theatre. For von Balthasar, the deepest resource of theatre is tragedy.[63] Neither the play of sociality nor its theatrical representation can undergird their own meaningfulness. Tragedy is underpinned by justice, the necessity of the gods. If there is no order which transcends this, we will be governed by an ineluctable immanent justice alone. If their ground does not stand beyond themselves, the phenomenological structures are 'closed'. Only when God enters the immanent world-play can its tragic logic be brought to a transcendent fulfilment.

The drama of the Incarnation is God's self-expression. This is the exhibition of free necessity. In it, God's immeasurable light and order coalesce to create a perfect logic which is yet directed by the transcendent freedom which only God can wield. The

New Testament's words for this interlocking are *prepei, prepon estin, dei, deon estin*. Von Balthasar says that, '*dei* . . . includes the hard law of the necessity of suffering . . . to the point of Cross and Hell, as the centre of God's free, salvific will.'[64] Three strands of thought are here combined. First, von Balthasar has considered the meaning of the early phenomenologists' fascination with a priori structures. Second, Scheler, like Barth, recognized that Anselm's 'arguments' do not probe the internal necessities of thought: they depict the advent of revelation. The self-illuminative 'Logic' descends from above. Third, the underlying picture is that of St Anselm's *Cur Deus Homo*. Here, the cosmos is upheld by an aesthetic order, out of which Christ's free decision in suffering to rectify the human relation to God emerges.[65] As von Balthasar says, 'the drama of God and man shows itself to be something "than which nothing greater can be thought".'[66] The logic of Incarnation is not a fixed wallpaper of univocal relations. Nor does it duplicate the supra-temporal connection of Divine and human 'essences'. It is the 'Theodrama' of Divine and human *personae*. Each have their reality, and their apprehensibility by being in relation.

The theological aesthetic is rooted in a Form within the Trinity. The Form issues from the mutual engagement of Father and Son, out of whose love the Spirit is breathed.[67] Christ is the *expression* of God. This is no static mirroring. It is an expressing of the Father by the eternal Son, in an movement which displays the nature of the Trinity. The eternal movement within the Trinity is a going out and a coming back, a 'sending' and a 'returning'. When the Son becomes incarnate, the shape of His mission extends the relation between Father and Son into the world. As von Balthasar says,

> if, as St Thomas has it, his mission in this world is the manifestation . . . of his being begotten . . . then his mode of being here on earth will . . . be . . . the translation into creatureliness, of this heavenly form of existence.[68]

Von Balthasar's Christology is Johannine.[69] What matters for him is John's presentation of glory.[70] In John, the glory of God is exchanged between the persons of the Trinity. It is the 'mutual indwelling' of Father and Son, of which the Spirit is the fruit, and through Whom it 'takes root on earth'. In John's gospel, the Incarnation is the making visible of glory, and that 'to the senses'. The movement issues in 'exaltation': upon the cross, and to the Father. Von Balthasar observes that 'The God of the "dazzling darkness" . . . is the Johannine God, in whom is no darkness at all.'[71]

The beauty of Christ is not that of a luminous icon, crystallized into immobile perfection. It is the beauty of an action. It shows the dramatic movement within the Trinity to us. Von Balthasar says that Christ traverses two 'circles': one is within the Trinity and the other between God and humanity.[72] The path of Christ's mission traces out the shape of the Trinity, expressing the relations between Father, Son and Spirit. The earthly mission follows the curve of the eternal Son. It entails submission, obedience and transparency to the Father.[73]

It also draws us into the circle. As both God and man, Christ integrates human experience into the transcendent reality. One cannot know any artistic object, let alone revelation, without entering its interior.[74] Christ's revelatory function is the inclusion of a human audience within the Trinity: 'Whoever is able to hear the Son as Logos of the Father . . . will also be listening to the interior dialogue between Father and Son wherein the Father utters His entire divinity . . . and His love to the Son.'[75]

Jesus' acts embrace an 'archetypal' human experience of God. If He 'embodies' the human experiential relation to God, then He also lives the fullest imaging of God.[76] His life shows what Christian experience of God should be like. It is known by an exercise of sympathetic mimesis, which takes part in His drama.

Phenomenology Upended

Phenomenology analyses meanings. Phenomenology of religion describes the expression of meaning in given religions.[77] Van der Leeuw suggests that the meaning of such expressions is released when they are construed as 'forms' or *gestalten*. This science speaks of 'appearances': that is, of the *subject's* experience of God.[78] Von Balthasar gives the exercise a transcendent dimension: religious experience emerges from imaginative empathy with Christ's archetypal experiences.[79] His description of religious experience is drawn from the typical case: the God-Man's movement through reality. The shape of our intentional relation to God is drawn from that of Christ to the Father. This is philosophical phenomenology turned upside down.

This enterprise requires a practical root in the personality. Religious experience is the fruit of connaturality with God. The whole person, and not just human feeling, or imagination or thought must participate. The person becomes the 'malleable material' which is remodelled as the image of Christ.[80] As von Balthasar argues:

> An existence is envisaged which is like an instrument tuned by the Spirit . . . This is an attunement (*Gestimmtsein*) which is a concordance (*Übereinstimmung*) with the rhythm of God himself, and therefore an assent . . . to God's being.[81]

The subject of religious experience is re-formed by its transcendent object. Human experience is synthesized – both internally and in what it faces outwardly – by receiving an accord with an objective, revealed Form, which it is to express.

The theological aesthetic has two dimensions, the 'fundamental' and the 'dogmatic'. Fundamental theology elucidates the experience of revelation. It is a 'theory of vision'. This phenomenological dimension is worked out in the first volumes of *The Glory*. Dogmatic theology presents God's seizing, or 'rapture' of the human self. It is laid out in the volumes which describe the biblical engagement of God and humankind. 'Rapture', or 'transport', are words for grace.[82] If with an aesthetic, and scriptural, eye for the image, one envisages the path of grace literally, it can be seen as an interchange of positions, a coming down and a going up. The plot opens out from Mount Sinai:

> The momentum of descent opens up a living relational space . . . that space of ascents and descents which is the . . . stage for all biblical revelation. The divine mountain on which God dwells . . . now becomes the . . . mountain

on which YHWH 'descends' in the form of fire . . . and up
to which he calls Moses . . . to ascend . . . and experience
a . . . meeting between heaven and earth . . .[83]

The stage is set for an absolutization of the momentum of
descent. The story is taken up by St Paul. The key text of *The
Glory of the Lord* is thus 2 Corinthians, 3–4:

> if . . . the children of Israel could not steadfastly behold
> the face of Moses for the glory of his countenance . . . And
> not as Moses, which put a veil over his face . . . which veil
> is done away in Christ . . . But we all with open face
> beholding as a glass the glory of the Lord, are changed
> into the same image from glory to glory even as by the
> Spirit of the Lord. For God . . . hath shined in our hearts
> to give the light of the glory of God in the face of Jesus
> Christ . . . Always bearing about in the body the dying of
> the Lord Jesus, that the life also of Jesus might be made
> manifest in our body. . . . While we look not at the things
> which are seen, but at the things which are not seen . . .

The perception of Christ is a turning toward divine nature: it is
a seeing which is mobilized by a divine 'I' Who lifts the human
'I' into His own Form. For St Paul, the theological experience is
carried by its ontological 'rope'. In speaking 'of a "vision of the
Lord's splendour with unveiled face", through which we are
transformed into the same image . . . Paul unites vision and
rapture as a single process.'[84]

The Being which engages us is, above all, personal. Von
Balthasar underlines the fact that the focus of the glory is the
'face' (*panim*) of Christ. This is a 'sensory' hearing and seeing. We
gaze upon the contours of real, visible face. Bultmann proposed a
somewhat rigid demarcation between the world of 'mechanical'
fact, and the sphere of faith. It entailed that the glory of the figure
of Christ is given only paradoxically. This is to confuse two
notions: that the object of faith is 'visible' and that it is 'capable of
scientific proof'. The facts upon which faith relies are lodged in
the given, physical world and yet go undetected by scientific
experimentation. Von Balthasar suggests an analogy between
the way in which we know another person and that in which we

know Christ. A person, like any 'worldly' fact, is understood first through our sensitive grasp of their physical features and gestures. At the same time the genuine communication of one self to another, and in which we gather more than empirical information, must be freely offered. Because it is personal, the real givenness of the glory of God in Christ transcends the opposition of 'direct' or 'indirect' vision.[85]

What of the 'we look . . . at the things which are not seen'? This is a radiance which emerges in confrontation with its opposite, with hideous suffering and the formlessness of death:

> It is only where Cross and Resurrection are kept in view together that Christ can be called the 'eikon of the hidden God' (Col 1.15). . . must not the visibility of what is essentially invisible also bear in itself an element of . . . hiddenness?[86]

The self-illumination of the *eikon* blinds as much as it enlightens. Christ attains 'full presence' not schematically, as the Logos of perfect meaning, but by embodying in the flesh both the cross of meaningless and the resurrection of meaning. We cannot have the one without the other.

Suffering belongs within Christ's archetypal relation to God.[87] St Paul speaks of Christian life as 'Always bearing about in the body the dying of the Lord Jesus'. Von Balthasar's examination of Bonaventure's fusion of vision and rapture illustrates this. Bonaventure's 'fundamental experience' is, first, surprise in the marvel of being, as it touches his self. Bonaventure is 'transported out' of himself by the wonder of the infinitude of being. Second, as Bonaventure depicts the stigmatization of St Francis, it is given to Francis to undergo an imitation of the crucifixion.[88] He could not have produced for himself this connaturality with the crucified Lord. Nonetheless, the objects of fundamental and dogmatic theology are conjoined, in this paradigmatic experience:

> The crucified seraph . . . expresses himself by impressing himself . . . in Francis . . . although the power of expression goes out from the crucified, the bodily sign is imprinted only because Francis . . . had . . . become in spirit an expression of the love of the crucified.[89]

Perfectionism

Does von Balthasar overemphasize the value of the existential assimilation of faith? Does he make saintliness the sole and sufficient qualification for the work of theology? Noel O'Donoghue has asked, with respect to *The Glory*, whether, if theology is based in the intuition of beauty rather than in the philosophical judgement of truth, it will not become the mouthpiece of the corporate praise of God: it will then cease rationally to communicate with those who have yet to join the chorus.[90] Fr O'Donoghue is always perceptive; never more so than when he noted that Chesterton's *Orthodoxy* is persuasive, not in its rational argument, but as an imaginative invocation of the philosophical experience of wonder.[91] The real question is whether one must tie the perception of the image to a subjective capacity which is impossible without sanctity, and which is rendered veridical by it. David Brown suggests that von Balthasar confuses the idea that sanctity is the basis of 'religious insight' with the more extensive claim that the rational and systematic work of theology can only be the task of the mystic.[92] John McDade links the issue to von Balthasar's vision of theology as issuing from the praying, Marian church. He rightly takes exception to von Balthasar's use of the visions of the mystics to supplement the Bible's depiction of Christ's life. This, as he says, is illegitimately to elaborate.[93] The results will be as tendentious as the 'embellishments' castigated by Kähler. Perhaps von Balthasar retaliates against the essentialist objectivism of Catholic theology between Trent and the First Vatican Council. At this time, as he considers, systematic theology shrivelled to a 'notional' skeleton, whilst piety evinced an unreasoning 'porridge' of devotion.[94] Many find his existential emphasis appealing. One may yet wonder whether the wish that theology be a perfect synthesis of objective revelation with subjective sanctity is not exaggerated.

That emphasis is prominent in the *Theo-Drama*. Von Balthasar says here that there is no 'orthodoxy' without 'orthopraxy'.[95] Unfortunately, as a brief self-examination may indicate, it is quite possible to hold orthodox credal propositions unmatched by one's behaviour. But, J. A. T. Robinson claimed that the South American theologians of praxis drew their inspiration from John's gospel, in which knowing and doing the truth are closely aligned.[96] A. E. Harvey showed that the central figure in John's gospel is the *witness*; its key words are 'giving evidence' and 'bearing witness'. One of the recurring scenes of this gospel is the *trial* (cf. John 5.1–18; 8.13–19; 10.24–33; 11.45–54; 18–19.16). Thus, in von Balthasar's Johannine Christology, the spectator can only sympathize with the 'play' because it touches the heart; one's understanding of the action is in the degree of one's willingness to become a witness. The believer must engage with the play from within, if he or she is to carry it forward.

Myth

It is only as experience revolves like the radar disc towards its transcendent centre that theological reasoning can find its voice. Although the beauty to which it is attuned transcends the 'phenomenal' imagination, the theological aesthetic finds an echo in the forms of human experience. Human experience is articulated in myth. Von Balthasar affirms mythology. He has no small respect for the 'gods'. He states, 'Art in the Christian era is possible as long as the sphere of mythology is still attainable, as long as there are still "gods in this world".'[97]

Nonetheless, he maintains the distinction between mythology and revelation, a distinction regarding which the Romantic Idealists were careless. When immanent myth is identified with transcendent revelation, theology becomes an extension of myth. The 'gods in this world' are real: but their forms are bound in with those of human experience. In reaction against the equation of myth and revelation, von Balthasar sometimes employs the disjunction: either the form is supernaturally impressed upon us, or it is just a projection.[98] Although he says that the great myths are gifts from above, he on occasion describes mythologizing as the 'dream-like' projection of the forms of human experience. He usually does so when he is contrasting myth with the gospel. He does not invert the human fabrication of images, as Bultmann does. He recognizes that some human myths are open to reality.

His reappropriation of 'myth' has a Romantic background. His precursors are the German Catholic traditionalists of nineteenth-century Tübingen, such as J. S. Drey and Adam Mohler. These men regarded mythopoeic speech as the original human language. They envisaged mythological legends as 'sacred tradition' which issued from God's revelation.[99] The myths come down from above. This is to construct an analogy between natural knowledge and revelation on the level of figurative, aesthetic understanding. Von Balthasar would find this appealing. A Christological reinterpretation of pagan myth is present in both the art of the catacombs and in some Pre-Nicene Fathers.[100] What is new in Mohler, and what von Balthasar may have learned from him, was the principle that myth is passed on in a historical community.[101]

The Tübingen traditionalists were inspired by Schelling.[102] For Schelling, art needs a mythology: the gods shelter the symbolic consciousness which art requires. But Schelling considers that Christianity is allegorical, not symbolical. He says that Christianity evacuates the symbol by realizing infinite deity in finite form in a mode which 'nullifies' the finite.[103]

In its alignment of freedom and necessity, tragedy is to be the highest art. Schelling writes that 'in order to allow necessity to overcome him without simultaneously overcoming it, the protagonist also had to atone voluntarily for this guilt – guilt imposed by fate itself. . .'[104] The tragic hero must transcend his suffering, for the symbol can have no trace of ugliness. Christ cannot belong in Schelling's mythological pantheon because he endures pain.[105]

Von Balthasar accepts Schelling's conception of the symbol as the interpenetration of finite and infinite and shares his tragic vision. But he avers that Christ is their ground. He affirms the myths of 'Antiquity' because they depict the suffering hero. The heroes of the *Iliad* are clearly delimited just because of their mortality, and painful finitude: 'Before the foil of Hades . . . the doomed form of the hero takes on its unprecedented sharpness of outline.'[106]

Like Lynch, von Balthasar believes that the reality of the

image turns upon its being contained within boundaries. As with Lynch, the narrow gateway of form is passable only in a death. A real death must precede the resurrection, or elevation, of form. Von Balthasar considers that the finitude of form is sealed and safeguarded by the bodily resurrection of Jesus of Nazareth. Now the literal and the particular are carried into transcendence. The resurrection of Christ upholds the balance of finite and infinite, of form and splendour. The desire of the poetic imagination to find meaning in definite, well-shaped facts is also safeguarded by it. For now the symbol takes root in the reality of being. Von Balthasar argues that 'the resurrection of the flesh vindicates the poets . . .; the aesthetic scheme . . . which allows us to possess the infinite within the finitude of form . . . is right.'[107]

Myth Fulfils Human Desire

The theological aesthetic gives poetic intuition back to itself because Christ's revealed form answers the specific question it had always asked. The mind was seeking the sense of reality. It looked for a description of how things are knowable and yet also 'other'. If the answer corresponds all too exactly to the question, we may only be dealing with a projection. A figure was needed which would step out of, or emerge from, the same concrete reality which we have tried to explain. But, at the same time, that figure must overflow every specific depiction of being. Christ's image appeared only after we had sought to the limits of human rationality. Von Balthasar suggests that

Biblical revelation occurs in the same . . . anthropological locus in which the mythopoeic imagination designed its images of the eternal . . . the living God of Abraham, Isaac and Jacob will . . . exhaust all philosophical theories about God, world and man even to the reversal of their meaning . . .; but this . . . occurs . . . at the point where man once looked over the last horizon of Being . . . the self-revelation of God . . . can only be the fulfilment of man's entire philosophical-mythical self questioning.[108]

The Actualization of the Myth

Myth corresponds to the shape of the world as we experience it. Heracles and Hera are bound in with the natural shapes of the human imagination. We need not infer that they are mere concretizations of human fantasy. The solid, myth-making imagination is interwoven with reality. But it produces figures which are in dialogical relation to itself. Myths exist only as they react upon immanent being. They form part of the immanent aesthetic. In the historical Christ the order is reversed. His Form turns toward the human form and actualizes it: the anchor is on the other side. The shapes of human imagining are not expunged. If they will admit it, they will be given a relation to the supernatural. Von Balthasar states,

> the uniqueness with which the form of Christ confronts us is the identity between myth and historical reality . . . the magic of the 'gods of Greece' . . . by entering the eschatological dimension, is . . . plunged into the radiance of God's glory.[109]

Myth is validated when we grasp that it has this eschatological horizon. We must then show how mythic imaginings have been avenues of approach to transcendence. Von Balthasar praises the Baroque era for having imaginatively realized the figures of Greek myth as 'types' of the historical Christ: 'this was done . . . in the work of Calderon, and . . . in . . . Baroque literature and art. Christ is the true Orpheus, the true Odysseus, the true Eros who meets the human psyche.'[110]

The Revealed Myth Is 'Poetry'

One of Maritain's dicta is that aesthetic beauty is a simultaneous delight for intellect and senses. Von Balthasar says that the Incarnation absolutizes the innate mythologizing instinct. Myths are double-pronged: they encapsulate *meaning* in a *figurative* form. Myth reaches both for complete rational meaning and a 'thisly' shape, vividly coloured. In its best forms, as

Ransom noted, an extensive and an intensive, an all-embracing and a unique God, interpenetrate.

The claim that God has a Form which has entered historical particularity means that the dynamics of myth are elicited by a real object. When we are approached by the infinite God, we need not leave off the poetic inclination to find meaning in a particular place and time, rather than spread everywhere, thinly and indifferently. Yet this Form has a universal import. This is why von Balthasar proposes that, because its God has both tactile shapeliness and infinitude, 'Christianity becomes the aesthetic religion par excellence.'[111]

Myth looks to individuals, philosophy to kinds. There are two ways in which we make sense of the world: in the concrete fact, and in universal truth. Both are necessary, and yet, historically, they have tended to drift apart. Von Balthasar speaks of myth and philosophy as the 'two piers', which ever reach toward one another, and never touch.[112] Each 'pier' tries to attain reality. Each is only partially successful.

Homer's mythical epics achieve a synthesis of the divergent levels of human life and of divinity. In the shield of Homer's *Iliad*, gods and men dwell together in a unified and yet differentiated world. The gods belong with the world of nature, but they do not coalesce with it. So, too, the conclusion of Aeschylus' *Oresteia* draws together chthonic powers and the transcendent, and yet humanizing impulse of Athena.[113] But the ineluctable growth of the philosophical impulse pushed myth toward the periphery of the human imagination. It continued to exist, but without philosophy, it ceased to be open to reality, shutting itself up in Gnostic fantasy.[114]

Philosophy is rather more deficient in von Balthasar's eyes. Its first step is to cut itself off from the faithful prayer which was instinctual to myth. Plato then enunciated a self-contained world, in which being participates in divinity, rather than relying on it, as the heroes of myth do upon their gods.[115] Where philosophy posits an analogical relation between immanent and transcendent being, it all too easily transforms it into an univocal relation. Von Balthasar believes that philosophy begins in what seems to be a kind of 'Titanism'. He overstates his case: the prowess of Western philosophy is partly due to the distance which it set between itself and the religious cult.

But he has discerned the problem of pure philosophy: it is tempted to abstraction from concrete reality. Philosophy requires the universality which, as he says, St Thomas gave it.[116] But this pursuit of generalizable truths drives it toward intellectualization. The revealed 'myth' of the resurrection reminds philosophy that it relies upon the *'conversio ad phantasma'*, the turning of the mind toward images of facts.[117]

When imaginative myth and philosophy fly apart, neither can touch real things. The one will project images which are not garnered from facts, while the other extrudes concepts, rather than examining existing objects. This is Tate's version of the disassociation of sensibility. For von Balthasar, the two 'piers' of myth and philosophy can only be conjoined by the resurrected body of Christ. The marriage of sensory myth and philosophical notion is achieved when both are given real and physical moorings by the literal, historical fulfilment of the myth-making tendency. The risen body of Christ is the bridge between image-making and universal understanding. This is the transcendent Object through which sensibility is unified.

Truth is the right relation between a reality and an affirmation someone makes about it. Theology cannot logically deny the possibility: if it does so, it has denied that it can do so. Von Balthasar does not reject propositional truth. But, he says, philosophy always comes back to the veridical quality of the thinker's perceptions. Myth turns on the vision, and subjects itself to it. Now the clouds open, and the sun of sublimity, or glory, streams through. In the myths which attain this light, the subject is pierced by something which transcends them, and for which they cannot account. Philosophy deploys myths when it wishes to speak of transcendent things – as in Plato's *Republic*. But it cannot consistently invoke them. Myth is thus its 'upper limit'.[118] Nevertheless, the glory which shines through myth upon philosophy confirms its truth as transcendental.

Tragic Dramas

Myths flower in revelation because they are images of reality. Von Balthasar regards Greek tragedy as the supreme prefiguration of Christian revelation. These dramas give a body both to the action of being and to the story of salvation. Sophocles' Oedipus is a proto-image of Christ.[119] Von Balthasar investigates those tragic figures whose fate imitates the reactions of transcendent upon created being.

The fate of the tragic hero is to step into the causal interflow between God and the world. He enters a chain of events which involve suffering: God's 'hammer' breaks in upon Oedipus and forces him to recognize a truth. Tragic heroes and heroines bear their guilt for others. Having been pulled apart, Oedipus becomes a suppliant. He is an image of passive dependence. Finally, in being healed, the hero becomes a source of 'sanctity'. Having undergone destruction, he is transposed into a higher realm, as in the last scenes of *Oedipus at Colonus*. This displays the elevation of being.

The tragic hero's travails open a window upon glory, and that in the apparent absence of God: 'Sophocles . . . had but one vision of man: silhouetted against the night-sky of an infinitely sublime and distant god, one who yet through this distance proclaims his presence.'[120]

Iphigenia at Aulis and Alcestis offer to die for another; Shakespeare's kings, as representatives, die to redress the 'balance of justice' in their kingdoms.[121] These errands of mercy break the bonds of the internal necessities of this world. Tragedy shows, von Balthasar says, that love is as strong as death.[122] The heroine or hero whose death is atoning dies both alone and encompassing another.[123]

Such tragedies contain, in germ, the inner necessities which govern Christ's mission. Christ's sending, His suffering, and His return are a figure of the movement of being. They 'let down a rope' from the transcendent Father into creation.[124] This makes transcendent being visible. Christ's concrete, finite form is broken. It has ventured into the territory of death and of sin, thence to reclaim those who have fallen there. The love which He manifests is not only justice: it is also forgiveness. He is bound, not by 'fate', but to his gentle Father. But when, 'in the form of Crucified love', He hangs between finite and infinite freedom, He is the figure of necessity.

Tragedy as a Univocal Genre

In the course of the first, 648-page volume of his five volume *Theo-Drama*, von Balthasar states his procedure thus: 'We have not space here to do justice to comedy. It will have to suffice to define it by reference to tragedy.'[125] He does not mention Aristophanes' comedies as vehicles of glory. He is right to draw the analogy of tragedy, as Lynch did. But, unlike Lynch, he sometimes presses analogy to univocity. When he does touch on a comic figure, such as Odysseus, he places him under the unsuitable palimpsest of the tragic theme. Many-pathed Odysseus becomes the 'man of Sorrows'.[126]

Von Balthasar composed a magnificent invective against 'the bad habit of interrupting the Word before it has finished speaking', so to interject one's own comments.[127] Does he protest too much? Like all great readers, he interprets almost as much as he hears. As *The Glory* imagines the Biblical history, a series of ever more shattered figures – David, Job, Ezekiel – must mark the path of the dissolution of the Old Covenant. His study of the biblical stories about David presses so heavily on his 'humiliation' that his lightness of foot is not registered. It seems strained to take David as an Oedipus at Colonus.[128] One may or may not quarrel with von Balthasar's finding in David 'a type of the Ecce Homo'. Some may accept his contention that God speaks to Job from the whirlwind only of his own 'absoluteness and eternity'.[129] I would say that Job's *character* disappears. Von Balthasar sees only the 'withdrawal' of God, the process of 'pulling apart'. When he imagines Job, as when he writes of Oedipus, he has before his mind the objective pattern of these characters' destiny. His interest in the diagram of the plot, at the expense of the characters who move it, can turn playwrights into choreographers. Oedipus is, he says, guiltless.[130] Is he? Von Balthasar would have preferred Oedipus to prefigure Christ more precisely than he does. He does not imagine that Christ had any comical precursors.

Christ as an Historical Symbol

Christ's form is historical. Time (and space) were the first victims of the relegation of facts to the ghetto of positivity: and likewise the historical mission of Christ. Von Balthasar thinks that Ehrenfels' conception of the Gestalt indicates that this occludes our everyday experience. In musical compositions, time flows into a musical form.[131] So does it in Christ's historical mission. An aesthetic apprehension can take seriously the Incarnation of Christ in a narrow expanse of time. Univocalist theology, which seeks Poe's 'wild beauty above', will allegorize Scripture, passing immediately from the biblical words to their fancied universal referent, without first attending to the historical detail. M.-D. Chenu showed that, when it is practised insensitively, allegorical reading fixes on isolated word-meanings – avoiding the many dimensions of the whole image, which require a nuanced, many-faceted response.[132] The allegorist loses himself among the multiplicity of parts when he lacks a sense of analogical form, with which to ingather the parts to an historical whole. The demythologization programmes of Bultmann and Shubert Ogden are also a form of allegorization and separative analysis. Bultmann combines positivistic literalism with respect to historical fact with an interiorized supernaturalism.[133] Both positivism and misused allegorism reduce human experience to only one level, whether the literalism of sense or that of intellectuality. As Tate proposed, one must bring a polyphony of levels of experience into play if one is to know historical objects in their fullness. If, as Lynch says, human understanding is historical, it needs to be guided into reality by fluent, temporal images. It is by embodying the multiple forms of time that Christ mobilizes human apprehension.

The unity between subject and historical object is created by affective connaturality. Historical knowledge depends, not upon analytic detachment, but upon practical immersion in the object. It is just by being submerged in the history through which Christ has moved – leaving a trail of images in His wake – that one can gain the synthetic perception through which adequately to know the concrete base of biblical history.

Thus, in his *Theology of History*, von Balthasar depicts Christ's slow, patient movement through the forms of time: 'He is not only the New Covenant realized; he has to realize it step by step.'[134] By waiting upon the Father's will, Christ binds himself to the anticipatory structure of temporality.[135]

The Historicality of the Incarnation in St Irenaeus

Both Lynch and von Balthasar value Irenaeus for his historical sense, gained in combat against Valentinian Gnosticism. Von Balthasar says that, if it is not to succumb to Gnosticism, the endeavour to make sense of historical humanity must be founded in a concrete subject.[136] The search for historical meaning must come down to earth in a real fact.

Lynch claimed that the phases of human life are so ordered as to evoke significance naturally, if properly lived through and imaged. Irenaeus knew that embodiment is temporality. Human beings realize God's image in themselves by passing through the medium of temporal form. Von Balthasar states that for Irenaeus, 'Man's essence is to experience, that is . . . by contrast to the . . . perfection of the gnostics, which is given from the outset, to be a person in the temporal process of becoming . . . one who receives, and is therefore a believer . . . "Thus does man advance forward slowly and softly, and he is elevated up to the Perfect".'[137]

Irenaeus aims to preserve the reality of temporal existence. So, he says that human kind needed slowly to be formed before the gospel could come: human beings were not created in perfection, as 'gods', but in an 'infantile' state.[138]

Christ treads through the whole of human history. This is the atoning labour of *anakephalaiosis*, by which all of the events of the human story are threaded together. The recapitulation is achieved in Christ's movement through human experience.[139]

As the re-formation of humanity, *anakephalaiosis* involves a struggle with death. Irenaeus imagines the conflict both historically, as the summation of the Old Covenant history, and mythically, as the archetype of Jonah's adventure within the whale.[140] Wingren describes his image of Christ's task:

> he forces his way through the Fall and emerges on the other side in God's sinless creation . . . the place of His emerging is His resurrection . . . between these two worlds . . . there lies the zone of death where the battle is waged. The entrance to this region of darkness is the Serpent's conquest of man; the way out is Christ's victory over the Serpent.[141]

Irenaeus pictures Christ as the new Adam. He is the generative type of a new humanity. He draws everything that is human into Himself. Christ draws all 'humanness' into His own unique person. He expands within all human time. In this conception of *anakephalaiosis*, the body of history is made beautiful by being lifted into Christ, its head. Historical humanity becomes a Gestalt: a whole wider than the numerical totality of its members.[142]

The Analogy of History

Martin Kahler wrote against the 'thin' conception of factuality deployed by many 'historical' reconstructions of Christ's life.[143] Not all historians have been positivists. Wilhelm Dilthey (1833–1911) perceived that the historian does not deal with discrete facts.[144] Rather, historical fact is grasped as the expression of the inner dynamic of a culture. For Dilthey, 'expressions' are human objectifications of meaning. Layer upon layer of meaning is to be found in the historical artefact. Historians re-create an epoch by classifying and interconnecting the set of meanings which governed it. In order to do this, they must find the 'focal-point' from which these meanings radiate, and in which they cohere. Dilthey says that the historian's task is possible because he belongs to the same historical world which his ancestors created, and which is still being created. This can be glossed:

those within a tradition can imaginatively reconstruct its meanings on a human, or non-reductionist, plane.

Thus far, we remain on the level of what Dilthey calls the 'immanent teleology' of human life, that is, of human self-definition through history. If we are to reach beyond the sphere of human meanings, we need a conception of transcendental intelligibility. At the same time, the conception of meaning as historical must be retained. The apprehension of the transcendentals may be related to human historicality without enclosing human beings in temporal process. I proposed that one argument for the existence of the transcendentals is that they infuse community with shared meanings. The Fugitives found their relation to the good by re-imagining the social traditions of the South. A theology which takes history seriously might discover transcendence in the concrete universal of humanity, in its emergence through time. This community of persons would be the wider analogate through which the transcendentals are known. There will be no such concrete universal unless we have adhered to beauty, truth and goodness. If it is not sustained by the transcendentals, community dies. Tate and von Balthasar believe that history has an intrinsic meaning – a 'mid-point' – because something else is acting alongside it. Human community is unified by a transcendent Form. The idea of humanity as a concrete universal might strike us as a bland and elastic concept, as one of Tate's 'long' perspectives on history. In order to have imaginative reality, it must be based in a clearly delimited fact. Since history consists of the acts of individuals, it must ground itself in a particular being: the historical person of Christ. He conjoins the webs of human sensibility and of community that they may apprehend the transcendentals which He frames and makes present.

Von Balthasar believes that philosophy inevitably takes the Hegelian 'Long View' of historical humanity. It envisages humanity in its universal 'essence', and so as a social form. But each person can only exist as a individual, 'here and now'. The conflict between the claims of philosophy and those of concrete existence is resolved by historical revelation. This does not rescind the claim of universality. The philosophical search for the human essence is founded in Christ as the 'norm' of humanity, just as the existential requirement for particularity gains credence from His facticity: 'He himself is the Idea made concrete, personal, historical: *universale concretum et personale.*'[145]

Those who live within His 'normative drama' turn away from the Cartesian ego, bending their persons toward universal humanity. Their lives are 'deprivatized'.[146] Each stands on the universal world stage, there to portray an aspect of the good.[147] If it is thus to be both unique and universal, Christian theology must be practised in the form of a reiteration of the drama. 'Lyric' theology, von Balthasar says, relates its interior repercussions.[148] It is theology as prayer. It tells of the committed subject. 'Epic' theology paints with a detached eye an objective panorama. 'Dramatic' theology rises above both. The theology which is worked out in the midst of the scenes of the play can explore the divine engagement with humankind.

The Titanic Epic

Metaphysics, Scheler said, 'tells no tales'.[149] This is a combatative statement, and one with which von Balthasar concurs. Having carefully distinguished the metaphysical and the religious act, he will have to define any theology which is not explicitly 'descendent' as 'metaphysics'. He sometimes rhetorically belies his recognition that theology needs its argumentative partner.[150] Noel O'Donoghue takes his exclusion of St Thomas from the ranks of the theological aestheticians to limit von Balthasar's enterprise.[151] Von Balthasar more than once designates St Thomas as philosopher, rather than theologian.[152] He means to assign to Thomas his proper place, as a 'metaphysician'. To differentiate is not to denigrate; but is the ascription correct? Nor does he always stand by the terms of his distinction: 'philosophy' is his repeated metaphor for abstract generalisation. This is really only true of one kind of philosophy: the Idealism with which he is embroiled in debate. For the Idealists, the 'originary genre' of poiesis is epic.[153]

The Romantic Idealists created a metaphysical narrative of epic proportions. In it, the human spirit's emergence into complete consciousness transforms it into Absolute Spirit.

For Hegel, human spirit is driven to ascend by history, for Fichte by ethics, and for Schelling by aesthetics. In each Idealist story, human spirit and God are not two characters but one.[154] The Idealist narrative is univocalist: the texture of the reality which it portrays is monovalent. It abolishes Kant's thing-in-itself, and with it the mysterious, unassimilable depths of existence. We know the Absolute by re-creating it. It is not surprising that, as Reardon says 'aesthetic idealism [is] the coping stone of the entire idealist system.'[155]

For Schelling, artistic activity enables the spirit, which is making its 'Odyssey' through nature, to realize itself. Art unites what thought had set apart, in an 'infinite contradiction'.[156] Aesthetic works engender the interplay between the finite and the Infinite. When it emerges, he says,

> it is as though the invisible curtain that separates the ideal from the real is raised . . .; it is . . . the opening through which the characters . . . of the world of fantasy, which shimmers . . . imperfectly through the real world . . . come upon the stage. Nature . . . is the imperfect reflection of a world that exists not only outside but within him.[157]

Where Maritain and the Southerners see the artistic object as an *analogue* of transcendence, Schelling makes an *univocal* equation of the two. For he is implicated in two immanent-isms. First, his epistemology includes no notion of a transcend-ing relation to an external object. As we noted with reference to the narcissistic aberrations of modern art, without this inten-tional relatedness, the known or imagined object is seen, not as an objective reality but as an interior, magical world. Myster-iously allied to this is Schelling's metaphysical immanentism, which makes no distinction between being as proportionate to the human mind, and transcendent Being. For Schelling, God and the work of art which He projects, are two views of one, ultimately identical reality.[158] He does not propose that God transcends the reality which He creates.

In this univocalist cosmology, the immanent drama of human existence coalesces with the 'theo-drama'. Schelling urges that a God who writes the play 'from the outside' would deprive its players of their freedom.[159] His God is no transcendent author, known through His interplay with human reality. He is the play's emergent theme. Which kinds of freedom and necessity coincide in tragedy? Schelling answers: immanent necessity and human freedom. But then, the play has no further horizon from which a resolution can issue.

Having set the world-play free of God's transcendent 'interference', we may succumb to the temptation to set language free of that interference which is the necessity of correlating words with the world. If it is made to stand alone, the beautiful word is an island, severed from being and truth. We recall that, for Schelling, the Christian incarnation of absolute meaning in one finite fact 'nullifies' the finite. If this is so, then the 'is' of poetic analogy, or the 'one and multiple identity' in which Beatrice remains in the flesh and yet symbolizes transcendental perfection, is equally impossible. Schelling stands here for the withdrawal of the simultaneity of mythic intuition and the philosophical judgement. The one grasps the unique fact, the woman before one's eyes, the other finds her universal correlation with other women. If the intention to name a specific woman cannot be implicit in the naming of their universal features, then the fact will continuously withdraw from the language which refers to it. This creates the self-defeating character of linguistic reference, upon which scholars such as Kevin Hart build postmodern theologies.[160]

Von Balthasar urges that Idealistic philosophy was 'aestheticized': it was founded in a beauty isolated from the other transcendentals. He goes on to say that, 'The light of the transcendentals, unity, truth, goodness and beauty . . . can only shine if it is undivided. A transcendence of beauty alone is not viable.'[161] He will try to build the beautiful back into the framework of *all* of the transcendentals.

The Communicability of Being

Kant employed two 'I's. One is the moral self, the other the virtual subject which unifies categorial constructions. The weaver behind our categorializing acts is not the personal self. Rather, knowledge is synthesized by the hypothetical 'virtual self'.[162] Left with the question of how to lend coherence to Kant's fissiparous categories, the Idealists identified the 'I' with the hypothetical self, which became the Absolute. The categories have a history. In its course, the self emerges from and sinks back into, the Absolute.[163] In this recrudescence of a Spinozistic pantheism, the individual 'I' was submerged. Against this, von Balthasar will claim that theology is founded in an irreducible personal form which exceeds the power of the human intellect to explain or destroy. He writes, in his Dissertation on German literature, 'God is dead; I have killed, sacrificed him. That is Nietzsche's conclusion. God is dead; he has sacrificed himself, but he has not stopped living. That is Kierkegaard's paradox.'[164]

For Kierkegaard, God's command to Abraham to sacrifice Isaac, and the 'preposterous' faith which accepts this duty, drives a wedge of finitude into Hegel's 'universal' generalizations.[165] Von Balthasar believes that Romanticism treats the self as an effluescent episode in an engulfing narrative. For Fichte, 'The object of the ethical law in me as an individual is not myself alone but the whole realm of reason.' In Hegel's writings, 'the nation, "the generalized individual" [is] the centre.'[166]

Although they eschew the Hegelian metanarrative, some Postmodernists still deduce the individual 'I' from a wider story. Critics of the Cartesian essentialist self have used the metaphor of language to recapture the truth that the self comes to awareness within a community. Hayden White argues that, although it has no 'plot', the 'hidden protagonist' of structuralist-functionalism is 'language'.[167] The 'I' is taken to be a spoken word, or an episode, within a story which is narrated by society as a whole. Lyotard says, 'even before he is born, the human child is already positioned as the referent in the story recounted by those around him, in relation to which he will chart his course.'[168]

Michael Edwards' *Christian Poetics* draws out the implications of the translation of the being of the self into the interplay of languages. The self as word is fallen: it suffers the disjoinedness of language itself. Just as the single arch in which word and thing once achieved their Edenic correlation is broken, leaving a multiplicity of half-built bridges, so the self has lost its unity. It plays a succession of roles amid a series of language games which tell no single story.[169]

The Christology which finds in the transcendentals the source of speech will prolong this tale somewhat further, and add a forgotten thread. The *Theo-drama* seeks the ground of the uniqueness of the human 'I': without it, God has no real partner in the play.[170] In the course of his quest, von Balthasar returns to the things themselves, that is, to the experience of 'I-ness'. 'Presence-to-myself' reveals three modalities.

In the first place, 'I' come upon the 'limitless expanse' of being.[171] The enclosed ego cannot meaningfully say 'I am'. For the self – in distinction to the material ego – is not just a slab of 'thereness', taking up physical space. 'I am' by transcending my self and participating in the intelligible action of infinite being. I can communicate with others because my unique 'I' is created by the self-communication of being.

But, secondly, my self is 'incommunicable'.[172] Each 'I' has its inaccessible loneliness. So much did the essentialists exaggerate it that it is discarded by Postliberals and Postmodernists alike. The self deserves a more nuanced clarification. On the one hand, it must make play with its destined social role. The words which others speak to it situate the self within a pre-given story. It will not find its identity in a still-point of uniqueness, outside all relations, and beneath the roles in which social beings must be costumed. The opposition between sincerity and role-playing is misplaced. The social world does not impinge upon the 'I' only to distort a genuine, private self. Such a 'centre within' fails to root the 'I' in reality. The given mask is not an arbitrary disguise. Actors successfully play those roles for which the depths, or shallows, of their personality are fitted.[173] Nor is a man or a woman who gives a sermon or a lecture simply 'being someone else'. To act well is to put aside all egotism. It is by losing itself in the role that the 'I' engages in reality. To acquiesce in being human is to accept one's predestined roles.

But, the roles do not wholly body forth their actors' 'I am'. The function shows the self, but it does not exhaust it. There is a distance between the person and the role which he or she conveys. Although the mask is necessary, it does not quite fit. We who insist against Cartesians and experiential-expressivists that the self is constructed in the language of others, know that we are not only the 'plumbers' or 'wives' which they make of us. As von Balthasar says, the gap between the 'I' and its role is a basic fact of human experience.[174]

The mislaid thread is human freedom. The role which I play is not only thrust upon me. It is in my freedom that I have both my inalienable transcendence of the social narrative and my ability to give to the drama new twists and turns. Because a measure of my co-operation in the drama is free, my entrance into the plot adds to it a fresh rhythm. If the social narrative alone created each human role, the narrative would return eternally upon itself. For Lyotard, language is an 'agonistics', in which each player adds fresh moves to the game.[175] But, how could a player go on to the attack without a moment of freedom in which she redefines the contest precisely because she has first so defined herself? This is the moment of 'loneliness'.

In the third place, however, the self which would conceal itself in an untouchable inner space could never become an 'I'. I am called to myself when some other speaks to me. One,

> can only be awakened to free self-awareness by some other free self-awareness: for example, the child by its mother. . . . Free self-awareness experiences itself as an 'I' only when it is addressed as a 'thou' – through word, gesture, smile, protection . . . the individual subject realizes that he is 'for-himself-with-others'.[176]

Von Balthasar's search for the 'I' culminates in the 'Biblical reflection' of Martin Buber and Franz Rosenzweig. Buber saw that the 'eternal Thou' never recedes into silence. Rosenzweig grasps the deeper theological truth: the insistent address of the divine Thou, drawing me out of immersion in generality and inviting decision, names my 'I'.[177] As Rosenzweig has it, 'personality', 'is man playing the role assigned to him by fate, one role among many in the polyphonic symphony of mankind.'[178]

'Personality' is a loose-fitting handed-down overcoat.[179] When the 'self' asserts itself above the role, it gains its solitude. But 'self' is 'defiant': locked up in itself, it is 'fixed' upon an unalterable path. God's gift of the proper name, to this specific 'I', turns it to its 'soul'. Now, Rosenzweig says: 'It is not fated but borne by volition.'[180]

Thus, von Balthasar, following Rosenzweig, also draws on the metaphor of language. But here, language is rooted, neither in the surging up of Absolute Spirit, as in the 'Titanic Epic', nor in the self-construction of human communities. Language is, first, the word of God, within the 'divine drama'.

The 'to be' of the self is caught up in the drama of being. Transcendent Being causes things to be. The creativity of Being is not an emanation, or a monologue, but a call and a rebounding. The self in relation to others and to God *is* because it is spoken to, and replies. It exists in dialogue. When our 'self-presence' show us our createdness, we 'give thanks'. Our freedom in uniqueness is the gift of God. The dialogical quality of human life, in its turn, is founded upon the community of Persons within the Trinity.[181] That divine relationality is an unbounded self-giving. The being of each Divine person is a handing over. There is a dialogue of Being within the Trinity itself: Father, Son and Spirit co-create themselves by giving themselves up to each other.[182]

The Form of Christ is obtained, not in self-subsistence, but in infinite self-emptying. Christ has His being in *kenosis*. He has those interior spaces which can contain the darkness of the other. The Word is held open to the breakdown of language. Natural form is creative because it has wrestled with formlessness. In the descent into hell, the supernatural form of Christ enters the fall of speech and reverses it:

> The Word of God becomes unheard, and no message forces its way upward to speak of its journey through the darkness: for it can do this only as not-word, as not-form, through a not-land, behind a sealed stone . . . The body that rises from the sealed grave is 'no longer Christ according to the flesh, but a new creature' (2 Corinthians 5.6 ff.).[183]

The drama is not only strung between Fall and future paradise: in entering death, Christ endures the chaos of wordlessness. Out of the abyss of un-meaning, the Word/Form accomplishes its resurrection. In this turn, speech has its *peripeteia*.

The Play

There is no communication in a vacuum. Meaningful relations among persons require a stage. Persons see and know one another by acting together: they name one another, and read the parts thus apportioned from a shared script. The stage is a meaning conferring space. The 'I' must stand on it, if it is communicate with other 'thous'. Its identity is integrated as it plays its scenes. Christ enters history in order to construct a stage upon which the Triune God and human beings can meet. The three scenes of His action are openings, in which the divine-human engagement is carried forward.

In the first scene, Christ announces the Kingdom.[184] The Kingdom has a dual temporal extension. Christ spoke of the apocalypse both as near and as distant. On the one side, it is already occurring in His ministry: He is the presence of the Kingdom. The Kingdom is attained, when He 'goes to the end of time', in his death. On the other side, the Kingdom has yet to come: the Christian Church is always seeking it. The drama will not end until Christ has 'put his enemies under his feet'.

The second scene stands at centre stage: this is His crucifixion. It is the moment of 'decision', in which He turns to face all that is opposed to God. This is the deepest opening within the 'supra-tragedy': Christ now creates the space in which all other characters will make their entrance. It is the moment of His greatest passivity. His autonomous 'I', his self-understanding, is taken from Him. He loses his name.

It is not for Him to 'reassemble' His broken identity. The third is thus a recognition scene: in the resurrection, Christ is given His 'exalted name' by the Father; the Holy Spirit witnesses to His identity. In the Spirit, the apostles will confirm that the pre-Easter Jesus and the post-Easter Christ are one and the same Messiah.

The Actors

The God-man is a true 'dramatic' persona. He is 'awakened' to a presage of who He is to be by a human Thou, who is His mother. She also teaches Him the story which forms His character: that is, the traditions of Israel.[185] His human character is earned in successive stages: as the performance unfolds, so does His identity. Von Balthasar draws upon the Patristic conception of Christ's two 'states': the *status exinanitionis* is the state of abasement; in the *status exaltationis*, He is given His 'grandeur'.[186]

To play a role is to represent someone. Christ's mission on earth is the concrete representation of the Father: it is the effective rendition of the Trinity. Christ's role is His mission. He has hold of His 'I' in the action which carries His persona.[187] In His earthly life, Christ knows Himself by knowing what He must do. He is tempted to discard the mission. He knows Himself in that which relates Him to others. It is the mission which is directly present to Him. It is thus the vehicle of His immediate knowledge of the Father. He has not taken the mission upon Himself. He is defined in His role by the Father, as the 'well-beloved Son'. His divine Sonship is not a static pregiven within a self-sufficient consciousness. This is a 'divinity received'. It is given to Him in mission, as an reciprocal relation, performed through the mediation of the Spirit. The person of Christ *is* His mission. In Christ, and in Him alone, 'role' and person have a single source. Von Balthasar often repeats St Thomas' statement of the matter: Christ's begetting (*processio*) within the Trinity is His sending (*missio*). The Father Who gives His 'only-begotten' Son is not an extrinsic 'Director', but the principle actor in the divine drama.

To enter the play to be 'in Christ'. Here von Balthasar cites Jacques Maritain: 'The (pure) Church is the only one on earth who carries out the role she presents . . . in her, both role and person come from God. The world . . . is a stage on which the roles and what they embody . . . are rarely in harmony.'[188] To assume the role which God imparts is to find the mask within. It can only be uncovered by discarding the masks behind which the ego takes shelter. In obedience to the call of God, the role and the 'I' become as one. When the representative role becomes the mission, the 'I' is freed to perform with infinite freedom.

The Personalizing of the Transcendentals

If our abstracted and generalizing minds undermine our belief in the Incarnation, then aesthetic and dramatic images should be our vehicles of analogy. These are more rounded analogates than philosophy can obtain. They display a rich reality through the actions of persons. Von Balthasar claims that an aesthetic apprisal of theology must be Trinitarian. With reference to Gerard Manley Hopkins, he says that,

> It is . . . the duty of the one who ascends to Christ . . . to interpret all the forms of God's revelation in Christ throughout the universe, and this task is achieved by Hopkins the poet. For what has to be interpreted is not concepts (of 'universal' truths), but images (of the unique, personal, divine-human truth), and here poetry is the . . . appropriate language.[189]

Where St Thomas spoke of the contingency of all nature, Hopkins grasps his personal createdness.[190] His 'taste of self'[191] is his evidence that he has been moulded into being, not by a general evolutionary process, but by One who is more idiosyncratic than he is. This mediates his knowledge of 'All things counter, original, spare, strange.'[192] Outward form is threaded through finite personality before it can be known. Hopkins asks whether he might not be an accident of a universal mind – such as that posited by Hegel? No, because 'the universal mind is outside of my innermost self . . . nor does it share . . . my moral standing or my fate. And for all that this universal mind may be at work in mine, it leaves me finite.'[193]

Hopkins exercises what Maritain takes to be the poetic prerogative of seizing upon the irreducibility of objects. He finds the finite image which he seeks in the Form of Christ. Christ brings about the particularity of the forms of nature

and, more perfectly, that of persons. He makes them act out
the is-ing peculiar to themselves. Thus from 'As kingfishers
catch fire',

> I say more: the just man justices;
> Keeps grace: that keeps all his goings graces;
> Acts out in God's eye what in God's eye he is –
> Christ – for Christ plays in ten thousand places,
> Lovely in limbs and lovely in eyes not his
> To the Father through the features of men's faces.[194]

Hopkins' sensuality is assimilated to his faith. His poetic sense is
founded in the personal and substantial ground of form. He sees
that the Creator is more specific than created nature.

The ebbing away of the cosmological imagination is no fall
into the quotidian. But it has to be imagined rightly. If not, it
will issue in an ever starker confrontation between God and
human self. That jeopardizes both the unity of being and the
unity of experience, on which incarnational theology rests. The
person is then reduced to just one of its agencies, whether
emotion, will, or the mind which becomes more general in the
degree of its abstraction from embodied action, and so from the
particular fact. Some, such as Bultmann, denude the subject of
external relations. Whether it remains a subject is an open
question. A subject is the agent of a continuous narrative:
existential decisions do not construct it. Others assert that
God's descent to the cross negates the ascending ladder of
philosophical analogy. Von Balthasar agrees that the cosmological model could not place the self-emptying of Christ at its
centre.[195] He also has his suspicions of the metaphysical
concourse between humankind and God. This stems from a
phenomenologist's focus on the unique form of each intentional
act.[196]

He thus argues, first, that the informing principle of the
religious act is personal. Transcendental beauty is real being,
confronting us from the outside. It is the manifestation of reality
in the 'double-sided' form of a Person. This Form binds being
into the narrow shape of the divine Person. As the light which
communicates the truth of being, the figure of the crucified
Christ is beautiful. A broken 'I' displays the meaning of being:

this form has opened itself to otherness. Envisaged in this way, this Person compels us to think realistically.

Because He is personal, He is free. Von Balthasar finds the Christian keystone within the classical analogy of being: it is the infinite freedom of God to accompany His creatures, and the free self-proportioning of the finite person to God.[197] The analogy of freedom is, on the side of creatures, a transparent self-disposing, or availability, to God. Through it, the self becomes His presence in the world. God is drawn into the earth through human presences. Thus could Ezekiel 'gesticulate with his whole existence'.[198] The Christian heroes perform ever new 'post-figurations' of Christ's drama. As an analogous, or ontological category, expression is representation. As the analogy of freedom, the analogy of being becomes the meeting place of infinite and finite freedom, in what Przywara called a 'point of exchange': the place where that which is represented is what it represents.[199] In Christ, created and Uncreated Being change places. Incarnational theology depends on the possibility of the convergence between finite and infinite being.

Such freedom requires that the infinite God can define his own terms. He transcends proportional being and meaning. Aesthetically beautiful forms are the effects of what St Thomas called *ens*, or created being. Von Balthasar says that, because St Thomas recognizes that God rises above *ens*, he preserves the place of 'glory' in metaphysics.[200] To distinguish aesthetic beauty from the glory of God is to be open to the Christological affirmation of the interpenetration of infinite and finite being. God's glory is His absolute actuality of being. Such a God is not constrained by fate: 'He will be what He will be'. His actuality of being is a complete availability. Von Balthasar's single focus on God's transcendence leads him to recover Nicolas of Cusa's designation of God as the Wholly Other in the Non-Other.[201] He says: 'A purely transcendent God would be an abstract mystery. But a God who, in His transcendence, can also be immanent, is a positive and concrete mystery . . .'[202]

Thus does he gather the universality of metaphysics into the free relation between God and the human 'I'. He recasts the cosmological ground of metaphysics, whilst retaining the medieval affirmation of the reality, truth, goodness and beauty of being.[203] He intends that reality radiate from the shape of the person, not that it be confined within it. In his work, the density of being is known as a Person. In the illumination of the transcendentals by beauty, we have a personalistic theology which includes the analogy of being. In Christ the panoply of being is made present through the 'face' of a Person. The revelation of the Crucified makes the reality of being stand out, and so clarifies the Being of the Wholly Other. The self-emptying of Christ ventures forth to recapture the meaningfull-ness, or truth, of being. His self-giving is the model of the human response to the call of the good. It is thus as Crucified beauty that Christ upholds the transcendentals.

The Shape of the Theological Aesthetic

The pattern of the theological aesthetic is the reception of an outward form by the self. Irenaeus describes the Word as an obdurate historical presence which impedes gnosticizing fantasy. Bonaventure and Hopkins speak of self-abandonment to an uncontrollable influx of reality. Having so let go of itself, the 'I' is given back. For Hopkins, Mary is the archetype of the self. In 'The Blessed Virgin Compared to the Air We Breathe' she translucently embodies the radiance of God. This is the assimilation of heroic humanity to God, or of the immanent aesthetic to transcendental beauty. As in some of Tate's poems, the human figure clothes, or makes tangible the relation between the poet and the object of his vision. A more naked relation is logically possible. But it will have been stripped of the gentle materiality which renders it accessible to the human self. Poets are the ablest guardians of this materiality. Mary signifies the physical and corporate lifting up – of the human, toward the transcendent. The theological aesthetic calls for an intuition of the supernatural ground of poetry within the body of the world. It cannot endure if the human is left out of the picture. As von Balthasar says, 'the whole of aesthetics . . . depends upon the inextricable linkage of Christ and Mary; on the interweaving, by grace, of the human act of assent into the redeemer's own act of

assent . . . Thus is Mary everywhere present in the work of
Hopkins . . . and without any dialectic 'as if' beautiful.'[204]

Von Balthasar's work is tragic. It is a 'descendent' theology,
whose theme is the imposition of the Form of God upon the self.
But the figure of the Virgin is present. Her contemplative seeing
presents an eschatological foretaste of the elevation of human
nature.[205] In her sinless humanity, the Fall of beauty is overturned. She exemplifies both the acceptance of transcendent
necessity and the boundless possibilities of humanity. Whilst
tragedy and comedy are separate modes of experience, they do
not exclude one another in existence.

The Tasks of Post-Kantian Christology

We live within images. They are the sources of our Christologies. The image by which empirical cultures are guided is
attentive to experiential data, to the plurality of cultures, and to
the 'unconditionality' of the human world. In his *Jesus Christ and
Modern Thought*, John Macquarrie proposes that a Christology
relevant to the post-Enlightenment mind must have five features. It should be ecumenical. It must begin 'from below'. It
should use a minimum of historical data about Christ. It ought
not to be unduly metaphysical. And it must not make atonement so objective that it 'takes place behind our backs'.[206]
Macquarrie joins part with the empirical venture. A second
image looks upward for its synthesis: as God reaches down from
heaven to shut the door of Noah's ark, so He puts into place the
centre-piece of this theology. This is how von Balthasar
imagines things. Both images are problematic. The former is
weighted toward what A. O. Dyson terms 'declension into
genre': that is, total immersion in the tenets of one's own
culture.[207] The latter tends toward what the same author calls
'declension into abstraction': the flight of theology to a place
'above' the society to which it should speak. We shall weigh von
Balthasar's theology against Macquarrie's criteria in order to
ask: what sort of Christology do we require?

Ecumenism – Analogy

Here we must distinguish the issue of *dialogue* from that of *methodology*. Macquarrie proposes that Christ is the 'climax' of a series of 'saviour figures', such as Lord Krishna.[208] This appears to be posed as an opening for ecumenical dialogue. Given that such benign inclusivism is vigorously rejected by Hindu theologians, it fails.[209] Eric Sharpe speaks of 'the well-meaning niceness of post-Vatican II writers on inter-religious dialogue'.[210] No one has accused von Balthasar of this. He believes that every religion must be judged before it is gathered around the Christ. Louis Dupré finds in his work a too predominant note of condemnation. The 'inclusive' strand is also a difficulty. John Cobb asks von Balthasar how Christianity can claim to fulfil religions whose goals are not its own, such as Buddhism.[211] It has to be said that the objective givenness of the Christian drama is so deeply dyed into von Balthasar's imagination that he can forget that every non-Christian thought-form is not a conscious contribution to that drama. Whilst, for example, he finds the anti-Semitisms of others abhorrent, he is himself capable of ugly insensitivity.[212]

Which methodology would enable Christian theology to make sense of the plethora of avataras, gurus, and messengers with which the study of religions confronts it? One ought immediately to be drawn to the fascinating particularities of the texts and rituals of each religion. It is only membership in a specific tradition which enables one genuinely to understand these phenomena. The neutral stance, outside all tradition, is blind. Van der Leeuw argues that even the phenomenologist of religion must belong to a believing community. He says: 'religions are not wares to be spread out on a table'.[213] The forms of the varying religions present themselves only to those who have faith in one. Burch Brown claimed that it is 'spurious' to base aesthetics in revelation.[214] The answer which we can now give is that if we commence by making a general survey of the *gestalten*, of each art form – or religion – we shall not imaginatively grasp the meaning of any. Understanding is by analogy: it must be orientated, or localized, by an accepted image. Whilst, on the level of *dialogue* von Balthasar does not give plurality its due, his *methodological* recognition that one only sees the forms through a form gives Christian ecumenicists a method of speaking with 'the faiths', through a faith.

Christology from Below and Above

Macquarrie's finest appeal for a Christology from below is that, if God could become human, inner-worldly reality must have the latent potential for incarnation. He seeks that potential in human thought, hope, and love. Von Balthasar sets out a Christology from above because the ground of his theology is the analogizing of being. Both agree that world and God are in analogical relation. The question is whether to initiate Christological reflection from the causal dynamic which sets that relation in motion, or from the mind which returns it. In von Balthasar's theology, as in any realistic metaphysic, it is the object which shapes the knowing mind. Human experience is completed by Christ. But it cannot by itself attain His transcendent figure. If Uncreated Being is the source and the analogical measure of created being, the measure of Christ, the concrete analogy of being, is the divine Word.[215] Christology 'from above' begins from within being, rather than within thought. As von Balthasar interprets it, the creative analogizing of being does not 'descend from the heights'. In His infinite freedom, God constructs a space of exchange within finite being. The interchange requires that He be 'already' within the created structures, without distorting them. In von Balthasar's analogy of freedom, God is both the transcending *Aliud* and the ascending, immanent *non-Aliud*. The Christologies which drew out these principles would know that being is not an impersonal emanation: in the analogy of freedom, being, coming from God, is riven with calls, spoken by God. Such Christologies would include decision: the call touches this person. They would not be voluntaristic: the call is inscribed within being. The heroes, von Balthasar says, had the 'enormous courage' and the 'piety' to affirm being.[216]

History – Mobility – Analogy

The 'empirical venture' is marked by its sense of historicity, a sense with which von Balthasar is not overly endowed. He depreciates time. He pictures Christ's mission as a *recirculatio* – a Latin term for *anakephalaiosis*. As we saw, the image of the circle governs Dionysius' theology: he handed it on to the medievals, who used it to depict the intra-Trinitarian life, and the emanation and return of being from God.[217] Von Balthasar rejects the distinction between Judaeo-Christian 'historical' faith and the 'cyclical' religions, whose festivals follow the round of nature. Both, he says, can be circular, in proceeding from God and returning to Him.[218] This assimilates the temporal reality of God's election of Israel, and of Incarnation, to an eternal action. Is the intrinsic significance of time upheld? Von Balthasar often seems to be looking down on history from above. His 'supra-temporal' perspective has rightly been criticized.[219]

His disregard for modern biblical scholarship has also been called into question.[220] This is less just. If anything dates the Old Covenant volume of *The Glory*, it may be its use of the now debatable 'document hypothesis'. There are persons who are empirically minded. They might minimize our knowledge of Christ by pointing out the discrepancies between the gospel narratives, or noticing their authors' eagerness to indicate that Old Testament prophecy is fulfilled in every detail by the life of Christ. It is clear that von Balthasar has not this temperament. On the other hand, there are those who choose to be constrained by an empiricist's understanding of what a fact can be. They would reduce our knowledge of Christ by subjecting the data to the canons of empirical science.

The critical historiography of theologians is often conditioned by Kant's dichotomy between the moral, or noumenal realm, and that of individual facts. The problem for Christology is not the ethical paradigm in itself, but that the good is conceived as a static pattern which lies outside the human reality. In order properly to appropriate the gospels, we must interpret the good dramatically. Does the reality of the drama depend upon its empirical self-containment? The minimizing of the gospel record is related to an intuition about what ought, or ought not, to be there. It is felt that, if Deity enters the story, it will break up its natural order: the noumenal and the phenomenal must be kept at a distance, if each is to retain its reality. Thus, Macquarrie considers that a Christ who foresaw His death could not be fully human. He cites Raymond Brown: 'a Jesus for whom the future was as much of a mystery as it is for us . . . is a Jesus who would have gone through life's real trials.'[221]

He would remove from the narrative those aspects which lead Karl Jaspers and George Steiner to contend that Christianity knows not tragedy: in it, they say, the ultimate triumph is a foregone conclusion.[222] Von Balthasar urges, to the contrary, first, that each scene of the drama has its inner integrity. In that case, resurrection does not make the desolation of the cross the less real. We cannot leap over the temporal extension of the story. That which is ahead does not cancel out that which is now.

Secondly, his 'supra-tragedy' is not a closed, inner-worldly drama. The good need only be perceived to negate human freedom if it is taken to bypass the geography of human action. The 'Christology of morals' which has been with us since the eighteenth century is drawn from an implicitly deistic metaphor. We need a new metaphor if we are not endlessly to question how the supernatural can 'get inside' the natural world. This is what we find in the *Theo-drama*. Von Balthasar claims here that 'infinite freedom accompanies man. . . . in God's plan for the world, the possibilities are not like places on a map, which the traveller can visit . . . the paths themselves journey and wander as, leading on those who walk along them.'[223] As that which underlies the drama of moral action, the good is a latent *persona* within all reality, not an extraneous *deus ex machina*. Such is the model of the contact of transcendent and created freedom: infinite freedom enables human freedom from within. This is a presupposition of incarnational Christology.

Von Balthasar is right to begin with a dramatic faith, rather than the positivist's hypothesis. But, in tragedy a necessary outcome is – slowly – imposed from above. We also need the comic sense of the contingent. Hans Frei adds a helpful comment, which von Balthasar does not think to make: 'each event in the story – passion, death, resurrection – has the sort of . . . integrity . . . one finds in lifelike reports . . . the bond between the events is such that each succeeding occurrence is . . . appropriate to what went before, and yet each has a certain accidental . . . rather than inevitable quality about it.'[224] Faith needs some imaginative irony. An ironic faith will neither dismiss the empirical evidence nor be so overwhelmed by it that it gives itself up to a reduced account of what a fact can be. It will perceive the comic drama, from which concrete human potentiality surges, and which reveals the superabundance of being out of which bread and fish proliferate, and a healing hand gives sight and life. The comic sense knows both the randomness of the human adventure to fill time and space, and the eternity of God. Such an image of faith holds doubt and certainty together. It has both feet on the ground.

Metaphysics – Analogy

Macquarrie voices a widespread feeling when he claims that, 'The New Testament managed to say all the important things about Jesus without getting into the niceties of metaphysical discussion.'[225] Metaphysics has had its part in Christian teaching since Nicea. Bernard Lonergan depicts the 'way to Nicea' as a journey which replaced 'dogmatic' – and imaginable – affirmations about Christ with 'critical' affirmations. The critical affirmation transcends the concrete image in order to overcome the subordinationism implicit in a literal picture of a Son's relation to a Father.[226] It thereby produced what Joseph O'Leary terms 'a word which defied imagination': the *homoousios*.[227]

And yet, how biblical is O'Leary's 'biblical phenomenality'? Van der Leeuw's 'movement and countermovement' of images seems closer to Scripture, which is long on events and short on interiority.[228] The affirmation of the universality of the Trinitarian belief is bound to the belief that *images* can be true. The theological quest for universal, *propositional* truth is not unproblematic. Where once theologians sought prematurely to designate the universal content of the biblical images, they have, more latterly, demythologized them. For von Balthasar, no theological concept can surpass the poetry of Scripture.[229] But he does not reverse the road to Nicea. The theological aesthetic, founded in beauty, draws out the imaginative meaning of the metaphysical affirmations of Christian tradition. Theological dramatics, founded in the good, moves with the narrative. This aesthetic theology, both particularizing and mobile, is well placed to respond to Macquarrie and O'Leary's just but partial contentions. The beautiful gives to the true its shape. In so doing, it shows its relation to experience. Those who read the Scriptures in the light of von Balthasar's work need not be tied to his sometimes too a priori schema, in its entirety. They could learn from him how to compose from Scripture a synthetically beautiful picture. Such a synthesis would be imaginative; that is, bounded by the forms of the biblical stories; and, second, metaphysical, that is, exalted by the splendour and the truth of those stories.

Atonement – Analogy

The reality portrayed in those stories is dialogical: its spaces and forms are created by the inter-relating of free persons. The interplay between transcendent and immanent persons is a 'Theo-drama'. This would be so whether or not it had become a struggle between good and evil. It now contains such a struggle. It has yet to be concluded. As von Balthasar says, 'The centre of this drama is in the Lamb "as though it had been slain", which has triumphed over "the Lion of Judah": the Lamb is depicted simultaneously in its eternal triumph . . . and in his continuing battle, riding out with his garment drenched in blood (Rev. 19.13).[230] The Christian takes part in this combat. This is made possible by the 'exchange of natures', in which Christ gives satisfaction for sinners through His human self-identification with them.[231] By entering the place of substitution, each human person gains a mission. His or her character gains its shape as it acts or fails to act upon the call of the good.

Although the cross is the *peripeteia* of history, the Theo-drama does not proceed 'mechanically' thenceforth to its conclusion. This is no objectivist view of atonement!

Metanarrative and Theodrama

We are led to two curious conclusions. First, that von Balthasar's strength is his ability to dwell upon the particular, and his weaknesses are his departures into outer space. He writes about German Idealism in the style of the German Idealists. More seriously, he has a proclivity to view the drama from 'the seat of the gods'. We have found fault both with his exaltation of the saintly subject, and with his objectivism. Both are the effects of the shadow cast by the human imagination: the fantasial effort to create a flawlessly coherent system. Von Balthasar's tragic realm needs to be shaken about by some comic turbulence.

Second, however, Macquarrie's Christology is the less flexible. His suspicion of miracle assumes that reality is determined from within by a single agency of causality, unfolding in unbroken unilinear succession. His response to the thorny issue of ecumenicism is that of the nineteenth-century Hegelians.[232] He subordinates non-Christian religions to the Christian world-plan, without recognizing that this is to judge them without saying so. To gather every religion into a smoothly inclusive framework is to bind theology to the metanarrative which the postmodernists so sternly reject. Von Balthasar's Christ says 'Behold, I make all things new'. His holding fast to Christ's humanity-in-divinity, to His power of miracle, prophecy, and judgement, is undergirded by an imaginative willingness to accept difference. There is tension and therefore drama, because many levels of causality and freedom are brought into play. The *personae* of his Theo-drama have both liberty and identity. The human self enters the stage, and re-creates the social narrative, by virtue of a God-given 'I-ness'. Persons who are imagined in this way can exercise historical creativity. The theme, or quest, of the drama is the correspondence between the infinite freedom of God and the finite freedom of men and women. Neither is negated when they meet in the divine and human wills of Christ. We have to do, not with a fixed – linguistic or metaphysical – structure, which defines the position of each character, but with the opacities of free action within a drama. This Christology speaks to the needs of an empirical culture, without being enslaved to its presuppositions.

Conclusion: The Works of Christ

We begin by talking about realistic phenomenology. This led us to the conception of transcendental beauty as Form illuminated by an indefinable Glory. This is the Form of Christ, as He acts within the Godhead, and in His incarnate life. His inner and outer light presents His person to human intuition. His splendour allows us to participate in Him, by converting the subjective structures of human apprehension into an objective Form. Here the 'double-sidedness' of beauty comes into its own for theology. It does so in an extension of the phenomenologists' questions about the shape of the relations between consciousness and its objects. The traditional idea of experiential knowledge as especially 'practical' is also enlarged: religious experience re-enacts the narrative of Christ's life.

The form of Christ turns outwardness toward human intuition. He turns human inwardness toward transcendent reality by giving it a pattern of action to repeat, or a shape to the imagination. The resurrected body of Christ allows poets and philosophers to uncover both specific images and absolute truths within the earth of this world. The notion of symbolical form clarifies how temporal facts, such as the Incarnation, contain meaning. Von Balthasar may not do justice to historical contingency. But his aim is to show that Christ makes the flow of time coherent. It is Christ's salvific labour to bind historical community into Himself. He lives within all 'metaphysical community'. Incarnational theology requires an objective ground. Von Balthasar suggests that, in breaking through our desires for a univocal concordance with the world, the crucified Christ gives us the sense of real being. Thus, as the Form of transcendent beauty, Christ gathers the reality of

being, the good, and the true around Himself. Now men
and women can begin to comprehend, and to act upon them.
I have employed three stages: the objectivity of an analogizing metaphysics, the emergence of the self in a poetics of the
image, and the transcendental revelation of the Form of the
personal God. By so doing, I have sought to create an image of
Christ as the ground of both 'originary experience' and outward
reality, and to show that the two converge upon Him. We must
now gather up the various threads of this study.

NOTES

1 Von Balthasar, *Glory: I*, p. 118.
2 Michael Waldstein; 'Hans Urs von Balthasar's Theological Aesthetics',
  Communio, 11 (Spring, 1984), pp. 15 and 20.
3 Von Balthasar mentions the group all together in *Glory: VI*, p. 21. On
  Dionysius' significance for von Balthasar: De Schrijver, *Merveilleux Accord*,
  pp. 62 and 297–306. On 'symmetry', see *On the Divine Names*, in *The
  Complete Works of Dionysius the Areopagite*, Ch. 1 (p. 50), Ch. 2(p. 64), on
  'Providence' as fitted to individuals, Ch. 4, (p. 95); on Dionysius'
  'Providence' as 'analogous' to the creature in von Balthasar, *Glory: II*,
  p. 171; on the 'missionary character' of this movement of being, ibid. p.
  201.
4 Dionysius, *On the Divine Names*, Ch. 3 (p. 68).
5 Dionysius, *Divine Names*, Ch. 4 (pp. 83–84); von Balthasar, *Glory: II*, pp.
  164–167, 180.
6 De Schrijver, *Merveilleux Accord*, p. 70.
7 Von Balthasar, *Glory: V*, pp. 548–549. Here von Balthasar cites the Fourth
  Lateran Council, as quoted in Denzinger 806.
8 On Plotinus, ibid, pp. 213–214, 307, and 435; on Schelling, ibid, p. 565
  and De Schrijver, *Merveilleux Accord*, p. 108.
9 Aidan Nichols notes that von Balthasar 'set out . . . to realise in
  Catholicism the kind of Christocentric revolution Barth had wrought
  in Protestantism', 'Balthasar and his Christology', *New Blackfriars* (July/
  August, 1985), p. 320.
10 Von Balthasar, *Glory: V*, p. 15.
11 Von Balthasar, *Barth*, p. 170.
12 Von Balthasar, *Glory: IV*, pp. 14 and 23–25.
13 Von Balthasar, *Theo-Drama: I*, p. 16.
14 Franz Rosenzweig, *The Star of Redemption*, translated from the second
  edition of 1930 by William W. Hallo, pp. 4 & 17. On Rosenzweig's work,
  see *Franz Rosenzweig: His Life and Thought*, presented by Nahum N. Glatzer.
15 For a brief survey of von Balthasar's philosophical studies in Vienna and
  Berlin, and his later theological work under Henri de Lubac in 1933–

186   *Christ the Form of Beauty*

1937, where he learned the typological method of Scriptural exegesis dear to the *Nouvelle Théologie Francais*: Medard Kehl, 'Hans Urs von Balthasar: A Portrait', Introduction to the *Hans Urs von Balthasar Reader*, edited by Medard Kehl and Werner Löser, pp. 3, 15 and 31.

16 Barry Smith writes that 'Brentano showed his students how to *notice* psychologically given distinctions . . . but he then showed also how to take these distinctions seriously as the basis of an ontology.' 'Gestalt Theory: An Essay in Philosophy', in Barry Smith, (ed.), *Foundations of Gestalt Theory*, p. 12.

17 Ibid, pp. 11–12 and William M. Johnston, *The Austrian Mind: An Intellectual and Social History, 1848–1938*, p. 302. On Ehrenfel's use of Brentano's theory of wholes, Johnston, pp. 294 and 304.

18 Christian von Ehrenfels, 'On Gestalt Qualities', (1922) translated by Barry Smith, in Smith (ed.), *Foundations of Gestalt*, pp. 90 & 98; von Ehrenfels, 'Gestalt Level and Gestalt Purity', in ibid. p. 118; von Ehrenfels, 'On Gestalt Qualities', (1932) ibid. p. 123.

19 Von Balthasar, 'Die Entwicklung der musikalischen Idee. Versuch einer Synthese der Musik', *Sammlung Bartels* 2 (1925), 3–38. [Braunschweig]; *Glory IV*, p. 30. In 'Die Entwicklung', von Balthasar draws out the concept of 'musical gestalt' in a way which I take to be clearly influenced by Ehrenfels: see my 'The Sound of the *Analogia Entis*: An Essay on the Ontological Difference as the Context of von Balthasar's Theology', *New Blackfriars*, November 1993, pp. 508–521

20 Edmund Husserl, *Logical Investigations*, Vol. I, p. 245.

21 Spiegelberg, *The Phenomenological Movement*, Vol. I, pp. 168–226 & 228–268; Edith Stein writes of the 'short flowering time of the Göttingen School of Phenomenology' (in 1905–1914) in her *Life in a Jewish Family: 1891–1916: An Autobiography*, pp. 239–293. Reinach examines the nature of phenomenology in 'Concerning Phenomenology' (a lecture given in 1914; published in 1921) translated by Dallas Willard, *The Personalist*, 50, (Spring, 1969), pp. 194–221.

22 Max Scheler, 'Problems of Religion', in *On the Eternal in Man* (1921), p. 282.

23 Max Scheler, *The Nature of Sympathy* [1913], pp. 217–218, 246–247, and 258.

24 Ibid. pp. 10, 40–46, 243–250.

25 Von Balthasar, *Glory: I*, pp. 390–393.

26 Von Balthasar, *The Glory of the Lord: A Theological Aesthetics: VII: Theology: The New Covenant*, p. 288.

27 In private conversation, von Balthasar said that expression is 'the centre of my construction': Michael Waldstein, 'Expression and Knowledge of Other Persons', *Aletheia* Vol. II (1981), p. 129. Von Balthasar also states: 'there is a parallel between [our theology] and the phenomenological method of Scheler, inasmuch as this method aims at allowing the object to give itself purely. However, the bracketing of existence is out of question in theology.': cited by Michael Waldstein, 'An Introduction to

Hans Urs von Balthasar's the Glory of the Lord', *Communio*, 14 (Spring, 1987), p. 14. Werner Löser calls von Balthasar's work a 'theological phenomenology'. He continues: 'With this two things are said: first it is a matter of phenomenological method. This concerns itself with the comprehension of forms. But forms are wholes, which are more than the sum of their parts. Historical forms cannot be comprehended unless . . . historical-critical method is brought to bear on them. Nevertheless the compilation of this historical information does not present the 'form'. While [exact] science . . . is analytic . . . the perception of the total form . . . is synthetic.' Quoted in Louis Roberts, *The Theological Aesthetics of Hans Urs von Balthasar*, p. 34.

28 Scheler, *The Nature of Sympathy*, pp. 84, 123–129, and 224.

29 Ibid. p. 86.

30 De Schrijver, *Merveilleux Accord*, pp. 31–32 and 260, 284.

31 Erich Przywara, *Analogia Entis* [1932], translated from the 1962 edition by Philibert Secretan, p. 10.

32 On the measured movement 'towards', ibid. pp. 100–105, 107, 110 and 127; on the 'caesura' in St Thomas, p. 156; on the 'Art of the Fugue', both 'sonorous' and 'silent', pp. 31 and 163; analogy as between 'reciprocal alterities', pp. 114–115; that the greater the similitude of the creature, the greater the dissimilitude of God, pp. 87 and 116. Here Przywara cites the Fourth Lateran Council (as mentioned in footnote 8).

33 Ibid. pp. 58 and 65–68.

34 Ibid. pp. 19–20. Secretan notes Przywara's involvement with the phenomenologists in his Forward, pp. 11–12 and 14.

35 Scheler, 'Problems of Religion', in *Eternal in Man*, p. 138; von Balthasar, *Glory: V*, pp. 613–615.

36 Von Balthasar, *Glory: V*, p. 615.

37 Scheler, 'Problems of Religion', in *Eternal in Man*, pp. 146–147, 163, 260–261, 273–274, 283–284.

38 Von Balthasar, *Theo-Drama: II*, p. 228.

39 Von Balthasar, *Glory: I*, p. 431, *Glory: IV*, pp. 30–31, 156, 307.

40 Przywara, *Analogia*, pp. 133 and 155. Von Balthasar notes Przywara's 'exaggerations', and that Przywara's '*tanta*' ('the *greater* the similitude) is not in Denzinger, in *la Dramatique Divine: II. Les personnes du drama: 2. les personnes dans le Christ*, p. 176.

41 Von Balthasar, *Theo-Drama: II*, p. 355.

42 Von Balthasar, *Glory: III*, p. 105ff.

43 S. T. Coleridge, *Biographia Literaria*, Volume I, pp. 261–262. G. N. G. Orsini thinks that Coleridge is drawing on Schelling's early essays: *German Idealism*, pp. 192–197.

44 S. T. Coleridge, *Aids to Reflection*, pp. 359–360.

45 Tate, 'Longinus and the New Criticism', in *Essays*, pp. 311–317.

46 R. W. Bretall, 'Kant's Theory of the Sublime', in *The Heritage of Kant*, edited by George Tapley Whitney and David F. Bowers, pp. 381–384.

47 Wesley Trimpi, *Muses of One Mind: The Literary Analysis of Experience and Its Continuity*, pp. 102–103.

48 Tate, 'Longinus and the New Criticism', *Essays*, p. 527.

49 Kant, *The Critique of Judgement*, Part I, Book II: Analytic of the Sublime, pp. 90–91.

50 Ibid. p. 127.

51 Bretall, 'Kant's Theory of the Sublime', pp. 397–398 and Kant, *Critique of Judgement*, Part I, pp. 104–105 and 114.

52 Jean-François Lyotard, *The Postmodern Condition: A Report on Knowledge*, p. 78

53 Coleridge, 'The Statesman's Manual: A Lay Sermon', in *Lay Sermons*, p. 30.

54 Anthony Thiselton, *The Two Horizons. New Testament Hermeneutics and Philosophical Description: with Special Reference to Heidegger, Bultmann, Gadamer and Wittgenstein* pp. 208–232; van Harvey *The Historian and the Believer* (pp. 139–146). The Liberal lives of Jesus of the eighteenth and nineteenth centuries take what is concrete in His life and teaching as a veil used in condescension to his Jewish audience.

55 Rudolf Bultmann, *Jesus Christ and Mythology*, pp. 61–62.

56 R. A. Johnson, *Origins*, pp. 79, 84–86 and 116–122. He cites Bultmann: 'the utter difference of human existence from all worldly existence was recognized for the first time in Gnosticism and Christianity and thus the world became foreign soil to the human self' (ibid). Cited from Bultmann's *Theology of the New Testament: I*, p. 165.

57 Eric Voeglin, 'The Gospel and Culture', in *Jesus and Man's Hope*, edited by Donald G. Miller and Dikran Y. Hadidian, 1971) pp. 98–100.

58 Bultmann, *New Testament: I*, pp. 6, 11, 42 and 67.

59 Ibid. p. 58.

60 Von Balthasar, *Glory: I*, p. 153.

61 Ibid. p. 118.

62 Ibid. p. 120–121.

63 Von Balthasar, *Theo-Drama: II*, p. 83.

64 Von Balthasar, *Glory: VII*, p. 316.

65 St Anselm, *Cur Deus Homo*, Book I, Chapter XV, in *St Anselm: Basic Writings. Proslogium, Monologium, Cur Deus Homo and Gaunilon's Reply in Behalf of the Fool.* Anselm is one of von Balthasar's theological aestheticians because he treats the grasping of truth as a 'visual illumination' of the proportionality of the parts of propositions and of realities. As von Balthasar says, 'From such apprehensibility there arises certainty.': *Glory: II*, p. 223. See also Glenn W. Olsen, 'Hans Urs von Balthasar and the Rehabilitation of St Anselm's Doctrine of Atonement', *Scottish Journal of Theology*, 34 (1981) pp. 49–61.

66 Von Balthasar, *Theo-Drama: II*, p. 117.

67 Von Balthasar, *Glory: I*, pp. 611–614, 322–324 and 609; *Engagement With God*, p. 40

68 Von Balthasar, *A Theology of History*, p. 27.

69 'He reads the Synoptic Gospels in the light of the Fourth Gospel . . .

Schillebeeckx's appeal for a revival of Synoptic Christological patterns holds little appeal for von Balthasar': John McDade, 'Reading von Balthasar', *The Month* (April, 1987), p. 140.

70 Von Balthasar, *Glory: VII*, pp. 246–249, 259–260, 279, 291, 357.

71 Von Balthasar, *Glory: II*, p. 205.

72 Von Balthasar, *Man in History: A Theological Study* p. 109.

73 Von Balthasar, *Glory: I*, pp. 324–330; *A Theology of History*, pp. 26–28.

74 Von Balthasar, *Glory I*, pp. 617–618.

75 Ibid. p. 614.

76 Ibid. p. 304

77 There are three kinds of phenomenology of religion: 1. Scheler's Platonistic phenomenology, for which God is luminously present in the religious act; 2. the study of the human expressions of the religious act, as in Van der Leeuw and Jacques Waardenburg: for the latter, phenomenology of religion is the uncovery of systems of meaning-intentions within acts such as the adoration of a statue in his *Reflections on the Study of Religion* pp. 88, 99, 108–110; 3. the work of Joachim Wach, on which see Eric Sharpe, *Comparative Religion: A History*, pp. 238–240, 248.

78 Van der Leeuw, *Religion in Essence*, pp. 87–90, where he draws on the same gestalt psychologists to whom von Balthasar is indebted; on phenomenology of religion as the study of appearances to a subject, pp. 23, 671, 675.

79 Von Balthasar, *Glory: I*, p. 252.

80 Ibid. pp. 221 and 248.

81 Ibid. p. 251.

82 Von Balthasar, *Glory: VI*, p. 9.

83 Ibid. p. 45.

84 Von Balthasar, *Glory: I*, pp. 126–127.

85 Von Balthasar, *Glory: VII*, pp. 471–472.

86 Ibid. p. 366.

87 Von Balthasar, *Glory: I*, p. 252.

88 Von Balthasar, *Glory: II*, pp. 267–270.

89 Ibid. p. 271.

90 Noel O'Donoghue, 'A Theology of Beauty', in John Riches (ed.), *The Analogy of Beauty: The Theology of Hans Urs von Balthasar* pp. 1–11.

91 Noel O'Donoghue, 'Discovering Orthodoxy: Chesterton and the Philosophical Imagination', *Chesterton Review*, Vol XII, No 4, November, 1987, 455–474.

92 David Brown, *Continental Philosophy and Modern Theology*, pp. 21–22.

93 John McDade, 'Reading von Balthasar', (138 and 142).

94 Von Balthasar, 'Theology and Sanctity', in *Word and Redemption: Essays in Theology 2*, pp. 49–86.

95 Von Balthasar, *Theo-Drama: I*, pp. 68–69.

96 J. A. T. Robinson, *The Priority of John*, pp. 375–378; A. E. Harvey, *Jesus on Trial: A Study in the Fourth Gospel*.

97 Von Balthasar, *Word and Revelation. Essays in Theology 1*, p. 139.

98 Von Balthasar, *Glory: I*, pp. 117, 173 and 177.
99 Bernard Reardon, *Religion in the Age of Romanticism: Studies in Early Nineteenth Century Theology*, pp. 137–141; Josef Rupert Geiselmann, *The Meaning of Tradition, pp. 49, 59 and 65–69.*
100 E. I. Watkin *Catholic Art and Culture*, p. 7; and Jean Danielou and Henri Marrou, *The Christian Centuries: the First Six Hundred Years*, translated by Vincent Cronin, p. 32. This is parallel to Jusin Martyr's '*Logos spermatikos*', as in Justin's *Apology* 1.46 and II.13, in *A New Eusebius*, edited by J. Stevenson, pp. 63–65 and Clement's *Stromateis* I. 5.28.1–3, in ibid, p. 196.
101 Geiselmann, *Tradition*, page 65.
102 Thomas O'Meara, *Romantic Idealism and German Catholicism: Schelling and the Theologians*, pp. 51–56, 92–99, and 102–103.
103 Von Schelling, *The Philosophy of Art*, pp. 61–64.
104 Ibid. p. 253–254.
105 Ibid. pp. 64, 89 and 149 and René Wellek, *A History of Modern Criticism: 1750–1950*: Vol. II, pp. 76–77.
106 Von Balthasar, *Glory: IV*, p. 47.
107 Von Balthasar, *Glory: I*, p. 155.
108 Ibid. p. 145.
109 Ibid. p. 503
110 Von Balthasar, *Science, Religion and Christianity*, p. 64.
111 Von Balthasar, *Glory: I*, p. 216.
112 Von Balthasar, *Glory: IV*, p. 216.
113 Ibid. pp. 71 and 119–120.
114 Ibid. p. 219.
115 Von Balthasar, *Glory: IV*, pp. 156, 164, and 181–183.
116 Von Balthasar, *Barth*, p. 254.
117 Von Balthasar, *Glory: I*, p. 146.
118 Von Balthasar *Glory: IV*, pp. 156+195
119 Von Balthasar, Ibid, pp. 109–111, 123, 129–131, 150.
120 Ibid. p. 122.
121 Von Balthasar, *Theo-Drama: I*, pp. 279 and 460.
122 Ibid. p. 388.
123 Ibid. p. 408.
124 Homer, *The Iliad*, Book Eight, pp. 182–183.
125 *Theodrama I*, p. 436.
126 Von Balthasar, *Glory: IV*, pp 54–55.
127 Von Balthasar, *Theodrama: II*, p. 125.
128 Von Balthasar, *Glory: VI*, pp. 112–113.
129 Ibid, pp. 289–290
130 Von Balthasar, *Theodrama: I*, p. 453.
131 Von Balthasar, *Glory: IV*, p. 33.
132 M.-D. Chenu, *Nature, Man and Society in the Twelfth Century*, p. 142.
133 Von Balthasar, *Glory I*, p. 52. Shubert Ogden argues, not unreasonably, that if, as Bultmann says, faith is a non-objective, 'non-mythic' occur-

rence, it need not be related to the historical fact of Jesus' life: *Christ Without Myth. A Study Based on the Theology of Rudolph Bultmann* p. 145.

134 Von Balthasar, *A Theology of History*, p. 52.

135 Ibid. pp. 29–32.

136 Von Balthasar, *Glory: II*, p. 70.

137 Von Balthasar, *Glory I*, p. 265.

138 Irenaeus, *Against Heresies*, Book IV, Chapter XXXVII, 'Why Man was Not Made Perfect from the Beginning', in *The Writings of Irenaeus: Volume II*, edited by Alexander Roberts and James Donaldson, pp. 42–45.

139 Irenaeus writes 'unless man had overcome the enemy . . . the enemy would not have been legitimately vanquished . . . Wherefore also he passed through every stage of life, restoring all to communion with God.' *Against Heresies*, Book III, Chapter XVIII, in *The Writings of Irenaeus: Volume I*, edited by Rev. Alexander Roberts and James Donaldson, p. 343.

140 Unlike some later Patristic authors, Irenaeus does not think of Christ's work as the payment of a ransom: F. W. Dillistone, *The Christian Understanding of Atonement*, pp. 92–98; H. E. W. Turner, *The Patristic Doctrine of Redemption*, pp. 49–58.

141 Gustaf Wingren, *Man and Incarnation*, p. 48

142 Von Balthasar, *Man in History*, pp. 107–108.

143 For Clifford Geertz, 'thin' anthropological description does not give the meaning of human acts: 'Thick Description: Toward an Interpretative Theory of Culture', in *The Interpretation of Cultures*, pp. 3–30.

144 Bernard Lonergan, *A Third Collection*, edited by F. E. Crowe, pp. 152–155; *Method in Theology*, pp. 198–199 and 208–212; Wilhelm Dilthey, 'The Construction of the Historical World in the Human Studies', in *Selected Writings*, edited and translated by H. P. Rickman, pp. 191–192, 197, and 201. Dilthey's conception of 'empathy' differs from Scheler's: he thinks that empathy is the 're-living' of an expressed meaning which occurs by virtue of an 'inference by analogy'. He speaks of a 'transposition' of the content of an external form into the consciousness of its audience, which has then to 're-experience' it: See Dilthey, ibid, pp. 222–231.

145 Von Balthasar, *A Theology of History*, pp. 8–10, and 89.

146 Von Balthasar, *Theo-Drama: II*, p. 50.

147 De Schrijver, *Merveilleux Accord*, pp. 68–69.

148 Von Balthasar, *Theo-Drama: II*, pp. 54–62.

149 Scheler, *Eternal in Man*, p. 235.

150 Von Balthasar, *Barth*, p. 295.

151 Noel O'Donoghue, review, *Glory: II*, *The Irish Theological Quarterly*, Volume 52, No 1/2 (1986), pp. 141–144.

152 Von Balthasar, *Glory: III*, p. 22, *Glory IV*, pp. 371–372.

153 Lacoue-Labarthe, *The Literary Absolute*, pp. 95–96.

154 Royce, *Idealism*, p. 160; Maritain, *Moral Philosophy*, pp. 119–120 and 185–187.

155 Reardon, *Religion in the Age of Romanticism*, p. 99.

156 Schelling, 'Conclusion to the System of Transcendental Idealism', in Simpson, (ed.), *The Origins of Modern Critical Thought*, pp. 227–228.
157 Ibid, p. 228.
158 Schelling, *The Philosophy of Art*, pp. 14–15 and 84.
159 Schelling states that 'If the Poet were . . . external to his play, we would be merely actors performing what he had written. Whereas if he is not independent of us but unveils . . . himself . . . through the play of our freedom . . . we are co-writers of the whole script.' From the *System of Transcendental Idealism*, quoted in von Balthasar, *Theo-Drama: I*, p. 181.
160 Hart, *The Trespass of the Sign*, pp. 12–20
161 Von Balthasar, 'Revelation and the Beautiful', in *Word and Revelation*, pp. 122–123 and 138. Romanticism, he says, 'foundered on a . . . aesthetic and religious monism.': *Glory: I*, p. 104.
162 Royce, *Idealism*, pp. 34, 48–49, 53–54 and 70–72.
163 McFarland, *Coleridge*, pp. 53, 91–92, 107–112.
164 Cited in Kehl, *Portrait*, p. 16.
165 Søren Kierkegaard, *Fear and Trembling and the Sickness unto Death*, pp. 64–77.
166 Cited by von Balthasar, *Theo-Drama: I*, pp. 561 and 579.
167 White, *Tropics of Discourse*, p. 234.
168 Jean-François Lyotard, *The Postmodern Condition*, p. 15.
169 Edwards, *Christian Poetics*, pp. 129, 137 and 141.
170 Von Balthasar, *Theo-Drama: I*, p. 645.
171 Von Balthasar, *Theo-Drama: II*, pp. 209–211.
172 Ibid. p. 388.
173 Von Balthasar, *Theo-Drama: I*, pp. 285–291.
174 Ibid. pp. 252–254.
175 Lyotard, *The Post-Modern Condition*, p. 10.
176 Von Balthasar, *Theo-Drama: II*, p. 388–389.
177 Von Balthasar, *Theo-Drama: I*, 626–637.
178 Rosenzweig, *The Star of Redemption*, p. 68.
179 Ibid. pp. 71, 164, 173–174, and 186–187.
180 Ibid. p. 213.
181 Von Balthasar, *Theo-Drama: II*, p. 206.
182 Ibid, p. 259.
183 Von Balthasar, *Glory: VII*, pp. 234–235.
184 On Christ's double temporal horizon, ibid, pp. 167–173; on 'Kingdom', 'Cross' and 'Resurrection', von Balthasar, *la Dramatique divine: II.2*, pp. 34–40, 89, 99–100 and 129–130.
185 Ibid. pp. 141–142.
186 Ibid. pp. 128–131.
187 Ibid. pp. 120–125, 133, 159–160, 165 and 419; *Theo-Drama: I*, pp. 645–647.
188 Von Balthasar, *Theo-Drama: II*, p. 14.
189 Von Balthasar, *Glory: III*, p. 391.
190 The novelty of the principle need not be exaggerated. St Thomas counters the 'Averroistic' idea that human thought participates in a

universal 'Possible Intellect' by saying that it is the act of *this* man thinking which is his individuating form: *Summa Contra Gentiles*, Bk. II, Chapter 73, Articles 4–6, 13–17, and 39–41.

191 Hopkins, 'The Principle or Foundation. An Address Based on the Opening of 'The Spiritual Exercises of Ignatius Loyola', in *Gerard Manley Hopkins: Poetry and Prose*, edited by W. H. Gardiner, pp. 145–150, p. 146.

192 Hopkins, 'Pied Beauty', in ibid, pp. 30–31.

193 Hopkins, 'The Principle or Foundation', p. 150.

194 Hopkins, Sonnet No. 34 in ibid, p. 51.

195 As in Jürgen Moltmann, *The Crucified God: The Cross as the Foundation and Criticism of Christian Theology*, Von Balthasar, *Glory: IV*, 340–341.

196 Compare Rudolph Otto on the 'sui generis' character of the numinous, in *The Idea of the Holy* (1917), pp. 21–22, 58–59 and 131–133. Scheler finds this significant.

197 Von Balthasar, *Glory: V*, p. 235, *Glory: VI*, p. 233, *Theo-Drama: II*, pp. 297 and 397.

198 Von Balthasar, *Glory: VI*, p. 270.

199 De Schrijver, *Merveilleux Accord*, p. 32.

200 Von Balthasar, *Glory: IV*, pp. 374 & 395.

201 Von Balthasar, *Glory: V*, p. 626.

202 Von Balthasar, *la Dramatique divine: II. 2*, p. 420.

203 Von Balthasar, *Glory: IV*, pp. 354–355.

204 Von Balthasar, *Glory: III*, p. 390.

205 Andrew Louth, *Mary and the Mystery of the Incarnation*, pp. 15–16.

206 John Macquarrie, 'What Would be Required in a Christology Today', Chapter 15 of *Jesus Christ in Modern Thought*.

207 A. O. Dyson, 'The Christian Religion', in *The British: Their Religious Beliefs and Practices: 1800–1886*, edited by Terence Thomas pp. 105ff.

208 Macquarrie, *Jesus Christ in Modern Thought*, p. 421.

209 See for example 'Vaishnavism on Hans Küng: A Hindu Theology of Religious Pluralism', by Bibhuti S. Yadav, in *Christianity Through Non-Christian Eyes*, edited by Paul J. Griffiths, pp. 234–246.

210 Eric J. Sharpe, *The Universal Gita: Western Images of the Bhagavadgita*, p. 144.

211 Louis Dupré, 'Hans Urs von Balthasar's Theology of Aesthetic Form', *Theological Studies*, No. 49 (June, 1988), p. 315; John Cobb, 'A Question for Hans Urs von Balthasar', *Communio* 5, (1978), p. 57.

212 Von Balthasar exercises his ironic gifts against the anti-semitism of the *Vengeance de Notre Seigneur (Theo-Drama: I*, p. 107); he finds *The Merchant of Venice* 'unbearable' (ibid, p. 463). He notes Hegel's anti-semitism (*Glory: V*, pp. 579 & 596). But his question 'In what sense is the Jew a person?' (*Theo-Drama: II*, p. 427) should not have been written, in any context.

213 Van der Leeuw, *Religion in Essence*, pp. 645–647.

214 Burch Brown, *Religious Aesthetics*, pp. 19–20.

215 Von Balthasar, *la Dramatique divine: II. 2*, p. 162.

216 Von Balthasar, *Glory: IV*, p. 354.

217 Ibid, pp. 108 and 244–246. On St Thomas' idea of 'circulation' see Jan Aertsen *Nature and Creature: Thomas Aquinas's Way of Thought*, pp. 40–42, and 379–382; Przywara, *Analogia*, p. 140; von Balthasar, *Glory: II*, p. 148.
218 Von Balthasar, *Man in History*, p. 116.
219 Gerard O'Hanlon, *The Immutability of God in the Theology of Hans Urs von Balthasar* pp. 22, 64; and, on the 'eternalizing' of Incarnation and Cross, pp. 101–102: the problem is that von Balthasar treats both history and Incarnation, as being 'pre-existent' within God. (cf. *A Theology of History*, pp. 61–62).
220 Dupré, 'Theological Aesthetics', p. 318; in defence of von Balthasar's exegetical method, Brian McNeil 'The Exegete as Iconographer' in Riches (ed.), *The Analogy of Beauty*, pp. 134–146. I find McNeil unconvincing: the Byzantine icon-maker aimed directly to imitate eternal truths, bypassing natural facts. Such are the roots of von Balthasar's imagination. R. N. Whybray's *The Making of the Pentateuch: A Methodological Study* has cast doubt on the document hypothesis. *Glory: VI* is dependent on von Rad's version of the document hypothesis. In Dionysian vein, Moses is 'caught up in a vision/non-vision': Von Balthasar identifies the 'dazzling' with the J 'fire' tradition and the 'darkness' with E's 'cloud'; he can then say that P's synthesis of the two fails to retain the 'dialectic' thus skillfully invented by himself: ibid p. 44.
221 Macquarrie, *Jesus Christ in Modern Thought*, p. 358.
222 Von Balthasar, *Theo-Drama: I*, p. 72, 327.
223 Von Balthasar, *Theo-Drama II*, p. 282.
224 Frei, *The Identity of Jesus Christ*, p. 57.
225 Macquarrie, *Jesus Christ in Modern Thought*, p. 344.
226 Bernard Lonergan, *The Way to Nicea: The Dialectical Development of Trinitarian Theology*, pp. 88–102 and 127–135.
227 O'Leary, *Questioning Back*, p. 146.
228 Ibid. p. 16; van der Leeuw, *Sacred and Profane Beauty: The Holy in Art* pp. 74–77.
229 Von Balthasar, *Glory VII*, p. 267.
230 Von Balthasar, *Theo-Drama: II*, pp. 61–62.
231 Von Balthasar, *la Dramatique divine: II. 2*, pp. 94–98, 190–193.
232 Macquarrie's view is not unlike J. N. Farquhar's *The Crown of Hinduism* (1903). For a critical evaluation of this approach see Eric J. Sharpe, 'The Fulfilment and Goal of all the Religions of the World', in *Faith Meets Faith: Some Christian Attitudes to Hinduism in the Nineteenth and Twentieth Centuries*, pp. 19–32.

Chapter 8

Conclusion

Christology becomes impossible once theologians cease to imagine facts as being important. Post-Kantian theology has excluded the domain of natural objects from the realm of meaning, and succumbed to what von Balthasar calls 'the fateful loss of sight which befalls whole generations'.[1] How do the authors who we have studied combine to redress this loss?

Negative Connections

None of these writers decry reason. But all reject the abstracted intellectualism which Ransom calls 'science', Tate 'angelism', Lynch the 'univocal mind', and Maritain and von Balthasar 'essentialism'. If reality is 'polyvalent', we must respond to it in kind. Nor, for any of these writers, do we know reality through the single 'faculty' of imagination. Imagination brings the entire personality to bear upon facts.

They criticize the Romantic absolutization of imagination. The Southerners' dislike of Romantic poetry is selective. Goethe deserves more than Lynch's label of 'Promethean'. Maritain is perhaps too inclined to attribute voluntarism to the whole of post-Cartesian philosophy. Von Balthasar is so involved in debate with Idealism that he occasionally echoes that which he denies. Theirs is not the whole story. But their negations help to explain why an incarnational theology needs

195

an external, meaning-bearing world. Thus, von Balthasar rejects Schelling's raising of beauty too far above the other transcendentals because it loosens its bonds with reality; Tate criticizes Shelley's imagination which intuits forms which shimmer in the Platonic heaven, but not on earth; he envisages Poe's quest for an all too purified beauty as a road leading to solipsism. Such figures become a negative backcloth, which these writers use to depict the conviction that an analogizing imagination must represent a given physical world.

By making metaphysics dependent on ethics, Kant gave rise to the voluntarism of later philosophy, and to the deworldedness of some modern theology. The will treats its objects as containers of power. This is the 'science' against which Ransom and his pupils take their stand. In turn, Lynch and von Balthasar disavow what begins as the idealistic projection of an inflated, power-driven world, and culminates in the demythologized theology which takes refuge from such facts in inwardness.

Convergences to the Way of Analogy

The first 'stage' is Maritain's idea of beauty as the threefold harmony of proportion, integrity and radiance. Proportion and integrity extend the form across space or time, and so into reality. Form is an intricate structure, for beauty is not just a blur. Radiance is here because beauty is impelling. An objective beauty, which inheres in reality, is the broad base of our pyramid. It flows from the beauty of Christ.

The Southerners present the 'second stage': the emergence of the self, in an aesthetic phenomenology of experience. Their notion of imagination is not 'psychological'. For what interests them is a certain conception of the image. This image is carefully bounded and 'finite'. It is a form which contains great complexity within the simplicity of limitation. In its compact apprehensibility, it represents the exact contours of the real world. The image has a double function. It embodies a set of realities and it is an entrance to outward reality. These authors speak of forms which transmit light. This conveys the image of finite form, carrying the self into participatory knowledge of objective being. Now the self becomes a person.

In the third stage, the Image is Christ. For Lynch, Christ is the bounded figure of analogy: He allows imagination to know the world realistically. Von Balthasar elaborates on this: Christ is a 'finite' Form, through Whom passes an infinite Glory. His indefinable mystery is yet visible. It translates us into itself, and thus directs us toward transcendentally objective being.

All of these writers say two things about the beautiful image. First, it is real. Tate's 'whole horse' resists the pragmatists' urge to transform it into an endlessly moving machine. Von Balthasar intends the factual image of Christ to obstruct infinite phantasizing. The image is real: it embodies and safeguards 'outwardness'. Second, we can see it. These writers employ the analogue of 'sight' because it is a direct grasping. They believe that reality is there and that we know that it is. What are the sources of these two concerns?

Form: Realism

It was sly to designate St Thomas' view of imagination as 'earthbound', and then to say that the image of the 'land' governed the Southerners' imagination. The Southerners had no first hand access to such metaphysics. They locate the source of their realism in the traditional society which nurtured them. They had a poetic realism because the images of land and of history loomed before them. The realism of Maritain, Lynch and von Balthasar is Thomistic. All think that reality is created by God; it is therefore good. Being bears witness to its transcendent source without being identified with it. Each believes that human nature is fulfilled by passing through a created nature.

Von Balthasar's praise for neo-scholasticism is sparing: he called it a 'desert'.[2] But, he adheres to those elements of the Thomistic synthesis which I have made basic for this study: acceptance of the analogy of being, rejection of voluntarism, and belief that imagining must be bound to the concrete image in order to know truth. Von Balthasar said that Thomas' metaphysics is

the philosophical reflection of the free glory of the living
God of the Bible. . . . It is a celebration of the reality of
the real, of that all-embracing mystery of being which
surpasses the powers of human thought . . . a mystery
which in its non-subsistence is shot through with the
freedom of the light of the creative principle.[3]

The search for poetic, philosophical and theological meaning
begins in the earth of physical facts.

Beauty displays the reality of being partly because these
writers draw upon the Romantics' re-animation of the idea
of aesthetic forms as organic wholes. In Maritain, the Southerners, Lynch and von Balthasar, the image draws us into a
formed external being. They learned from the Romantics that
the relation to the given world has actively to be constructed
through images. They envisage metaphysical doctrines through
the coloured glass of Romantic literature – as when von
Balthasar considers the idea of substance through Goethe's
'morphology'.

Light: Apprehensibility and Boundlessness

'Poetic Intuition' is Maritain's term for our apprehension of
facts: it includes artistic connaturality. The Southerners and
Lynch simply say 'imagination'. Von Balthasar describes a
sympathetic connaturality, imitating, as it 'sees', the Form of
Christ. They all call upon an activity which draws on reason,
emotion, and sense – that is, the whole self – in order to engage
in the idiosyncratic meaning of a real, concrete object.

Despite the importance of the idea of connaturality,
St Thomas is not responsible for these writers' interest in
how we reach outward being. Nor, I imagine, was the Old
South much exercised by the question of how the self is related
to the world. The source of this concern was the early
phenomenologists' examination of types of direct access to
finite realities.

Maritain rejected the element of materialism in Bergson's
thought. But Bergson had introduced him to the notion of

intentionality and had shown him that consciousness transcends itself by espousing an 'intuitive' attitude. This 'intuition' shows Maritain why the artist is moved by this *particular* woman, or city, or war. Poetic intuition is an affective transformation of the self into the veins and textures of a specific fact.

Bergson taught Ransom that the quality of experience depends on its particular focus. His pupils affirm that experience is unified when it is guided by finite form. Aesthetic form becomes a communicating medium between inner and outer worlds.

Tate gave Lynch the means of expressing the problem of how the subject may find meaning *in* the world: it must join itself with limited objects. Although these objects are 'there', it takes an imaginative act to know them as finite.

The Austro-German phenomenologists, such as Ehrenfels and Scheler, showed von Balthasar how formed objects communicate their shape to a mind. A form evokes a certain intentionality.

Bergson's anti-rationalism sets him apart from the German phenomenologists. But, when Husserl first heard of his work, in 1913, he said 'We are the true Bergsonians'.[4] Scheler initiated German translations of Bergson's works – whilst rejecting their 'monism'.[5] What is shared is not Bergson's metaphysics but his notion of intuition, as an immediate concourse with facts.[6] As von Balthasar puts it: 'Bergson's abiding merit is to have shown this simple and direct relation to reality (which Husserl . . . was . . . to work through in his own fashion) as the pristine impulse in all the sciences.'[7]

The phenomenology of the religious act delineates the experience of being encountered by the Wholly Other. Scheler says that the object of religious experience cannot be defined. He likens the method of the phenomenologist who gives pointers to this uncategorizable region of light to negative theology.[8] For von Balthasar, the Platonic tradition, carried forward by Plotinus, Pseudo-Dionysius and Nicolas of Cusa, represents the apprisal of the otherness of God. Or, as Albert the Great says in his Commentary on Dionysius' *Mystical Theology*,

the sort of vision by which we . . . see God without . . .
reference to His effects 'reveal[s] the hidden beauty' (of
God) . . . by having everything denied of it, the transcendence of the beauty of God is represented as by a formal
image.[9]

'Light' is not only that aspect of being which curves toward the
human eye. The light of Being gives of itself because it exists
beyond conceptual construction. To reduce it to that which
illuminates humans is to empty it of its glory.[10] For von
Balthasar, it is pre-eminently St Augustine

who takes over the metaphysics of Being-Light . . . into
Christianity and who determines it . . . by the . . . decision
of man for or against this light . . . The light in which our
spirit sees is not directly God . . . it is truth which holds
sway as the openness of God, in accordance with which it
thinks in orientation towards God, and in turning away
from which it loses God.[11]

We have described the metaphysical presuppositions of Christology. The acceptance of those presuppositions depends upon
conversion. This is an interior turning. But it is the converse of a
'psychological' act. It is the turning of the self to the otherness of
being.

Form and Light

There are two strata in these writers' work: first, a broadly
Thomistic realism, and second an epistemology which is drawn
from the phenomenologists. The second is linked to a Plotinian
and Augustinian metaphysics of light. We need both in order to
explain how facts are important. Once we have them, we may
say that the Incarnation occurs through expressive Form. These
authors speak of the shaped otherness of reality, and of the
illumined bonds between persons and that outwardness. In so
doing, they repair the loss of objectivity and of transcendence.
The means of engagement with finite particularity which they
have found is the creative perception which knows facts as
forms.

To recreate the fact as form is to make it represent the dynamism of meaning, circling in upon its source. Caroline Gordon's Heracles, the mighty hunter, gives us an image of the human leaping up toward the divine. The theologians attend to Athena's recreation of justice. To reflect upon such images is to take the first step of the Christic imagination. All of these writers have the analogizing imagination: they seek convergences between the physical underworld and the ethereal sky. The effort to represent those convergences is the imaginative and metaphysical task of Christology. Christology is a work of the imagination. It is the interpretation of human things as places in which God could be present. It means finding things interesting, or significant enough to be open to God.

Forms entwine to create an analogous order. The transcendental perfections are the cables of the analogy of being. Being, truth, goodness and beauty are creative likeness between God and the world. Maritain argues for the transcendentals, whereas the theologians believe that Christ reveals them. Although von Balthasar states that we require a natural conviction of the transcendentals, his central concern is faith. But, does not Maritain's conception of thought as 'enracinated' in being also rely on faith? This is not a faith which posits its object by an act of the will. It is a faith which allows something other to flood the mind. One has to be within a field in order to perceive the inner analogies between its objects. In order to apprehend the transcendentals, which uphold the analogy of being, one must be inside it. An act of faith in being carries human beings into a shared theatre of meaning. This is to enter a sphere which is permeated by mystery. If Allen Tate and von Balthasar both return to the Augustinian image of the child sheltered by its mother, that may be because one's faith in being is given through the hands of another person.

The Person

We moved from Maritain's philosophical metaphysics toward the concretion of being in an historical person. The reality of metaphysics is carried into the second and third stages, but it becomes ever more condensed. Maritain's history of poetic intuition depicts the emergence of the self. He singles out Tate and Hopkins as interiorized modern poets, for whom finitude is known as it rebounds on an 'I'. Lynch's *Christ and Prometheus* suggests that the advance of empirical method must be related to the good of human persons. Finally, von Balthasar's 'up-ended phenomenology' reveals the face of a Person.

The formed emotion, or sensitive affectivity through which one grasps a personal expression of form also roots the self in reality. And so, although the Personal God is the 'mid-point' of the reality which the theological aesthetic grasps, the God of metaphysics is not discarded. He is 'impacted' within the Form of historical revelation as the 'concrete analogy of being'.[12] The fact whose story is the inbinding force of metaphysics, myth and history also binds a self to their world.

Comedy and Tragedy

I call some of the authors 'tragedians' and others 'comedians' because their work has that 'plot'. This is not a matter of what one says about either genre. It is a matter of how one envisages the action of reality. Von Balthasar's plot is tragic: the Form descends upon us. In his story, the Form of Christ contains in itself the meaning of human experience. Lynch's equally Johannine Christology is comic because his theme is the ascent into reality. Here Christ 'internally' enters the conditions of human life and fulfills them. The tragic analogue belongs to the greater theologian; Lynch's comic analogies better preserve the unconditionality of human experience.

No writer automatically belongs to either genre. In order to do so, one must render one of the actions of being. One must show what life is actually like. In the nineteenth century, the absence of a realistic conception of reality threatened the existence of both comedy and tragedy. As Robert Dupree suggests,

The avoidance of tragedy is the substitution of . . . certainties of the mind's invention for the terrifying

certainties of the cosmos . . . For the great pessimistic
nineteenth century thinkers, tragedy is attractive . . .
because its theme is knowledge of the unchanging . . .
from the Storm und Drang generation to Nietzche,
tragedy was the occasion for some brilliant . . . reflection. Yet tragedy as an imaginative act was no longer
available to European culture . . . the comedy of pleni-
tude was equally unavailable.[13]

Resting in conceptual or univocal certainty gives us only the
appearance of tragedy. If one elevates nature toward the
supernatural without accepting its grossest depths, one's comedy will grow ever thinner. So, too, will one's Christology.

Christ engenders the mythic act in which Heracles briefly
lifted the world in his arms. Both comedy and tragedy incorporate gods and humanity into the common life of a single
'cosmos', in which heroic acts spring toward divinity. If drama
cannot play out this myth, transcendental and immanent being
will cease to face one another. There will be no imaginative
space for the incarnation of transcendent deity.

Lynch speaks of Christ's being 'lifted up upon the Cross': this
action effects the unity of being. Lynch says that this act
reconciles contraries. The Romantic imagination aimed to
do this. But where it wrestled with the necessities of the logical
understanding, Lynch speaks of the diversity within facts. The
one eventually overrides the empirical; the other incorporates it.

Beauty as the Expression of the Transcendentals

We attended first to beauty because we consider that the
Christological dilemma is an imaginative one. Theology also
needs to speak of the truth of the analogy of being, and of the
good which guides the community. The restatement of these
realities has often lacked materiality. It is because the beautiful
replenishes the imagination that it has come first for us. It
enables us to envisage the transcendentals of being, truth and
goodness.

The beautiful is the presence of being. As such, it is

pleasurable. This is not the aesthete's escapist pleasure. It includes a fact which Rosenzweig noted about the Bible: '. . . reading it certainly cannot be called a pleasure.'[14] To accept the transcendentality of beauty is to make an act of faith in the giveness of being no matter how appalling or terrifying or repulsive. Like the image which displays it, being is there, beyond all projections.

The Biblical Christ as True, Good or Beautiful?

Proceeding, as it hoped, directly to the *truth* of Scripture, biblical criticism dismembered both text and narrative. Biblical criticism went in search of the truth: but it was not entirely sure what it meant by the term. Did it want the truth *behind* the text, in intentions taken as 'inward' to their authors, or did it want the truth *beyond* the text, taken as that to which the text, once denuded of its form, referred?

Since the work of Brevard Childs, Hans Frei, and Robert Alter, it has become evident that many of those in search of the 'truth' behind or beyond Scripture did not know how to *read*. Childs taught us once again to read the many levels of the canonical Scriptures as a given whole; Hans Frei pointed us to the Christ presented by the narrative: the story, as he noted, is the full expression of authorial 'intention'; Alter practised, and to splendid effect, the careful literary study of the Hebrew Bible, taken as 'historical prose fiction'. In the Academy, literary sensitivity and charisma were swiftly institutionalized: the quest for the 'true' Christ gave way to the examination of 'Mark's story of Jesus'. Questions about referential truth have come to seem rather vulgar in some quarters. Although it is somewhat lacking in gratitude to those who have once more made that study a literate discipline, one must suggest that the cumulative effect of their work has been to 'aestheticize' the Bible. This is because the nature of truth and beauty are, as we have noted, somewhat unclear in our culture. The embattled parties of Biblical 'truth' (or falsity) and narrative beauty find little common ground on which to join issue. A third party is perhaps more numerous, since it includes many of those outside the clerical elite of the academy: those who look for *moral* inspiration from the stories of Scripture. I shall attempt, in conclusion, to suggest how the imagined form of Christ draws together the lines leading to his truth, his beauty, and his goodness.

The Biblical Christ as True and as Beautiful

Supposing, with Alter and Frei, that the authors of the Bible intended to produce a work of beauty. What would this entail? And what follows from the claim that the truth of the text is to be found within its beauty? We shall return briefly to the question of what literary truth and beauty are.

The statement that beauty illuminates truth must include two diverse intuitions. On the one hand, the worst apology for bad art is that it is 'true to life'. An artistic work is not 'true' because it reports successfully upon a social milieu or a moral or philosophical idea. On the other hand, even the first great 'formalist' novel in English, *Tristam Shandy*, is funny because there *are* people like Uncle Toby. Even artistic fiction is valuable in the degree of its palpability to reality.

The artist creates truth in three acts. First, he or she must know something well. Caroline Gordon was able to describe Heracles' labours with an attentive detail because of her earlier novels and stories about the sporting exploits of Aleck Maury, who was drawn from her father.[15] 'Poetic intuition' is an – imitative – knowing of a particular reality, and it conveys this insight. Second, this knowledge is refashioned as a little world, or representative structure. Once so transformed, it is a new creation: we must now look, not to the facts from which it was drawn, but to its form, in order to understand it. To this extent, the formalist is correct. But, third, this artistic form guides its audience back into the real world. Refashioned by creative intuition, the form becomes an analogue of a given reality. Its audience can repeat that process, through its representative patterning of images. The artistic structure imitates reality not by referring to it, but by *representing* it.

We have made two claims about the 'truth' of the artistic

work. The first is negative: the purpose of the artistic work is not directly to refer to facts, or to be descriptively realistic. The second claim is that the truth of the artistic work is bound to its structure, or form. Now, metaphysical works also have structure: the good philosopher does not adduce arguments at random. It might appear that, in this case, the structure is secondary. It is only there to clarify the truth which the writer intends to demonstrate. The structure should be transparent: what should be present to the reader's mind is the truth itself. If the parable of a world in which scientific knowledge is half-forgotten had concluded MacIntyre's *After Virtue*, rather than setting it in motion, the book might have less impact.[16] But it would say the same thing. As Thomas says, the philosopher's images and illustrations may be translated, or paraphrased without altering their meaning.

On the other hand, where the story begins, and how it unravels, tells us something of the truth at which a philosophical or theological work aims. The conception of the *Summa Theologiae* would be as much altered if the process of discovery were inverted – say, beginning with the revelation of the Trinity, proceeding to ethics, and concluding with arguments for the existence of God – as would one of Jane Austen's novels, if the order were reversed, to commence with the marriages, and work back through the complications of courtship. For, although the intention to truth can use variant images, its judgements are often synthesized by a latent metaphor. Thus, sight has a paradigmatic value for Plato, as does the exemplar of the circle for St Thomas' theology.

Nonetheless, those who seek truth must prove their metaphor, by analysing its individual components. I suggest that the intention to a direct relation with individual facts is an intention to truth. When our primary aim is to say something true, the referential description comes first. This direct relation to reality subsequently generates a synthesis. In the case of works whose primary intention is to be beautiful, the truth is achieved by showing the fact within a creative representation of form. The intention to a synthetic representation is referred to beauty, and that whether we find it in metaphysics, morals, mathematics, or art. The truth is now dependent upon the representation. The 'truth' of *The Glory of the Hera* is not the veracity of its hunting scenes, but that of the myth in which they are embodied. The 'truth' of the beautiful image raises a set of facts toward an analogous synthesis, which denies the reductionist caricature.

What follows for the reading of the work of art which is Scripture? Simply, I think, that referential and representative aims are not wholly at odds. This is because the form of the text has its context in an inherent palpability to a world beyond itself. As Rosenzweig noted, the genuinely beautiful provides no escapist fantasy, but that which breaks into the perfect text which we might prefer to maintain as a barrier between self and world. Beauty as form is not a self-generating engine, but, rather, *re-presentation*.

Thus, on the one hand, the canon critics are right to say that the given symbolic forms found within John and the Synoptics are the focusing mediums through which we must imagine Christ. On the other hand, the truth of his person continually breaks in, ever to deconstruct the absolutization of perfect form.

The Biblical Christ as the Good

If one is speaking of either the truth or the beauty of the work of art, it is 'fallacious' to refer to authorial 'intentions'. The author has shot her arrows (the intentions): once the intentions form a unity within the work, they are quasi-autonomous. But, if and when one chooses to consider the work in relation to the *good*, the author becomes a factor. Considered ethically, the creator is an integrative persona who is in some sense *inside* the artistic work. The author makes the moral judgement which enables his or her invented characters to make sense as characters, their actions threaded together across the narrative so that each forms a ethical unity.

If the good is conceived as a static absolute, it will have no place in the ways of the world. Beauty reminds us to interpret the good dramatically, or to seek it within the outlines of a plot. It is the reference to the good which reminds Christology that the transcendent author is immanent within His story. This entails that that story is understood best by the witnesses. The meaning of the biblical stories is best drawn out by those who act them out.

These authors create a picture of the Incarnation as the archetypal manifestation of beauty. Their combination overcomes Kant's 'complication': they show how the fact can be important. But in the end, it is not that 'Christology' requires a given world, but that Christ creates one.

NOTES

1 Von Balthasar, *Glory V*, p. 624.
2 Von Balthasar, 'In Retrospect', in *The Analogy of Beauty*, edited by John Riches, p. 219
3 Von Balthasar, *Glory: IV*, pp. 406–407.
4 Spiegelberg, *Phenomenological Movement*, Vol. II, p. 398.
5 Ibid. Vol. I, p. 236 and Max Scheler, *The Nature of Sympathy*, pp. 56 and 74.
6 The statement which heads the German *Year Book for Philosophy and Phenomenology* (of 1913) shows the divergence and the affinity: 'What unites [the editors] is the common conviction that it is only by a return to the primary sources of direct intuition and into insights into essential structures derived from them that we shall be able to put to use the great traditions of philosophy.' Composed by E. Husserl, M. Scheler, M. Geiger, A. Pfander and A. Reinach: Spiegelberg, *Phenomenological Movement*, Vol. I, p. 5.
7 Von Balthasar, *Glory: III*, pp. 422–423.
8 Scheler, 'Problems of Religion', in *On the Eternal in Man*, pp. 171–172.
9 Albert the Great, 'Commentary on Dionysius' Mystical Theology', in *Albert and Thomas: Selected Writings*, edited by Simon Tugwell p. 169.
10 This with reference to Goethe: von Balthasar, *Glory V*, p. 391.
11 Ibid. p. 639–640.
12 Von Balthasar, *A Theology of History*, p. 74.
13 Robert Dupree, 'The Copious Inventory of Comedy', in *The Terrain of Comedy* edited by Louise Cowan pp. 169–170.
14 Rosenzweig, cited in *Franz Rosenzweig: His Life and Thought*, edited by Nahum N. Glatzer, p. 160.
15 Radcliffe Squires, 'The Underground Stream: A Note on Caroline Gordon's Fiction', *The Southern Review*, n.s. 7 (I) (Spring, 1971), p. 468); Caroline Gordon, *Aleck Maury: Sportsman*; and *The Collected Short Stories of Caroline Gordon*.
16 MacIntyre, *After Virtue*, pp. 1–5.

Appendix 1: Patristic and Medieval Theories of Beauty

1. 'That which Pleases when Seen'

I have said that the scholastics define the beautiful as 'that which pleases when seen'. This is Maritain's interpretation of the formula. Umberto Eco dissents. Noting that St Thomas actually said '*pulchra dicuntur quae visa placent*', he claims that Maritain turns a 'sociological finding' into a 'dogmatic' definition.[1] He thinks that St Thomas' use of the phrase *dicuntur* ('is called') shows that he is commenting on how people tend to use the term 'beauty'. A grammatical point can be made in defence of Maritain's interpretation: how does St Thomas use the phrase *dicuntur* elsewhere? Each of his arguments for the existence of God concludes with a similar phrase, e.g., 'one is bound to arrive at some first cause . . . and this is what everybody understands by God'.[2] Whilst distinguishing finite being from the self-subsistent being of God, St Thomas says: 'the first cause is above being insofar as it is infinite being; "being" (*ens*), however, is called that which participates in being in a finite way, and this being is proportionate to our intellect.' [*'Secundum rei veritatem causa prima est supra ens in quantum est ipsum esse infinitum, ens autem* dicuntur *id quod finite participat esse, et hoc proportionatum intellectui nostro'*].[3] One would hesitate to conclude that this is the product of a sociological survey. Eco hangs too much on the use of the present passive plural. St Thomas uses the present passive singular and the gerundive, (*dicitur, dicendum*) more often. This is because, in the scholastic *Quaestio*, the master's reply to the 'problem' set (*quaeritur*, 'it is asked') usually commences with *dicendum*, 'it ought to be said'.[4] But the meaning of the verb appears to be interchangeable. Thus, St Thomas writes elsewhere: 'let that be called beauty, the very perception of which pleases.' (*'pulchrum autem dicitur id cuis ipsa apprehensio placet.'*)[5]

Two other facts emerge from this definition. First, that the Scholastics defined beauty with reference to pleasure did not render their interpretation less objective. As William of Auvergne puts it 'we call beautiful for the eyes that which *of itself* is able to please those who see it.'[6]

Second, as Tatarkiewicz notes, whilst St Thomas took sight to be primary in the perception of beauty, he did not restrict the perception of beauty to the visual senses.[7]

2. Form and Light

The Fathers and the Scholastics drew on two conceptions of beauty. One comes from the Neoplatonists: here the main property of beauty is light. The second is an aesthetic of proportion. Whilst one or other property may predominate in different Church Fathers, and in the various medieval schools, most writers seem to have combined the two aesthetics.[8]

The aesthetic of light springs from Plotinus and Pseudo-Dionysus.[9] Light is the predominant feature of the aesthetics of Robert Grosseteste and of St Bonaventure.[10] For both, light is a metaphysical principle, not just a quality or a brilliant colour. Grosseteste defined light as identity: God is its sovereign form. The unity of created being flows from God's emanation of light.[11] Bonaventure speaks of light in three ways: in its purest form, as *lux*; as the medium of bodies, as *lumen*; and as the 'accidental', qualitative refraction of material light in bodies, as 'color'.[12] As *lux*, light is the activating essence of material bodies. Bonaventure says: 'Light [*lux*] is the most beautiful, the most pleasant and the best among physical things.'[13]

The aesthetic of proportion has two forms. One is mathematical, the other qualitative. The quantitative interpretation comes from the Pythagoreans. It is less important for the scholastics, although it may have affected Grosseteste.[14] The qualitative notion of proportion was invented by Cicero. He says that beauty is a measured relation between the parts of a body. He writes '*corporis est quaedam apta figura membrorum cum coloris quadam suavitate, eaque dicitur pulchritudo.*[15] Augustine took this up, defining beauty as the harmony between the various elements of an object.[16] His aesthetic lies behind that of the *Summa Fratres Alexandri*, which was compiled in the thirteenth century by three Franciscan friars, Jean de La Rochelle, Considerans, and Alexander of Hales. It defines beauty as measure, order and form, with a special emphasis upon form, or species.[17] It says that 'A thing is said to be beautiful . . . when it observes the proper measure, form and order.'[18] Measure (*modus*) is taken as the limiting, or boundary principle; order (*ordo*) is the principle of internal coherence, and species as the differentiating characteristic. The introduction of Aristotle's *Metaphysics*, in the thirteenth century, changed the picture of beauty. In Albert the Great's writings, light and form are seen as act and potentiality, or as form and matter. Light is interpreted as the substantiating form of beauty, while proportion stands for matter.[19]

Albert gave the most well-known scholastic definition of beauty: 'Beauty consists in the gleaming of substantial or actual form over proportionally arranged parts of matter.'[20] Light is the actualizing, or structuring principle within facts. The beauty of an object consists in the perfect coherence of structure with the matter which it informs. Beautiful matter is the expressive presence of light. Ulrich of Strassburg and St Thomas attended Albert's lectures on *The Divine Names* in Cologne, in 1248–1252.[21] Ulrich of Strassburg takes up Albert's definition of beauty, treating it as the intelligible light within matter.[22] For St Thomas, a thing is beautiful 'if it possesses the spiritual and physical lustre proper to its kind, and if it is constructed in proper proportion.'[23] By the lustre 'proper to its kind', St Thomas means the actuality due to a specific form.

3. Relationism

The first 'relational' definition of beauty comes from Basil of Caesarea's attempt to reconcile Plotinus' identification of beauty with light with the 'proportional' aesthetic of Cicero and the Stoics. Basil argued that, in the case of beauty, the proportion lies in the relation of light to the human eye. He states that 'If physical beauty derives from a mutual proportion of parts and from good colour, can such a conception of beauty be applied to light, which is single and homogeneous? Can it not be applied because the proportionality of light occurs not between its parts, but in relation to the sight, for which light is joyous and pleasant.'[24]

For Tatarkiewicz, 'relationalism' is a distinguishing characteristic of the definitions of beauty which issue from the thirteenth century. He cites William of Auvergne: 'Just as we call beautiful for the eyes that which of itself is able to please those who see it and which affords visual delight, so also we call internal beauty that which delights the minds of those who see it and inclines them to love it.'[25] The authors of the *Summa Fratres Alexandri* also define beauty with reference to intention.[26] St Bonaventure states: 'There is no beauty except where there is a harmony of perceived with perceiver.[27] Edgar de Bruyne disagrees with Tatarkiewicz. He claims that such relationalism is Aquinas' discovery (or recovery, from Alexander of Hales).[28] Pouillon, mediating between the two, considers that the new element in Thomas is that beauty is defined with reference to knowledge, in distinction from the good, which is known in desire.[29]

4. Beauty and the Good

Beauty is subordinate in patristic and Scholastic thought because it is often absorbed into the good. Like the identification of beauty with proportion, this is the work of the Stoics.[30] Cicero translated Καλόν in Aristotle's *Rhetoric*, as *honestas*.[31] The Scholastics imitate this usage. For William of Auvergne, beauty is the inner beauty of soul which is reflected in moral action.[32] St Thomas speaks of beauty as the '*bonum honestas*': 'honesty,' he says, 'is a kind of spiritual beauty'.[33] Yet both Jean de la Rochelle and St Thomas distinguish the good and the beautiful. The good is the final cause, to be achieved through desire; the beautiful relates to the formal cause: for St Thomas, this is grasped intellectually.[34]

5. Beauty and Truth

The interpretation of beauty as form led to its also being connected with truth. For Considerans, in the *Summa Fratres Alexandri*, truth is the interior coherence of form, beauty its exterior disposition, or appearing. Here again, beauty is distinguished by its relation to an apprehender.[35]

6. Is Beauty a Transcendental?

Philip the Chancellor, writing in the early thirteenth century, is the first to *list* the transcendentals.[36] He names truth and good as universal properties of every existent reality: they are thereby convertible with being, and so 'transcendental'. Beauty is missing. Jean de la Rochelle and Considerans seem to be the first to treat the beautiful as a separate reality from the good. 'Timidly', it seems, they take the first steps toward recognizing the beautiful as a universal property of being.[37] St Bonaventure is the first amongst the Franciscans to *list* beauty as a transcendental property of being.[38] He lists four transcendentals: being, truth, goodness and beauty. Beauty never appears in the lists of transcendentals composed by the Dominican scholastics, Albert the Great and St Thomas Aquinas.[39] However, whilst both Albert and Thomas say little of beauty in the main body of their writings, they both succumb to its lure in their respective Commentaries on *The Divine Names* of Pseudo-Dionysus. In these texts, each of these writers speaks of the universal extent of beauty, and names God as its first cause.[40] In *The Divine Names*, Dionysius defines the beautiful as one of the sources of being:

> Beauty . . . is the great creating cause which bestirs the world and holds all things in existence by the longing inside them to have beauty . . . it is . . . the Cause toward which all things move, since it is the longing for beauty which brings them into existence. . . . The Beautiful is . . . the same as the Good, for everything looks to the Beautiful and the Good as the cause of being, and there is nothing in

the world without a share of the beautiful and the good
. . . This – the One, the Good, the Beautiful – is in its
uniqueness the cause of the multitudes of the good and the
beautiful.[41]

NOTES

1 Umberto Eco, *Art and Beauty in the Middle Ages*, Bredin p. 128.
2 Thomas Aquinas, *Summa Theologiae*, Ia, Q. 2, Art. 3, resp.
3 St Thomas Aquinas, *In De Causis*, lect. 6, Quoted in Jan Aertsen, *Nature and Creature*, p. 222.
4 John Marenbon, *Later Medieval Philosophy (1150–135): An Introduction*, pp. 28–29.
5 St Thomas Aquinas, *Summa Theologiae*, Ia IIae, Q. 7, Art. 1, and 3.
6 William of Auvergne, *De Bono et Malo* 206, quoted in Tatarkiewicz, *A History of Aesthetics, Vol. II: Medieval Aesthetics*, p. 206.
7 Tatarkiewicz, *Medieval Aesthetics*, p. 247.
8 Henri Pouillon, 'La Beauté, Propriété Transcendantale chez les Scholastiques: 1220–1270 (*Archives D'Histoire Doctrinale et Littéraire*, 21 (1946), p. 296.
9 Tatarkiewicz, *Medieval Aesthetics*, pp. 28–30 and 214.
10 Edgar de Bruyne, *Études d'Ésthétique Médiévale: III: Le XIIIe Siecle*, p. 23.
11 Eco, *Art and Beauty*, p. 49.
12 Ibid. p. 50.
13 Tatarkiewicz, *Medieval Aesthetics*, p. 237.
14 Ibid. p. 226.
15 Cicero, *Tusculan Disputations* IV, 31, quoted in Henri Pouillon, *La Beauté* p. 276.
16 Tatarkiewicz, *Medieval Aesthetics*, p. 51.
17 Ibid. p. 217–218.
18 Ibid. p. 224.
19 Tatarkiewicz, *Medieval Aesthetics*, p. 240, Pouillon *La Beauté*, p. 296.
20 Albert the Great, *Opusculum de pulchro et bono*, V., 456, quoted in Tatarkiewicz, *Medieval Aesthetics*, p. 243.
21 Pouillon, *La Beauté*, p. 294.
22 Ibid. pp. 302–303.
23 St Thomas Aquinas, *Commentary on The Divine Names*, IV, Lecture V, quoted in Tatarkiewicz, *Medieval Aesthetics*, p. 259.
24 Basil of Caesarea, *Homilia in Hexaim.*, II, 7, (P. G. 29, c. 45), quoted in Tatarkiewicz, *Medieval Aesthetics*, p. 22.
25 William of Auvergne, *De Bono et Malo*, 206, quoted in ibid. p. 227.
26 Eco, *Art and Beauty*, p. 24.
27 Bonaventure, quoted in Tatarkiewicz, *Medieval Aesthetics*, p. 238.
28 De Bruyne, *Études*, pp. 281–282.
29 Pouillon, *La Beauté*, pp. 307–308.

30 Eco, *Art and Beauty*, p. 22
31 Pouillon, *La Beauté, p. 270.*
32 Ibid, pp. 267–269.
33 St Thomas Aquinas, *Summa Theologiae*, IIa IIae, Q. 145, Art. 3, resp.
34 Pouillon *La Beauté* pp. 275 and 308–310, St Thomas Aquinas, *Summa Theologiae*, Ia, Q.5, Art. 4, ad1.
35 Eco, *Art and Beauty*, pp. 23–24 and Pouillon *La Beauté p. 278.*
36 Eco *Art and Beauty*, pp. 20–21.
37 Pouillon, *La Beauté*, pp. 278–279.
38 Ibid, p. 281.
39 Ibid pp. 294 and 305; Armand Maurer, *About Beauty: A Thomistic Interpretation.*
40 Pouillon *La Beauté*, pp. 293–294, 305 and 308.
41 Dionysius the Areopagite, *Divine Names*, Ch. 4, p. 77.

Appendix 2: The Scholastic Use of the Term 'Transcendental'

The great scholastic triumvirate of transcendentals was Being-Truth-Goodness. Being was aligned to the Father, Truth to the Son and Goodness to the Holy Spirit.[1] For Kant, transcendental ideas regulate human thought. For the Scholastics, the transcendent properties regulate reality. Suarez first used the term 'transcendental': it designates that which is convertible with Being.[2] But the schoolmen speak of 'transcendent' or universal properties of being. As our discussion of beauty indicates, we find the notion, if not the term, in many medieval authors. Duns Scotus effectively defines the transcendentals, albeit with a different emphasis to that given here.[3] Aristotle names ten categories.[4] As it is used in the thirteenth century, 'transcendent' means an aspect of reality which extends beyond such categorial divisions. It is part of reality 'before' it is separated into categories. It overflows all categorial distinctions between things. As such, it is a property common to every existent.

The first such 'transcendent' property is being. Being belongs to every thing: as St Thomas says: 'Being is said of everything that is'.[5] 'Things are not distinguished from each other in having being, for in that respect they agree.'[6]

Being is the first transcendental, since it is the primary act of all things. The transcendent properties are not 'lumps' that sit in things, alongside their qualities. They are moving, actualizing causes. To be is the basic act of all existents.[7] Transcendent properties can be called 'transcendent perfections.' For the scholastics, an object is 'perfected' by becoming what it is meant to be. The transcendentals are perfections: they are the causes through which things achieve their fullness. Each thing's being is actualized in a way proper to it. Being is proportioned to the scope of each category. There is an analogy between each existent's act of being.[8]

For St Thomas, created things 'participate' in the transcendental property of being: their being is something 'other', which flows through them, but which is not their own.[9] Only in God, the First Cause of Being, are nature and being identical. 'He is, St Thomas says, 'the cause of all things of which being is predicated.'[10]

The transcendental perfection of being exists in its most perfect form in God. 'Being' is said analogically of God and of creatures.[11] It is the analogical 'extension' of being from God to the created world which allows us to name God through His effects. The transcendental perfections are thus both universal attributes of reality and the best names for God.

If other properties exist which reappear as themselves within an infinite number of determinations, these would be convertible with – have as wide an extension as – Being. As existentially causative bonds between God and the essential forms of creatures, they would be appropriate names for God. We could name God by analogy through them. Such properties are truth, goodness, and, occasionally, beauty. The true and the good are the two relational transcendentals. Both are identical with being, in reality: but they add something to it which is not expressed by the term 'being'. They are thus conceptually distinct from it.

Truth is the relation of being to a mind. It is a transcendental perfection of being because existents achieve a perfection when they are known. All things 'want' to be known, to be brought into harmony with an intellect. When they are grasped intellectually, the perfection of 'truth' is actualized in them. 'Truth' thus expresses the universal intelligibility of being, or being as knowable. As St Thomas says, 'some [things] are said to add to being because the mode they express is . . . consequent upon every being in so far as it follows . . . upon every being considered in relation to another . . . Truth expresses the correspondence of being to the knowing power.'[12] Truth is primarily in the mind, and only secondarily in things.[13]

Would the transcendental property of truth disappear, if there were no human knowers? Not for St Thomas, for he considers that the first truth of objects is their relation to the mind of God.[14]

The good has an unchallenged place amongst the transcendentals. For one motive for the medieval discussion of the transcendent properties was the need to combat Catharism. The Scholastics emphasized the universal goodness of created nature, against the spirit/matter dualism which characterized such medieval sects.[15] It is the second 'relational' transcendental. Where the true is perfected by conformity with a mind, the good is actualized in desire, or in relation to an appetite.[16] The object is primary: the good actualizes the appetite, bringing it into conformity with itself.[17] The good is being as desirable. The good pulls, or attracts all things into itself: it is the final cause of all existents. It brings realities to fruition, or complete actuality. As such, it is a transcendent perfection.[18] God is named Good in His capacity as Cause of all being. To be is to be from the self-communicating goodness of God. Being and goodness are thus identical. 'That', St Thomas said, 'settles the Manichees'.[19]

NOTES

1 Aertsen, *Nature and Creature*, p. 381.
2 Joseph Owens, *An Elementary Christian Metaphysics*, p. 111.
3 Allen Wolter, *The Transcendentals and their Function in the Metaphysics of Duns Scotus* p. 4.
4 Aristotle, *Categories*, Chapter 4, 1b 24–27.
5 St Thomas Aquinas, *Summa Contra Gentiles*, II. 15, 2.
6 Ibid, Book I, Chapter 26, Section 3.
7 Joseph Owens, pp. 24, 29, 59–62.
8 Ibid, p. 112; Aertsen, *Nature and Creature*, p. 61.
9 Ibid, pp. 83 and 125–126.
10 St Thomas Aquinas, *Summa Contra Gentiles*, Book II, Chapter 15, Section 3.
11 Aertsen, *Nature and Creature*, p. 86.
12 St Thomas Aquinas, *The Disputed Questions on Truth*, Volume I: Questions I–IX, Question 1, Article 1.
13 Ibid. Article 2, Reply.
14 Aertsen, *Nature and Creature*, pp. 161, and 167.
15 Eco, *Art and Beauty*, p. 20.
16 Aertsen, *Nature and Creature*, pp. 145 and 338–339.
17 St Thomas Aquinas, *Summa Theologiae*, Ia, Q.5, Art. 5, resp.
18 Aertsen, *Nature and Creature*, p. 338.
19 G. K. Chesterton, *St Thomas Aquinas: The Dumb Ox*, p. 101. See also the *Summa Contra Gentiles*, Book II, Chapters 37 and 38.

Bibliography

Abrams, M. H. *The Mirror and the Lamp: Romantic Theory and the Critical Tradition*, (Oxford University Press, Oxford, 1953, 1972).

Aertsen, Jan, *Nature and Creature: Thomas Aquinas's Way of Thought*, translated by Herbert Donald Morton (E. J. Brill, Leiden, 1988).

Albert the Great, O.P., 'Commentary on Dionysius' Mystical Theology', in *Albert and Thomas: Selected Writings*, translated and edited by Simon Tugwell, (Paulist Press, New Jersey, 1988).

Alvis, J., 'The Miltonic Argument in Caroline Gordon's The Glory of Hera', *The Southern Review* 16 (1980), pp. 560–573.

Anselm, St of Canterbury, *Basic Writings: Proslogion, Monologion, Cur Deus Homo and Gaunilion's Response in Behalf of the Fool*, edited and translated by S. N. Deane (Open Court, La Salle, Illinois, second edition, 1962, tenth printing, 1982).

Amato, Joseph, *Mounier and Maritain: A French Catholic Understanding of the Modern World*, (University of Alabama Press, Alabama, 1975).

Aristotle, *The Basic Works of Aristotle*, edited by Richard McKeon (Random House, New York, 1941, thirty second printing).

Aquinas, St Thomas O.P., *The Disputed Questions on Truth: Questions I–IX*, translated by Robert Mulligan, S. J. (Henry Regnery Company, Chicago, 1952).

—,The Disputed Questions on Truth: Questions *X–XX*, translated by James V. McGlynn, S. J. (Henry Regnery Company, Chicago, 1953).

—,*The Division and Method of the Sciences: Questions V and VI of the Commentary on the De Trinitatae of Boethius*, translated by Armand Maurer (The Pontifical Institute of Mediaeval Studies, Toronto, Third, revised, edition, 1963).

—,*Summa Contra Gentiles*: Book One: God, translated by Anton C. Pegis (Doubleday and Co., 1955, University of Notre Dame Press, Notre Dame, 1975).

—, *Summa Contra Gentiles*: Book Two: Creation, translated by James F. Anderson (Doubleday and Co., 1956, University of Notre Dame Press, Notre Dame, 1975).

—, *Summa Theologiae*, General Editor Thomas Gilby (Eyre and Spottiswoode, London, 1964).

Augustine, St *The Confessions*, translated by E. B. Pusey (Thomas Nelson and Sons, Ltd, London, undated).

Balthasar Hans Urs von, *Science, Religion and Christianity*, translated by Hilda Graef (Burns and Oates, London, 1958).

—, *A Theology of History*, (Sheed and Ward, London, 1964) [No translator given]

220   *Bibliography*

—, *Word and Revelation. Essays in Theology 1*, translated by A. V. Littledale and Alexander Dru (Herder and Herder, New York, 1964).

—, *Word and Redemption. Essays in Theology 2*, translated by A. V. Littledale and Alexander Dru (Herder and Herder, New York, 1965).

—, *Man in History. A Theological Study*, [No translator given] (Sheed and Ward, London, 1968, 1982).

—, *Engagement with God*, translated by John Halliburton (SPCK, London, 1971).

—, *The Theology of Karl Barth*, translated by John Dury (Holt, Rinehart and Winston, New York, 1971).

—, *The Glory of the Lord: A Theological Aesthetics: I: Seeing the Form*, edited by Joseph Fessio and John Riches, translated by Erasmo Leiva-Merikakis (Ignatius Press, San Francisco, 1982).

—, *The Glory of the Lord: A Theological Aesthetics: II: Studies in Theological Style: Clerical Styles*, edited by John Riches, translated by Andrew Louth, Francis McDonagh and Brian McNeil (T. & T. Clark, Edinburgh, 1984).

—, *The Glory of the Lord: A Theological Aesthetics: III: Studies in Theological Style: Lay Styles*, edited by John Riches, translated by Andrew Louth, John Saward, Martin Simon and Rowan Williams (T. & T. Clark, Edinburgh, 1986).

—, *The Glory of the Lord: A Theological Aesthetics: IV: The Realm of Metaphysics in Antiquity*, edited by John Riches, translated by Oliver Davies, Andrew Louth, Brian McNeil, John Saward and Rowan Williams (T. & T. Clark, Edinburgh, 1989).

—, *The Glory of the Lord: A Theological Aesthetics: V: The Realm of Metaphysics in the Modern Age*, edited by Brian McNeil and John Riches, translated by Oliver Davies, Andrew Louth, Brian McNeil, John Saward and Rowan Williams (T. & T. Clark, Edinburgh, 1991)

—, *The Glory of the Lord: A Theological Aesthetics: VI: Theology: The Old Covenant*, edited by John Riches, translated by Brian McNeil and Erasmo Leiva-Merikakis (T. & T. Clark, Edinburgh, 1991).

—, *The Glory of the Lord: A Theological Aesthetics: VII: Theology: The New Covenant*, edited by John Riches, translated by Brian McNeil (T. & T. Clark, Edinburgh, 1989).

—, 'On the Concept of the Person', *Communio*, 13, (Spring, 1986), pp. 18–26.

—, *Theo-Drama. Theological Dramatic Theory: I: Prologomena*, translated by Graham Harrison (Ignatius Press, San Francisco, 1988).

—, *Theo-Drama. Theological Dramatic Theory. II: 1 Dramatis Personae: Man in God*, translated by Graham Harrison (Ignatius Press, San Francisco, 1990).

—, *la Dramatique divine II. Les personnes du drame: 2 Les personnes dans le Christ*, translated by Robert Givord (Lethielleux, Paris, 1988).

Baker, Howard, 'The Stratagems of Caroline Gordon, or, The Art of the Novel and the Novelty of Myth', *The Southern Review*, n.s. 9, (II), (1973), pp. 523–549.

Bakhtin, M. M., *The Dialogic Imagination: Four Essays*, edited by Michael Holquist, translated by Caryl Emerson and Michael Holquist (University of Texas Press, Austin, 1981).

Barth, Karl, *Anselm: Fides Quaerens Intellectum. Anselm's Proof of the Existence of God in the Context of his Theological Scheme*, translated by Ian W. Robertson, (SCM Press, London, 1960).

—, *Protestant Theology in the Nineteenth Century: Its Background and History*, translated by Brian Cozens and John Bowden (SCM Press, London, 1972).

Beardsley, Monroe C., *Aesthetics from Classical Greece to the Present: A Short History*, (Macmillan, New York, 1966, University of Alabama Press, Tuscaloosa and London, 1975, 1978).

Bergson, Henri, *An Introduction to Metaphysics*, translated by T. E. Hulme (Macmillan, London, 1913).

Blondel, Maurice, *Letter on Apologetics and History and Dogma*, translated by Alexander Dru and Illtyd Trethowan (Harvill Press, London, 1964).

Bouyer, Louis, *Life and Liturgy*, (Sheed and Ward, London, 1955, 4th impression, 1978).

Brentano, Franz, 'The Distinction Between Mental and Physical Phenomena', translated by D. B. Terrell, in *Realism and the Background of Phenomenology*, edited by Roderick Chisholm (The Free Press, New York, 1960).

Bretall, R. W., 'Kant's Theory of the Sublime', in *The Heritage of Kant*, edited by George Tapley Whitney and David F. Bowers (Russell and Russell, New York, 1962).

Brown Ashley, 'A Note on God Without Thunder', *Shenandoah*, 3 (1952), pp. 34–37.

Brown, David, *Continental Philosophy and Modern Theology*, (Basil Blackwell, Oxford, 1987.

Brown, Frank Burch, *Religious Aesthetics: A Theological Study of Making and Meaning*, (Macmillan, London, 1990).

Bruyne, Edgar de, *Études D'Esthétique Médiévale: III: Le XIIIe Siècle*, (Bruges, 1947, Slatkine Reprints, Geneva, 1975).

Buffington, Robert, 'Allen Tate: Society, Vocation and Communion', *Southern Review*, n.s. 18 (Winter, 1982), pp. 62–72.

Bultmann, Rudolf, *Theology of the New Testament*: I, (SCM Press, London, 1952, 1978).

—, 'New Testament and Mythology', in *Kerygma and Myth*, edited by Hans Werner Bartsch, translated by Reginald Fuller (SPCK, London, 1953), pp. 1–44.

—, 'Bultmann Replies to His Critics', in *Kerygma and Myth*, edited by Hans Werner Bartsch, translated by Reginald Fuller (SPCK., London, 1953), pp. 191–211.

—, *Essays: Philosophical and Theological*, (SCM Press, London, 1955).

—, *Jesus Christ and Mythology*, (Charles Scribner's Sons, New York, 1958).

Bundy, Murray Wright, 'The Theory of Imagination in Classical and Medieval Thought', in *University of Illinois Studies in Language and Literature*, Urbana 12 (1927), pp. 6–280.

Casey, Edward S., *Imagining: A Phenomenological Study*, (Indiana University Press, Bloomington, 1976, 1979).

Chenu, Marie-Dominique, O. P., *Nature, Man and Society in the Twelfth Century*, edited and translated by Jerome Taylor and Lester K. Little (University of Chicago Press, Chicago, 1968).

Chesterton, G. K., *St Francis of Assisi*, (Hodder and Stoughton, London, undated).

—, *St Thomas Aquinas: The Dumb Ox*, (Doubleday, Image Books, New York, 1956).

Cobb, James B., 'A Question for Hans Urs von Balthasar', *Communio*, 5 (1978), pp. 53–59.

Coleridge, Samuel Taylor, *Aids to Reflection: In the Formation of a Manly Character: On the Several Grounds of Prudence, Morality, and Religion*, edited by Edward Howell (London, 1883).

—, *Biographia Literaria: or Biographical Sketches of My Literary Life and Opinions*, edited by James Engell and W. Jackson Bate, Bollingen Series LXXV (Routledge and Kegan Paul, London, 1983), Volumes I and II.

—, *Confessions of an Inquiring Spirit*, edited by Henry Nelson Coleridge (Edward Moxton, London, third edition, 1853).

—, *On the Constitution of Church and State: According to the Idea of Each*, Bollingen Series LXXV, edited by John Colmer (Routledge and Kegan Paul, London, 1976).

—, *The Friend*, Two Volumes, edited by Barbara E. Rooke, Bollingen Series LXXV (Routledge and Kegan Paul, London, 1976).

—, 'On Poesy or Art', in *Biographia Literaria, Volume II*, edited by J. Shawcross (Oxford University Press, Oxford, 1983), pp. 253–263.

—, 'On the Principles of Genial Criticism', in *Biographia Literaria, Volume II*, edited by J. Shawcross, (Oxford University Press, Oxford, 1983), pp. 219–243.

—, 'The Statesman's Manual: A Lay Sermon', in *Lay Sermons*, edited by R. J. White, Bollingen Series LXXV (Routledge and Kegan Paul, London, 1972).

Cowan, Bainard, 'The Serpent's Coils: How to Read Caroline Gordon's Later Fiction', *The Southern Review*, n.s. 16 (II) (1980), 281–298.

—, 'Nature and Grace in Caroline Gordon', *Critique*, Vol 1, No. 1 (Winter, 1956), pp. 11–27.

Cowan, Louise, *The Fugitive Group: A Literary History*, (Louisiana State University Press, Baton Rouge, 1959).

—, *The Southern Critics*, (The University of Dallas Press, Irving, 1981).

Cowan Louise, (ed.), *The Terrain of Comedy*, (Element Books, Dallas, 1986).

Cupitt, Don, *Taking Leave of God*, (SCM Press, 1980).

Danielou, Jean, and Marrou, Henri, *The Christian Centuries: The First Six Hundred Years*, translated by Vincent Cronin (Darton, Longman and Todd, London, 1964).

Dante, *The Divine Comedy*: Hell, translated by Dorothy Sayers, (Penguin Middlesex, 1949, 1981).

Davidson, Donald, *Southern Writers in the Modern World*, (University of Georgia Press, Athens, 1958).

Davidson, Donald and Tate, Allen, *The Literary Correspondence of Donald Davidson and Allen Tate*, edited by John Tyree and Thomas Daniel Young (University of Georgia Press, Athens, 1975).

Dillistone, F. W. *The Christian Understanding of Atonement*, (SPCK, London, 1968, 1984).

Dilthey, Wilhelm, *Selected Writings*, edited and translated by H. P. Rickman (Cambridge University Press, Cambridge, 1976).

Dionysius, Pseudo, *The Complete Works*, translated by Colm Luibheid (SPCK, London, 1987).

Duke, Paul, *Irony in the Fourth Gospel*, (John Knox Press, Atlanta, 1989).

Dunlop, Francis, *Max Scheler*, (Claridge Press, London, 1991).

Dupré, Louis, 'Hans Urs von Balthasar's Theology of Aesthetic Form', *Theological Studies* (No. 49, June, 1988), pp. 299–318.

Dupree, Robert S., *Allen Tate and the Augustinian Imagination: A Study of the Poetry*, (Louisiana State University Press, Baton Rouge, 1983.

—, 'The Copious Inventory of Comedy', in Louise Cowan (ed.), *The Terrain of Comedy*, (Element Books, Dallas, 1986).

Dyson, A. O., 'The Christian Religion', in *The British: Their Religious Beliefs and Practices 1800–1986*, edited by Terence Thomas, (Routledge, London, 1988).

Edwards, Michael, *Towards A Christian Poetics*, (Macmillan Press, London, 1984).

Ehrenfels, Christian von, 'Gestalt Level and Gestalt Purity', in Barry Smith (ed.), *Foundations of Gestalt Theory*, (Philosophia Verlag, Munich, 1988), pp. 118–120.

—, 'On Gestalt Qualities', (1890) in Barry Smith (ed.), *Foundations of Gestalt Theory* (Philosophia Verlag, Munich, 1988), pp. 82–117.

—, 'On Gestalt Qualities', (1932) in Barry Smith (ed.), *Foundations of Gestalt Theory* (Philosophia Verlag, Munich, 1988), pp. 121–123.

Eco, Umberto, *Art and Beauty in the Middle Ages*, translated by Hugh Bredin, (Yale University Press, New Haven, 1986).

Engell, James, *The Creative Imagination: Enlightenment to Romanticism*, (Harvard University Press, Cambridge, 1981).

Fergusson, Francis, *The Idea of a Theatre. A Study of Ten Plays; The Art of Drama in Changing Perspective*, (Princeton University Press, 1949).

Fichte, Johann Gottlieb, *The Vocation of Man*, translated by William Smith (The Open Court Publishing Company, Chicago, 1906).

Ford, David F. (ed.), *The Modern Theologians: An Introduction, to Christian Theology in the Twentieth Century. Volume I and II*, (Basil Blackwell, Oxford, 1989, 1990).

Fraistat, Rose Anne, *Caroline Gordon as Novelist and Woman of Letters*, (Louisiana State University Press, Baton Rouge, 1984).

Frei, Hans, *The Identity of Jesus Christ: The Hermeneutical Bases of Dogmatic Theology*, (Fortress Press, Philadelphia, 1975).

Frye, Northrop, *The Anatomy of Criticism*, (Princeton University Press, New Jersey, 1957).

—, *The Secular Scripture: A Study of the Structure of Romance*, (Harvard University Press, Cambridge, 1976).

—, *The Great Code*, (Routledge and Kegan Paul, London, 1981).

Geertz, Clifford, *The Interpretation of Cultures: Selected Essays*, (Basic Books, New York, 1973).

Geiselmann, Josef Rupert, *The Meaning of Tradition*, translated by W. J. O'Hara (Herder and Herder, New York, 1966).

Gilson, Etienne, *The Unity of Philosophical Experience*, (Sheed and Ward, London, 1938).

Gimpel, Jean, *Against Art and Artists*, (Polygon, Edinburgh, 1991, revised British edn

Glick, Nathan, 'Sidney Hook: Embattled Philosopher', *Encounter*, Vol. 65 (June, 1985), pp. 28–32.

Goethe, Johann Wolfgang von, *Theory of Colours*, [1810] translated by Charles Lock Eastlake, (Frank Cass & Co, London, 1967).

Gordon, Caroline, *Aleck Maury: Sportsman*, (Charles Scribner's Sons, New York, 1934, reprinted Southern Illinois University Press, 1980).

—, 'Some Readings and Misreadings', *Sewanee Review*, 61 (Summer, 1953), pp. 384–407.

—, *How To Read a Novel*, (Viking Press, New York, 1957).

—, 'Cock-Crow', *Southern Review*, n.s. I, (July, 1965), pp. 554–569.

—, *The Glory of Hera*, (Doubleday and Co., New York, 1972).

—, *The Collected Short Stories*, introduction by Robert Penn Warren (Farrar, Straus, Giroux, New York, 1981).

—, 'A Master Class: From the Correspondence of Caroline Gordon and Flannery O'Connor', edited by Sally Fitzgerald, *Georgia Review*, 33 (1986), 827–846

Goulder, Michael (ed.), *Incarnation and Myth: The Debate Continued* (SCM Press, London, 1979).

Gray, Richard, *The Literature of Memory: Modern Writers of the American South* (Edward Arnold, London, 1977).

Greene, Theodore M., 'Kant's Theory of Aesthetic Form', in *The Heritage of Kant*, edited by George Tapley Whitney and David F. Bowers (Russell and Russell, New York, 1962).

Grillmeier, Alois S. J., *Christ in Christian Tradition: From the Apostolic Age to Chalcedon (451)*, translated by J. S. Bowden (Mowbray and Co., London, 1965).

Gunton, Colin E., *Enlightenment and Alienation: An Essay Towards a Trinitarian Theology*, (Marshall Morgan and Scott, Hants, 1985).

Halévy, Daniel, *Péguy and Les Cahiers de la Quinzaine*, (Dennis Dobson, London, 1946).

Handy, William J., *Kant and the Southern New Critics*, (University of Texas Press, Austin, 1963).

Hart, Kevin, *The Trespass of the Sign: deconstruction, theology and Philosophy*, (CUP, Cambridge, 1989)

Harvey, Austen van, *The Historian and the Believer: The Morality of Historical Knowledge and Christian Belief*, (SCM Press, London, 1967)

Hayen, André, *L'Intentionnel Selon Saint Thomas*, second, revised edition, (Desclee de Brouwer, Paris, 1954).

Heilman, Robert Bechtold, *The Ways of the World: Comedy and Society*, (University of Washington Press, Seattle, 1978).

Heller, Erich, *The Disinherited Mind*, (Bowes and Bowes, London, 1957).

Henderson, Ian, *Myth in the New Testament*, (SCM Press, London, 1952).

Hengel, Martin, *The Atonement. A Study of the Origins of the Doctrine in the New Testament*, (SCM Press, London, 1981).

Herodotus, *The Histories*, translated by Aubrey de Selincourt (Penguin, London, 1954, 1976).

Hick, John (ed.), *The Myth of God Incarnate*, (SCM Press, London, 1977, 1978).

Hoffdung, Harald, *A History of Modern Philosophy: A Sketch of the History of Philosophy from the Close of the Renaissance to Our Own Day*, translated by B. E. Meyer (Macmillan & Co., London, 1900).

Homer, *The Iliad*, Book Eight, translated by Richmond Lattimore (Chicago University Press, Chicago, 1951).

Hook, Sidney, 'The Integral Humanism of Jacques Maritain', *Partisan Review*, 7, (1940), pp. 204–229.

Hopkins, Gerard Manley, S. J., *Poems and Prose*, Selected and Edited by W. H. Gardiner (Penguin books, London, 1953, 20th 1978).

Hume, David, *A Treatise of Human Nature: Being an Attempt to Introduce the Experimental Method of Reasoning into Moral Subjects. Volume I. Of the Understanding*, Edited with an analytical index by L. A. Selby-Bigge. Second Edition, revised, etc. by P. H. Nidditch (Oxford University Press, Oxford, 1978).

Hume, Robert, 'Kant and Coleridge on Imagination', *Journal of Aesthetics and Art Criticism*, 28 (1969/1970), pp. 485–496.

Husserl, Edmund, *Logical Investigations* (two volumes), translated by J. N. Findlay, from the second German edition [1913] (Routledge and Kegan Paul, London, 1970, 1982).

Ingarden, Roman, *The Cognition of the Literary Work of Art*, translated by Ruth Ann Crowley and Kenneth R. Olson (Northwestern University Press, Evanston, 1973).

—, *The Literary Work of Art. An Investigation on the Borderlines of Ontology, Logic, and Theory of Literature*, translated by George Brabowicz (Northwestern University Press, Evanston 1973, 1980).

—, *Selected Papers in Aesthetics*, edited by Peter J. McCormick (Catholic University of America Press; Philosophia Verlag, Munich, 1985).

Irenaeus, St, *Against Heresies*, in the *Ante-Nicene Christian Library*, Volumes V & IX, translated by Alexander Roberts and W. H. Rambaut, edited by Alexander Roberts and James Donaldson.

Jarvis, F. P., 'F. H. Bradley's *Appearance and Reality* and the Critical Theory of John Crowe Ransom', in *John Crowe Ransom: Critical Essays and a Bibliography*, edited by Thomas Daniel Young (Louisiana State University Press, Baton Rouge, 1968).

Johnson, Roger A., *The Origins of Demythologizing: Philosophy and Historiography in the Theology of Rudolf Bultmann*, (E. J. Brill, Leiden, 1974).

Johnston, William M., *The Austrian Mind: An Intellectual and Social History. 1848–1938*, (University of California Press, Berkeley, 1972).

Jonas, Hans, *The Phenomenon of Life: Towards a Philosophical Biology*, (University of Chicago Press, Chicago, 1966).

Kahler, Martin, *The So-Called Historical Jesus and the Historic Biblical Christ*, translated by Carl E. Braaten, (Fortress Press, Philadelphia, 1964).

Kant, Immanuel, *The Critique of Judgement*, translated by J. C. Meredith, (Clarendon Press, Oxford, 1928, 1988).

—, *The Critique of Pure Reason*, translated by J. M. D. Meiklejohn, Introduction by A. D. Lindsay, (Dent, London, 1934, 1988).

—, *Prolegomena to any Future Metaphysics that Will Be Able to Present itself as a Science*, translated by P. Gray Lucas (Manchester University Press, 1953, 1978).

—, *Religion Within the Limits of Reason Alone*, translated by Theodore M. Greene and Hoyt H. Hudson (Harper and Row, New York, 1934, 1960).

Keefe, Dennis J., 'A Methodological Critique of Hans Urs von Balthasar', *Communio*, 5 (1978), pp. 23–43.

Kehl, Medard, S. J., 'Hans Urs von Balthasar: A Portrait', in *The Hans Urs von Balthasar Reader*, edited by Medard Kehl, S. J. and Werner Loser, S. J., translated by Robert J. Daly S. J. and Fred Lawrence (Crossroad, New York, 1982).

Kerr, Fergus, O. P., *Theology After Wittgenstein*, (Basil Blackwell, Oxford, 1986).

Kerrane, Kevin, 'Nineteenth-Century Backgrounds of Modern Aesthetic Criticism', in *The Quest for Imagination: Essays in Twentieth Century Aesthetic Criticism*, edited by O. B. Hardison Jr (Case Western Reserve University Press, Cleveland and London, 1971), pp. 3–25.

Kierkegaard, Søren, *Fear and Trembling and the Sickness Unto Death*, translated by Walter Lowrie (Princeton University Press, Princeton, 1941, 1974).

Kirk, G. S., *The Nature of Greek Myths*, (Penguin, London, 1974, 1988).

Knight, Karl F., *The Poetry of John Crowe Ransom: A Study of Diction, Metaphor and Symbol*, (Mouton & Co., The Hague, 1964).

Lacoue-Labarthe, Philippe and Jean-Luc Nancy, *The Literary Absolute: The Theory of Literature in German Romanticism*, translated by Philip Barnard and Cheryl Lester (State University of New York Press, New York, 1988).

Landess, Thomas, 'The Function of Ritual in Caroline Gordon's Green Centuries', in *The Southern Review*, n.s. 1 (1971), pp. 495–508.

Langer, Suzanne, *Feeling and Form*, (Routledge and Kegan Paul, London, 1953, 1979).

Leeuw, Gerardus van der, *Religion in Essence and Manifestation: A Study in Phenomenology*, [1933] translated by J. E. Turner (George Allen and Unwin, London, 1938).

—, *Sacred and Profane Beauty: The Holy in Art*, (Holt, Rinehart and Winston, New York, 1963).

Lentricchia, Frank, 'Four Types of Nineteenth Century Poetic', *Journal of Aesthetics and Art Criticism*, Vol 26, No. 3 (Spring, 1968), pp. 351–366.

Lewis, C. S., *The Discarded Image*, (Cambridge University Press, Cambridge, 1964, twelfth impression 1983).

Lewis, Janet, 'The Glory of Hera', *Sewanee Review*, 67, (1973), pp. 185–194.

Lindbeck, George A., *The Nature of Doctrine: Religion and Theology in a Postliberal Age*, (S.P.C.K., London, 1984).

Lonergan, Bernard S. J., *Insight: A Study of Human Understanding*, (Longmans, Green and Co., London, 1957, 1958).

—, *The Subject*, (Marquette University Press, Milwaukee, 1968).

—, *Verbum: Word and Idea in Aquinas*, Edited by David Burrell, C.S.C. (Darton, Longman and Todd, London, 1968).

—, *Method in Theology*, (Darton, Longman and Todd, London, 1972, second edition 1973, reprinted 1975).

—, *A Second Collection*, edited by W. F. J. Ryan and Bernard J. Tyrrell, (Darton, Longman & Todd, London, 1974).

—, *The Way to Nicea: The Dialectical Development of Trinitarian Theology*, translated by Conn O'Donovan from the first part of *De Deo Trino* (Darton, Longman and Todd, 1976).

—, *A Third Collection*, edited by F. E. Crowe, S. J., (G. Chapman, London, 1985).

Louth, Andrew, *Mary and the Mystery of the Incarnation*, (S. L. G. Press, Oxford, 1977, 1983).

Lovejoy, Arthur O., *Essays in the History of Ideas*, (Johns Hopkins University Press, Baltimore, 1948).

Lynch, William F. S. J., *Christ and Apollo: The Dimensions of the Literary Imagination*, (Sheed and Ward, London, 1960, Notre Dame University Press, Notre Dame, 1975).

—, *Christ and Prometheus: A New Image of the Secular*, (University of Notre Dame Press, 1970).

—, 'Confusion in Our Theatre', *Thought*, Vol. 26, No. 102 (Autumn, 1951), pp. 342–360.

—, *The Integrating Mind*, (Sheed and Ward, London 1952).

—, 'Theology and the Imagination', *Thought* Vol. 29, No. 112 (Spring, 1954), pp. 61–86.

—, 'Theology and the Imagination II: The Evocative Symbol', *Thought* Vol. 29, No. 115 (Winter, 1954–1955), pp. 529–554.

—, 'Theology and the Imagination III: The Problem of Comedy', *Thought*, Vol. 30, No. 116 (Spring, 1955), pp. 18–36.

—, 'The Imagination and the Finite', *Thought* Vol. 33, No. 129 (Summer, 1958), pp. 205–228.

—, *The Image Industries*, (Sheed and Ward, London, 1960).

—, *Images of Hope: Imagination as Healer of the Hopeless*, (Helicon Press, 1965, University of Notre Dame Press, Notre Dame and London, 1973).

—, *Images of Faith: An Exploration of the Ironic Imagination*, (University of Notre Dame Press, Notre Dame and London, 1973).

Lyotard, Jean-François, *The Post-Modern Condition: A Report on Knowledge*, translated by Geoff Bennington and Brian Massumi (Manchester University Press, 1984, 1989).

Lytle, Andrew Nelson, 'Caroline Gordon and the Historic Image', in *The Hero with the Private Parts*, (Louisiana State University Press, Baton Rouge, 1966).

Mackey, James P. (ed.), *Religious Imagination* (Edinburgh University Press, Edinburgh, 1986).

Macquarrie, John, *Jesus Christ in Modern Thought*, (SCM Press, London, 1990).

Marenbon, John, *Later Medieval Philosophy (1150–1350): An Introduction*, (Routledge and Kegan Paul, London, 1987).

Marcel, Gabriel, *Coleridge et Schelling*, (Aubier, Paris, 1971).

Maritain, Jacques, *Art and Scholasticism and Other Essays*, translated by J. F. Scanlan (Sheed and Ward, London, 1930, revised edition 1943).

—, *The Degrees of Knowledge*, translated from the second, revised French edition by Bernard Wall and Margot Adamson (Geoffrey Bles, London, 1937).

—, *The Dream of Descartes*, translated by Mabelle Andison (Nicholson and Watson, London, 1946).

—, *Creative Intuition in Art and Poetry*, Princeton University Press, New Jersey, 1953).

—, *Moral Philosophy*, (Charles Scribner's Sons, New York, 1964).

—, *Bergsonian Philosophy and Thomism*, translated by Mabelle Andison, second edition (Greenwood Press, New York, 1968).

Maritain, Raissa, *We Have Been Friends Together: Memoirs*, translated by Julie Kernan (Longmans Green and Co., New York, 1943).

Mascall, Eric, *Existence and Analogy*, (Longman, Green and Co., London, 1949).

—, *Words and Images: A Study in the Possibility of Religious Discourse*, (Darton, Longman and Todd, 1949, reprinted 1968).

MacIntyre, Alasdair, *After Virtue: A Study in Moral Theory*, (Duckworth, London, 1981, second edition 1985, 1987).

—, *Three Rival Versions of Moral Enquiry*, (Duckworth, London, 1990).

Maurer, Armand, C. S. B., *About Beauty: A Thomistic Theory*, (Centre for Thomistic Studies, Houston, Texas, 1983).

McDade, John, S. J., 'Reading von Balthasar', *The Month*, April, 1987, pp. 136–143.

McFarland, Thomas, *Coleridge and the Pantheist Tradition*, (Clarendon Press, Oxford, 1969).

—, 'The Moral Theory of the Atonement: A Historical and Theological Critique', *The Scottish Journal of Theology*, (Volume 30, 1985), pp. 205–220.

McGrath, Alister, *The Making of Modern German Christology: From the Enlightenment to Pannenberg*, (Basil Blackwell, Oxford, 1986).

McRae, Robert, *The Problem of the Unity of the Sciences: Bacon to Kant*, (University of Toronto Press, Montreal, 1961).

Meiners, R. K., *The Last Alternatives: A Study of the Works of Allen Tate*, (Allen Swallow, Denver, 1963).

Millar, Kenneth, *The Inward Eye: A Revaluation of Coleridge's Psychological Criticism*, Doctoral Dissertation. University of Michigan, 1952.

Milner, Marion, *On Not Being Able to Paint*, (Heinemann, London, 1950, 1971, 1987).

Moltmann, Jürgen, *The Crucified God: The Cross as the Foundation and Criticism of Christian Theology*, translated by R. A. Wilson and John Bowden (SCM Press, London, 1974, 1979).

Bibliography 229

Moore, G. E., 'The Refutation of Idealism', *Mind*, Volume 12 (October, 1903), 1–30.

Newbigin, Lesslie, *The Other Side of 1984: Questions for the Churches*, (World Council of Churches, 1983, 1986).

Newman, J. H., *An Essay in Aid of a Grammar of Assent* (1870), (Notre Dame University Press, Notre Dame, 1979).

Newton Smith, D., 'Jacques Maritain's Aesthetics: To Distinguish, To Unite', in *The Quest for Imagination: Essays in Twentieth Century Aesthetic Criticism*, edited by O. B. Hardison Jr. (Case Western Reserve University Press, Cleveland, 1971).

Nicoll, Allardyce, *The Theatre and Dramatic Theory*, (George G. Harrap & Co, London, 1962).

Nichols, Aidan O. P., *The Art of God Incarnate: Theology and Image in Christian Tradition*, (Darton, Longman and Todd, London, 1980).

—, 'Balthasar and his Christology,' *New Blackfriars*, July/August (1985), pp. 317–324.

O'Connor, Flannery, *Mystery and Manners: Occasional Prose*, edited by Sally Fitzgerald (Faber and Faber, London, 1972).

O'Connor, Mary, 'On Caroline Gordon', *Southern Review*, n.s., 7, (Spring, 1971), pp. 462–466.

O'Donnell, John J., 'The Doctrine of the Trinity in Recent German Theology', *Heythrop Journal*, 23 (1982), pp. 153–167.

—, Review, 'The Glory of the Lord: A Theological Aesthetics, Vol. II', *The Irish Theological Quarterly*, Vol. 52., No. 1/2, (1986), pp. 141–144.

O'Donoghue, Noel, O. D. C., 'Discovering Orthodoxy: Chesterton and the Philosophical Imagination', *Chesterton Review*, Vol. XIII, No. 4 (November, 1987), pp. 455–474.

Ogden, Schubert, *Christ Without Myth. A Study Based on the Theology of Rudolph Bultmann*, (Collins, London, 1962).

O'Hanlon, G. F., S. J., *The Immutability of God in the Theology of Hans Urs von Balthasar*, (Cambridge University Press, Cambridge, 1990).

O'Leary, Joseph, *Questioning Back: The Overcoming of Metaphysics in Christian Tradition*, (Winston Press, Minneapolis, 1985).

Olsen, Glenn W., 'Hans Urs von Balthasar and the Rehabilitation of St Anselm's Doctrine of the Atonement', *Scottish Journal of Theology*, 34 (1981), pp. 49–61.

O'Meara, Thomas F., O. P., *Romantic Idealism and German Catholicism: Schelling and the Theologians*, (Notre Dame University Press, Notre Dame, 1982).

Orsini, G. N. G., *Coleridge and German Idealism: A Study in the History of Philosophy*, (Southern Illinois University Press, Carbondale and Edwardsville, 1969).

Otto, Rudolf, *The Idea of the Holy*, [1917], translated by John W. Harvey (Oxford University Press, 1932, Pelican, London, 1959).

Owens, Joseph C. Ss. R., *The Doctrine of Being in the Aristotelian Metaphysics*, (Pontifical Institute of Mediaeval Studies, Toronto, 1952, second printing 1957).

—, *An Elementary Christian Metaphysics*, (Centre for Thomistic Studies, Houston, 1985).

Patocka, Jan, *Philosophy and Selected Writings*, ed. Erazim Kohak (University of Chicago Press, Chicago, 1990), pp. 139–144.

Pelikan, Jaroslav, *Jesus Through the Centuries: His Place in the History of Culture*, (Yale University Press, New Haven, 1985).

Pouillon, Henri, O. S. B., 'La Beauté, Propriété Transcendantale chez les Scholastiques', *Archives D'Histoire Doctrinale et Littéraire*, 21, (1946), pp. 263–329.

Prickett, Stephen, *Romanticism and Religion: The Tradition of Coleridge and Wordsworth in the Victorian Church*, (Cambridge University Press, Cambridge, 1976).

Przywara, Erich, *Analogia Entis* [1932], translated from the 1962 edition by Philibert Secretan (Presses Universitaires de France, Paris, 1990).

Rahner, Hugo, S. J., *Greek Myths and Christian Mystery*, translated by Brian Buttershaw (Burns and Oates, London, 1963).

Ransom, John Crowe, *God Without Thunder. An Unorthodox Defence of Orthodoxy*, (Harcourt, Brace and World, 1930, Archon Books, Hamden, Conn. 1965).

—, *The World's Body*, (Charles Scribner's Sons, New York, 1938).

—, *Beating the Bushes: Selected Essays 1941–1970*, (New Directions Press, New York, 1941, 1972).

—, 'Poetry: I. The Formal Analysis', *The Kenyon Review*, Vol. 19, No 3 (Summer, 1947), pp. 436–456.

—, 'Poetry: II: The Final Cause', *The Kenyon Review*, Vol. 19, No 4, (Autumn, 1947), pp. 640–658.

—, 'The Concrete Universal: Observations on the Understanding of Poetry', *The Kenyon Review*, Vol. 16 (Autumn, 1954), pp. 554–564.

—, 'Art as Adventure in Form: Letters of John Crowe Ransom to Allen Tate', Edited by Thomas Daniel Young and George Core. *The Southern Review* 12, (Autumn, 1976), pp. 776–798.

—, *Selected Letters of John Crowe Ransom*, edited with an introduction by Thomas Daniel Young and George Core (Louisiana State University Press, Baton Rouge, 1985).

Reardon, Bernard M. G., *Religion in the Age of Romanticism. Studies in Early Nineteenth Century Theology*, (Cambridge University Press, Cambridge, 1985).

Reinach, Adolph, 'Concerning Phenomenology', translated by Dallas Willard, *The Personalist*, 50 (Spring, 1969), pp. 194–221.

Riches, John, (ed.), *The Analogy of Beauty: The Theology of Hans Urs von Balthasar* (T. & T. Clark, Edinburgh, 1986).

Roberts, Louis, *The Theological Aesthetics of Hans Urs von Balthasar*, (Catholic University of America Press, Washington, 1987).

Rosenzweig, Franz, *Franz Rosenzweig: His Life and Thought*, presented by Nahum N. Glatzer (Schocken Press, New York, 1953).

—, *The Star of Redemption*, translated by William W. Hallo (Holt, Rinehart and Winston, 1970, Notre Dame University Press, Notre Dame, 1985).

Royce, Josiah, *Lectures on Modern Idealism*, (Yale University Press, New Haven, 1919).

Rubin, Louis, Jr., *The Wary Fugitives: Four Poets and the South*, (Louisiana State University Press, Baton Rouge, 1978).

Sartre, Jean-Paul, *The Psychology of the Imagination*, (The Philosophical Library, New York, 1948, Methuen and Co., London, 1972).

Schaper, Eva, *Studies in Kant's Aesthetics*, (Edinburgh University Press, Edinburgh, 1979).

——, *The Nature of Sympathy*, translated by Peter Heath (Routledge and Kegan Paul, London, 1954).

Scheler, Max, *On The Eternal in Man*, translated by Bernard Noble (SCM Press, London, 1960).

Schelling, F. W. J. von, *The Philosophy of Art*, translated by Douglas Stott (University of Minneapolis Press, Minneapolis, 1988).

Schillebeeckx, Edward, O. P., *Jesus: An Experiment in Christology*, translated by Hubert Hoskins (Collins, London, 1979).

Schleiermacher, Friedrich, *The Christian Faith*, trans. of 2nd German edn., edited by H. R. Mackintosh and I. S. Stewart (T. G. T. Clark, Edinburgh, 1928, 1968).

Schrijver, G. de, *Le Merveilleux Accord de l'homme et de Dieu: Etude de l'analogie de l'être chez Hans Urs von Balthasar*, (Louvain University Press, Louvain, 1983).

Schuhmann, Karl and Smith, Barry, 'Adolf Reinach: An Intellectual Biography', in Kevin Mulligan, (ed.), *Speech Act and Sachverhalt: Reinach and the Foundations of Realist Phenomenology*, (Dordrecht, Nijhoff, 1987), pp. 1–27.

Schweitzer, Albert, *The Quest of the Historical Jesus. A Critical Study of its Progress from Reimarus to Wrede*, (Adam and Charles Black, London, 1910, third edition, 1954, reprinted 1963).

Sharpe, Eric J., *Comparative Religion: A History* (Duckworth, London, 1975, 1986).

——, *Faith Meets Faith: Some Christian Attitudes to Hinduism in the Nineteenth and Twentieth Centuries*, (SCM Press, London, 1977).

——, *The Universal Gita: Western Images of the Bhagavadgita*, (Duckworth, London, 1985).

Shelley, Percy Bysshe, *Poetry and Prose*, edited by Donald H. Reinman and Sharon B. Powers, (W. W. Norton, New York, 1977).

Simpson, David, (ed.), *The Origins of Modern Critical Thought: German Aesthetic and Literary Criticism from Lessing to Hegel*, (Cambridge University Press, Cambridge, 1988).

Smith, Barry, 'Kafka and Brentano: A Study in Descriptive Psychology. Appendix: Christian von Ehrenfels and the Theory of Gestalt Qualities', pp. 145–159, in Barry Smith, (ed.), *Structure and Gestalt: Philosophy and Literature in Austria-Hungary and her Successor States*, (John Benjamins, Amsterdam, 1981).

——, (ed.), *Parts and Moments: Studies in Logic and Formal Ontology*, (Philosophia Verlag, Munich, 1982).

Smith, Barry, (ed.), *Foundations of Gestalt Theory*, (Philosophia Verlag, Munich, 1988).

Spiegelberg, Herbert, *The Phenomenological Movement: A Historical Introduction* [two volumes], (Martinus Nijhoff, the Hague, second edition 1969).

Squires, Radcliffe, *Allen Tate: A Literary Biography*, (Bobbs-Merrill, New York,

232   *Bibliography*

232   *Bibliography*

232 *Bibliography*

232   *Bibliography*

1971).

—, The Underground Stream: A Note on Caroline Gordon's Fiction', *The Southern Review*, n.s., 7, (I) (Spring, 1971), pp. 467–479.

Squires, Radcliffe, (ed.), *Allen Tate and His Work: Critical Evaluations*, (University of Minnesota Press, Minneapolis, 1972).

—, Allen Tate and the Pastoral Vision', *The Southern Review*, n.s., 12 (Autumn, 1976), pp. 733–743.

—, *On the Problem of Empathy*, translated by Waltraut Stein (Martinus Nijhoff, the Hague, 1970).

Stein, Edith, *Life in a Jewish Family: 1891–1916: An Autobiography*, translated by Josephine Koeppel (I.C.S. Publications, Washington, 1986).

Stevenson, J., *A New Eusebius*, (SPCK, London, 1957, 1978).

Swiatecka, M. Jadwiga, *The Idea of the Symbol: Some Nineteenth Century Comparisons with Coleridge*, (Cambridge University Press, Cambridge, 1980).

Tatarkiewicz, Wladyslaw, *History of Aesthetics: Volume II: Medieval Aesthetics*, translated by R. M. Montgomery (Polish Scientific Publishers, Warsaw, 1970).

—, 'Poetry and the Absolute', *Sewanee Review*, 35 (1927), pp. 41–52.

—, *Stonewall Jackson: The Good Soldier: A Narrative*, (Minton, Balch and Co., New York, 1928).

—, *The Fathers*, (G. P. Putnam's Sons, New York, 1938, Cedric Chivers, Bath, 1977)

—, 'Religion and the Intellectuals', (Contribution to symposium of this title), *Partisan Review*, 17, (1950), pp. 250–253.

—, *The Man of Letters in the Modern World: Selected Essays: 1928–1955*, (Meridian Books, New York, 1955).

Tate, Allen, 'Christ and the Unicorn', *Sewanee Review*, 63, (1955), pp. 175–181.

—, *Collected Essays*, (Allan Swallow, Denver, 1959).

—, 'The Unliteral Imagination, or, I, too, Dislike It', *The Southern Review*, n.s. 1, (Summer, 1965), pp. 530–542.

—, *Memories and Essays: Old and New: 1926–1977*, (Carcanet Press, Manchester, 1976).

—, *Collected Poems*, (Farrar Straus and Giroux, New York, 1977).

—, 'The Migration', in *The Fathers and Other Fiction*, (Louisiana State University Press, Baton Rouge, 1977).

—, *The Poetry Reviews of Allen Tate*, edited by Ashley Brown and Frances Neel Cheney (Louisiana State University Press, Baton Rouge, 1983).

Thiselton, Anthony, *The Two Horizons: New Testament Hermeneutics and Philosophical Description: with Special Reference to Heidegger, Bultmann, Gadamer and Wittgenstein*, (The Paternoster Press, Exeter, 1980).

Trimpi, Wesley, *Muses of One Mind: The Literary Analysis of Experience and its Continuity*, (Princeton University Press, New Jersey, 1983).

Turner, H. E. W., *The Patristic Doctrine of Redemption*, (A. R. Mowbray, London, 1952).

Twelve Southerners, *I'll Take My Stand. The South and the Agrarian Tradition*, (Harper & Brothers, 1930, Harper and Row, New York, 1962).

Tyree, John and Young, Thomas Daniel (eds.), *The Literary Correspondence of Donald Davidson and Allen Tate,* (University of Georgia Press, Athens, 1974).

Uehling, Theodore Edward Jr, *The Notion of Form in Kant's Critique of Aesthetic Judgement,* (Mouton, the Hague, 1971).

Voeglin, Eric, 'The Gospel and Culture', in *Jesus and Man's Hope,* edited by Donald G. Miller and Dikran Y. Hadidian (Pittsburgh Theological Seminary, Pittsburgh, 1971).

Waardenburg, Jacques, *Reflections on the Study of Religion,* (Mouton, the Hague, 1978).

Walsh, W. H., *Kant's Criticism of Metaphysics,* (Edinburgh University Press, 1975).

—, 'Expression and Knowledge of Other Persons', *Aletheia,* Volume II (1981), pp. 124–129

Waldstein, Michael, 'Hans Urs von Balthasar's Theological Aesthetics', *Communio,* 11, (Spring, 1984), pp. 13–27.

—, 'An Introduction to von Balthasar's The Glory of the Lord', *Communio,* 14 (Spring, 1987), pp. 12–33.

—, 'John Crowe Ransom: A Study in Irony', in the *Virgina Quarterly Review,* 11, (January, 1935), pp. 93–112.

Warren, Robert Penn, *All the King's Men,* (Harcourt, Brace and Co., New York, 1946, reprinted New English Library, 1974).

—, *Selected Essays,* (Random House, New York, 1951).

—, 'Knowledge and the Image of Man', *Sewanee Review,* 63, (Spring, 1955), pp. 182–192.

—, *New and Selected Poems,* (Random House, New York, 1985).

Watkin, E. I., *Catholic Art and Culture,* (Hollis and Carter, London, 1942, second, illustrated edition, 1947).

Watson, Gerard, 'Imagination: The Greek Background', *Irish Theological Quarterly,* 52, 1/2, (1986), pp. 54–65.

Weatherby, Harold, *The Keen Delight: The Christian Poet in the Modern World,* (University of Georgia Press, Athens, 1975).

Weaver, Richard, *Ideas Have Consequences,* (University of Chicago Press, Chicago, 1948, 1984).

—, 'The Tennessee Agrarians', *Shenandoah,* 3 (1952), pp. 3–10.

—, *The Ethics of Rhetoric,* (Gateway Editions, Southbend, Indiana, 1953).

—, *The Southern Tradition at Bay: A History of Postbellum Thought,* (Arlington House, New York, 1968).

—, *A History of Modern Criticism: 1750–1950: Volume 2: The Romantic Age,* (Jonathan Cape, London, 1955, Cambridge University Press, Cambridge, 1981).

Wellek, René, *Concepts of Criticism,* edited by Stephen G. Nichols Jr. (Yale University Press, New Haven and London, 1963, 1973).

White, Hayden, *Tropics of Discourse: Essays in Cultural Criticism,* (Johns Hopkins University Press, Baltimore, 1978, 1987).

White, Victor, O. P., *God and the Unconscious,* (Harvill Press, London, 1952, Fontana, Glasgow, 1960, second impression, 1964).

Whitehead, Alfred North, *Science and the Modern World*, (University of Cambridge, 1926, Free Association Books, London, 1985).

Whybray, R. N., *The Making of the Pentateuch: A Methodological Study*, (Sheffield Academic Press, 1987).

Willey, Basil, *Samuel Taylor Coleridge*, (Chatto and Windus, London, 1972).

Williamson, Allen, 'Allen Tate and the Personal Epic', *The Southern Review*, 12 (Autumn, 1976), pp. 714–732.

Wittgenstein, Ludwig, *Culture and Value*, (Basil Blackwell, Oxford, 1980, 1989).

Wingren, Gustaf, *Man and the Incarnation: A Study of the Biblical Theology of Irenaeus*, translated by Ross MacKenzie, (Huhlenberg Press, Philadelphia, 1959).

Wolter, Allan, *The Transcendentals and Their Function in the Metaphysics of Duns Scotus*, (Franciscan Institute, Chicago, 1946).

Yadav, Bibhuti S., 'Vaishnavism on Hans Kung: A Hindu Theology of Religious Pluralism', in *Christianity through Non-Christian Eyes*, edited by Paul J. Griffiths, (Orbis Books, New York, 1990).

Young, Thomas Daniel, *Gentleman in a Dustcoat: A Biography of John Crowe Ransom*, (Louisiana State University Press, Baton Rouge, 1976).

Young, Thomas Daniel, (ed.), *John Crowe Ransom: Critical Essays and a Bibliography*, (Louisiana State University Press, Baton Rouge, 1968).

Zimmerman, Robert, 'Kant: The Aesthetic Judgement', in *Kant: A Collection of Critical Essays*, edited by Robert Paul Wolff (Macmillan, London, 1968).

Index